Jennie's Diary

To Michele
Love from
Jennie
Sept. 2019

Jennie's Diary
The Aussie from Posi

János

By Jennifer Hanlon

Table of Contents

Saving Stories

· Personal Historian ·
Researcher · Book Designer

Editing and book design by Chris Wisniewski of Saving Stories.
www.saving-stories.com

Back cover illustration by János Zigmond.

A Note from Jennie

In 2017, I decided I would call my book *Jennifer's Diary*. It really is a diary, a jotting down of dates and events so as not to forget certain things. Calling it a diary is also an excuse for me to relate my story without being worried that I am not a writer. I feel quite relieved about revealing this fact before I begin telling my stories. The book's subtitle, The Aussie from Posi, comes from a name that many people in Positano call me.

Old age seemed to have hit me over night. Suddenly my joints, which had always been quite strong and athletic, began to ache. Wrinkles started appearing on my face and my tummy and hindquarters seemed to get bigger. It is difficult for me to believe that the photo on the cover of this book was taken about 30 years ago! I started to go downhill in 2011 when I flew down a staircase in a villa in Positano. I would like to point out the fall happened before cocktail time! After that fall my doctors started to give me medicine for depression and panic attacks. Living in a town which is built on steps and stairs, did make me rather anxious every time I went out in town or even when I was within my house. I just wanted to stay in and get my body together again. With little else to do, I thought it was a good time to sit down and bring the past back to life.

My mind is still very lucid and I remember so much. Yet, going back can be emotional and my brain often says, 'Give it up, the past is the past', yet I can't seem to do that. Being a double Cancer, the past is very important to me. I just have to hear certain music, look at a photo or remember a conversation from the past and suddenly I am back there once again.

There will be many people and animals from my life who may not be mentioned here. I would like to apologise beforehand, to all of them. I have never forgotten any of of you—not one of you. My stories will be thrown together like a mixed salad, an *insalata mista*, as we say in Italian. That is rather like the pattern of my life.

Jennie, Joan, Alan and Peggy, 1939.

A Bonsai tree in Oz

I've always thought if I had to chose a tree to represent my family it would be a bonsai. We are just a small cluster of branches with very few leaves, I suppose that's because our family tree kept losing branches and getting smaller.

My mother's family lived in Nottinghamshire, England. I was told my great-grandmother died when my grandmother Mary was only four years old. Mary was sent off to work in the mills about four years later. My grandfather Stafford Caldwell was a cartage hauler in the coal mines. Being a cartage hauler was considered a good job, but it was dangerous. I remember he had a blue scar on his forehead from an injury he received when a cable had broke at work and cut his head. He said any cuts the men got in the mines healed with a blue tinge, because of the coal dust.

Mary and Stafford's first child, Fred, died a few months after he was born. Then came Amy, Florence Maude, who was my mother, followed by Alf, Evelyn and Mary. My mother worked in a milliners shop learning to make hats. When she was 18 years old her parents decided to leave England and move their family to Australia. My grandfather wanted to get out of the mines. Perhaps, it was the accident which had caused the blue scar which helped them decide to leave when they did. By the time the family was planning to leave, my Aunty Amy was already married and had a son, who was named Stafford after my grandfather. Amy had decided to stay in England. Then at the last minute, she left her husband, took the child and went with her parents on the ship. I had heard my grandfather Stafford had two sisters who also came to Australia. I don't think I ever met them and I don't even know their names. You see, our tree kept losing the few branches it had.

On **24 November 1925**, the Caldwell family left England on the steamship *Hobson's Bay* bound for Melbourne, Australia. I still have a copy of their ticket showing that the total fare they paid for the whole family was £181.

When the family arrived in Australia, they stayed with George Harrison, a cousin of my grandparents. Grandad soon bought a house on Sussex Street in Coburg just outside of Melbourne. I still remember that dark little house. We used to visit my grandparents there when I was a very small child. Their house was right next to the Pentridge Prison. There were cracks in the high walls of the prison where you could look through to the courtyard where they did executions. Fortunately I never saw anyone actually being hung by the neck any of the times I looked through.

My father's side of the family was from Ireland and England. There may have also been a bit of Norwegian going way back, which would account for my square jaw and blonde hair. My father was born on Greening Street in Plumstead just outside of London. He was the youngest child of Sarah Ann Elizabeth and Fred Hanlon. Even though his family was not wealthy, my father was quite well educated. He attended the Bostall Lane School in Abbey Woods followed by the Great Yarmouth School of Applied Arts and then the College of Art and Wood Carving at 39 Thurloe Place in South Kensington, London.

The branches on my father's side of our tree don't really exist for me. I have no memory of any of them myself. My eldest sister, Joan, told me all she knew about the family. Apparently Dad had a number of siblings. The eldest in his family was Fred, then came Syd, Doris, Glad, Roy and finally my father, Leslie Burton Hanlon. He was born on **12 September 1904**. Joan remembers our grandparents on our dad's side. Apparently my grandfather was a real Londoner and reminded her of the English actor Stanley Holloway. Syd was a ballroom dancer and never married. The two sisters, Doris and Gladys, both married and Gladys had two children. Uncle Roy married very late in life. Joan told me there were some people back in Dad's family who had a vaudeville act, which had performed in theatres in London. Joan thought

Mary and Stafford.

the comedian Tommy Hanlon was perhaps a distant relative of ours too.

Dad's family must have gone to Australia around the same time as the Caldwell family. Joan told me our mum and dad had met at a dance. They were married in the Church of England in Coburg on **6 August 1927**. By that time, Dad had a good job making furniture. I remember we had several beautiful pieces of his furniture in our house when I was growing up.

My sister Joan was born about ten months after their wedding—just in time, people would have said back then. Sometime before my other sister Peggy was born, the business Dad worked for went broke, most likely due to the worldwide economic Depression. He lost his job and the family had to leave their house. My father, who was always clever with his hands, built an extension on Mum's parents' house on Sussex Street, and the family moved in there. A couple of years later my brother, Alan, came along. At that point, I believe my parents felt their family was complete.

Times were hard and everyone seemed to be out of work, so Dad and Grandad decided to travel to Mildura, a small town on the Murray

River, to pick grapes. Anything to make money, even a little money, had to be done. Mildura was a little oasis. It had been founded by the Chaffey brothers of Canada, when they discovered it had the same climate as California, which was perfect for growing grapes for wine. When the harvest was over, Dad and Grandad came back to Melbourne with a big Hessian bag full of dried grapes for the family and a few coins in their pockets.

Dad thought there might be a better chance to find work in Mildura, so the family packed up their few belongings and left, hoping for a brighter future. As it often happens with immigrants, they found a friend in Mildura. In their case it was a man who had travelled on the same ship from England as they had. The family stayed the first night with him before they found a guesthouse to rent. They stayed at the guesthouse until they found a cottage on Magnolia Avenue. At first, they had to make do with wooden crates for tables and chairs until their furniture arrived from Coburg. Not long after the family had settled into the cottage, Grandma, Grandad and Stafford arrived. The three of them moved in to the little house at 115 Magnolia Avenue too and they stayed for about six years. Mum and Dad later invited their friend who had let them stay their first night to come live with them as well. It was quite a small cottage. How they all fitted, I can't imagine.

Dad would take any work he could find. When he met a man who wanted a house built, Dad said he could do the job, even though he had never built a whole house before. Somehow Dad figured out how to build it and he must have done a decent job because the house still stands today. When that job was done, Dad and Grandad decided to go to Ballarat, a gold mining town north-west of Melbourne, to try their luck there. That wasn't a very successful venture. They returned with only a small bottle of gold dust.

Even though the family was very poor, my brother and sisters had a good childhood. It didn't matter that they had no money, since everyone else they knew was in the same situation. My siblings were always well dressed, well mannered and received good grades in school. My brother and sisters were taught to sketch from the Brodie Mack *How To Draw* booklets which Dad had sent to the house by mail. Dad was a very good violinist and he used to entertain our family and friends in the evenings. Peggy also played the violin and Alan also had lessons too. Peggy ended up playing in the town orchestra.

Dad eventually managed to get a job with the City Council to design Henderson Park in Mildura. He went on to become a draughtsman, drawing plans of houses for builders and he also worked as a commercial artist. The family had a little more money as the years passed and their lives seemed happy.

As I said, I think my parents felt their family was already complete. I wasn't even a thought. Then surprise, surprise—quite a few years later I came along! When Joan was eleven years old, she was in the kitchen watching our mother prepare a meal. She told Mum she should stop eating, because she was getting too fat. That was when my parents decided they had to tell my siblings they were going to get a new baby from the hospital. Peggy, Alan and Joan had a little meeting and decided they didn't want any more babies. They reported their decision back to Mum and Dad and tried to convince them it would save money if they didn't have to buy another baby. My parents had to explain that wasn't how it worked and they really didn't have an option at that point.

It was **July 1939** and Australia was just months away from entering World War II. Dad was in the military at that time and was stationed full-time at the Mildura Drill Hall, which is how I ended up being born in the bathroom of the Mildura Base Hospital on **3 July 1939**. As soon as my brother and sisters saw me, they quickly changed their attitude about having a new baby in the family. The three of them started to fight over which of them could look after me. Perhaps that was because I was a cute baby. When I was three months old, I won a baby contest and was given a dress as a prize.

Australia entered the war that September. It was a time of unrest in the world and it began a time of unrest in my family. Dad was the social organiser for the troops, which meant he never saw any action during his six years in the military. He was commissioned to Lieutenant and then to Captain. Our family had more money then, since Dad was on officers' pay. While Dad was in the military, our house became a drop-in place for the officers. In turn the officers, many of whom were well to do businessmen, would ask our family to their huge houses. Dad was often away with the military when I was a baby. Throughout the war he was posted in various locations around Australia and was briefly posted in New Guinea. Whenever he had free time, he came home to be with us. Whenever he did, my brother and sisters would go to the station and wait for the troop train to come in early in the morning to greet him.

It was in New Guinea that Dad met Anne, a woman from Queensland who was working for the troops. Joan told me our mum and dad never argued, yet I suppose six years apart changes things between a man and a woman. Dad wasn't a womaniser, but he was very ambitious and Mum was reluctant to take chances. Anne was a socialite, had a good position and came from a wealthy family. Perhaps, she fit more closely with Dad's ambitions. One day Mum got word that Dad wasn't coming home again. Naturally it broke my mother's heart and it deeply upset the rest of us. Somehow Mum managed to carry on. She was a young woman who now had to adapt to a new life alone with her four children.

I missed out on the good times when our family was poor, but united. When we had a good father at home who kept the family laughing, even during the hardest years of the Depression. My mother's family had always approved of dad. They said he was cheerful and made the hard years easier for them with his music and stories. Almost as soon as I came around that family didn't exist anymore.

Dad came home on leave when I was nine months old. Perhaps that was the last time he came back before he left us. While he was home, I began walking. That must have been a very important occasion for me. I can actually remember it even though I was so very young. I was bald headed and wearing a little smocked dress, which had probably been made by my grandmother. I toddled across the front lawn into the outstretched arms of my father. He was dressed in his army uniform. I can still see the pride on his face and I feel the joy in my heart, as I reached my destination. Dad always liked attention, so he

Jennie and her mom.

took me walking all over the town with him. He brought me into all the shops, giving everyone a show of his little daughter. It was a short visit and soon he was gone. That was the most important contact I had with my Dad for a very long time. My father soon became only a vivid memory with his outstretched arms, as I took my first steps.

Even though Dad was gone, I continued singing, dancing and playing. After all, I was still just a little child. I loved to entertain my sisters and brother. Maybe I was channeling that vaudeville past in our family. However, even though I was cheerful on the outside, I did develop some nervous habits. I began sucking my wrists. I would do it so much that the skin would break. My mother put a bitter lotion on my arms to try to stop me, but I sucked that off as well. Then she started bandaging my wrists up every night. Each time

she did, I just sucked higher above the bandages. I ended up with both my arms bandaged all the way up to my shoulders. I also bit my nails. Each night my poor mother had to bandage both of my arms and put bitter aloes on my nails as well. Still nothing stopped me.

Joan and Peggy had always looked after their toys and kept them as good as new. That only lasted until I came along and wrecked the lot. I killed Rose Marie, Joan's celluloid doll. Joan said I had murdered her! I pulled the legs and arms off each one of their dolls—I disjointed them all.

Joan and Alan had very similar personalities, both were quite serious about life. Peggy and I were a bit different. We were always having fun and were busy with one thing or another. Peggy said we had 'monkey minds'. Peggy was a good artist, the top of her class. She was also good at sports and loved horseback riding. It was Peggy who bought me one of the few dolls which became part of my small family. It was a funny sort of knitted one, which Peggy had bought at a school fete. At Christmas time, Peggy would take me into a fantasyland. I would write a letter to Father Christmas and she would put it in one of the pink flowers on the hollyhock bush in our front garden. She and I would dance around the hollyhock as we chanted magical words. Then lo and behold, when I looked in the flower, the note had vanished! Year after year I desperately tried to stay awake on Christmas Eve so I could see Father Christmas, but I was never able to succeed. Then on Christmas morning I would find a pillowcase stuffed with presents, which he had left at the end of my bed. When I found out that Father Christmas didn't really exist, my whole world fell apart. I felt I would never believe in anyone ever again. When a child loses Father Christmas, that's when they stop being a child. Not long after that, I found out the actors in the cinema weren't really there either. So many of my childhood illusions were being destroyed!

When I was about one and a half years old, my mother took me to visit my father in an army barrack somewhere. It may have been in Melbourne. I know we had a long train journey to get to him. I was wearing my Scottish kilt, so I would look nice for my father, but on the journey

I got train sick and vomited all over my kilt. A kind soldier helped my mother clean me up. When we arrived at the barracks, my parents must have had important things to talk about together. They sat me down on a bunk bed where I watched them talk in whispers. Even though I was so young, I had the feeling they were discussing the future of our family. That was my second and my last memory of my father for many years.

Around this time, I wanted a dog who could be my friend to confide in, but no one else seemed to think we should have one. Then when I was three years old, a dog came to me on the street one day. He was a stray who was full of mange with patches of missing fur on his back, but to me he was beautiful. He was also very big, which I liked. The bigger the better, I thought. I called him Bob and my mother agreed to let me keep him. Bob and I became inseparable. My sister used to say, 'Wherever Bob was, there was Jennifer', but our friendship was short-lived. Bob mysteriously disappeared not long after I found him.

When I was young, my most traumatic memories were of being left alone at night. Looking back now, I realise my mother was a young woman in need of a private life and a break from all the responsibility she had of raising us alone. However back then, I was terrified at the thought of being alone after dark. I used to beg her not to leave me. The minute I was alone, I began looking around the house for a place to hide which felt safe. I would usually end up falling asleep in some strange corner of the house. Later, I would be woken up by the voices of my mother and sister saying, 'Try the wardrobes, under the beds or in the cupboard. She could be anywhere…'

On the first day I started primary school, the teacher greeted me saying, 'So, you are Peggy Hanlon's young sister. She was a brilliant student. We hope you will carry on in the same way.' That was quite a standard for a little girl to live up to. I don't know if I was truly a bright student or if I became bright to make up for all the other things I didn't have. I sailed through school with little effort and even won a prize offered by the State of Victoria for a Temperance exam when I was young. That makes me chuckle today! If I didn't make top or second from the top in my exams, my

Jennie as a young girl.

mother would want to know why. Although little praise was given to me personally, I knew Mum was proud of me, because all the neighbours knew about Maude Hanlon's bright little girl.

Our house on Magnolia Avenue was pretty shabby and I was rather ashamed of it. Actually our house was the third shabbiest on the street. There were a couple of families who were known among the kids as 'the dirty families', but our mother made sure our house was spotless. The inside was always kept clean and I was forever mowing the front lawn and weeding the garden. Still I remember seeing adults walk by our house shaking their heads and saying, 'It's such a pity the man left his wife and four children.' Some of the neighbourhood kids were cruel and whispered things about me not having a father. I think it was then I started my own secret battle. I began bottling everything up inside myself. Actually, I suppose my battle had begun with my arm sucking and nail bitting years before. As I got older and made more friends, I never wanted them to know my father had left us. I would make up stories about my father being a commercial traveller who had been travelling for many years. I fantasised about a world which didn't exist and I never shared my thoughts or feelings with anyone. When kids walked down our street on the way to school, I would stand in front of the fence two doors down and pretend that was where I lived instead.

I did have fun growing up on Magnolia Avenue. Every household had a few kids. Our back yard was enormous and it was used for hanging out the wash, repairing bicycles and storing things that could be of use one day. Our huge, iron rainwater tank was situated at the back of the house and the only vegetation was an apricot tree and a few not so productive grape vines. To waste a drop of precious water from the rainwater tank was a sin. It was the purest God-sent water in the world, to be consumed by the privileged ones, wrigglers and all. No one seemed to mind finding wriggling caterpillars at the bottom of their glass. The grape vines were home to many caterpillars. These poor creatures became the victims for me and my little friends when we turned ourselves into The Caterpillar Gang. We set up a small guillotine using one of my mother's kitchen knives or a small hatchet. The traitors, the eaters of the vine leaves, would be lined up on a slab of cement and sent wriggling towards the beheading line. When they arrived it was, 'Off with their heads!' Their squirming beheaded bodies would be put into empty marmalade jars, emitting an odour I still remember today. After we judged and beheaded the criminals, we would then proceed to take wing and become angels, probably to purify ourselves. We had an old corrugated iron shed where we

stored wood, bikes and rubbish. Beneath the shed we put an old mattress. We would scramble up onto the roof with open umbrellas and jump off, pretending we could fly. Our landing on the mattress was often quite rough, but we had fun. My friends and I were poor and didn't have many real toys except for a bike, so we made the most of anything we could lay our hands on.

Our family had an ice chest near the back of our house. I seem to remember our first one was covered in Hessian cloth before it was replaced by a more modern, wooden contraption. An old Chinese man delivered slabs of ice to fill the ice chest. As he would start his truck off toward the next house up the street, The Caterpillar Gang would spring out of a hiding place behind a hedge. We would charge after his truck calling out 'Ching Chong Chinaman'. He would stop his truck, jump out and come charging toward us with his huge, menacing ice pick.

We had several clubs in addition to The Caterpillar Gang. The most exciting one was The White Hooded Gang. Our meetings took place in a small room in the back yard of the McKinnon residence. It was an elite club for girls only and it was difficult to become a member. There were only about five of us in total. I was one of the directors, which meant I could draw up plans and give orders. We all had to wear hoods made from pillowcases with two holes for the eyes and one for the mouth. The usual topic at our meetings was to choose whose house would be haunted that week. We had our reasons for picking the house we chose, believing they deserved our punishment. The poor Cook family always seemed to be on the top of the list. They lived in a large run-down house at the end of the street. Plans were drawn up for the haunting with times, dates, locations and which scary sounds we would use. However all our hard work came to no avail. We never actually used our white hoods to scare anyone. We only used them in that little room. The fun was all in making the plans.

On Sundays, our group of Beheaders and Haunters all sacredly went to Sunday school and church. We had to divide up since we were a mixture of Church of Englanders, Methodists, Salvation Army, Presbyterians and Catholics.

Scenes from Jennie's life story by János Zigmond.

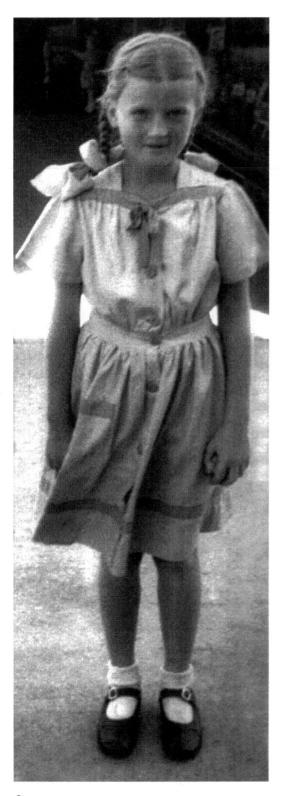

I enjoyed Sunday School, because I could wear my Sunday hat. We discovered if we put the hat on backwards, we were transformed into fireman. After being pardoned by God for a few hours early Sunday morning, we were then free to play firemen all the way home—helping people out of burning houses, rescuing children from make believe buildings and tending to their wounds.

I was actually quite involved in church and religion from a young age. I was baptised and confirmed in the Church of England. I grew up saying my prayers before going to bed every night. I began with *The Lord's Prayer* and ended with…

AND God bless Mum and Dad,
wherever he may be
God bless Joan, Peggy and Alan
God bless all the people in the world and make the bad ones good
God bless all the animals
God bless all the sick people and make them better
AND God bless me and make me a good girl… Amen

As a toddler I had come up with an image of Jesus up there in his long white robes, with a large pudding bowl cradled in his arms. He was constantly stirring a custard-like substance, which was the preparation of the babies he was about to make. He had a beautiful face and I always felt happy and at peace when I saw this image. Sometimes he would drop some chocolate coloured powder into the bowl, so I presumed he was preparing to make an aboriginal baby. I don't know where this idea came from, but back then I believed it. I seemed to have never ending questions for our local priest. He answered them all, but I was never entirely satisfied with his responses, so I continued down my own fantasy road.

My first ten years were fairly normal apart from my private inner torments. From an early age I always had my chores to do in the house and there was school five days a week. After supper, I would be allowed to play in the streets until bedtime. Saturday morning was shopping in the town with my mother and Sunday was taken up with Sunday school and church. My mother tried hard to make as much of a family life for us as she could, although I didn't see much of her. She would leave for work at the factory before I left for school. Because she was a working mum, she could never come to any of my school functions. I missed not having anyone from my family at these special occasions. One afternoon I was so surprised when my mother did appear at school. I still remember her arrival so clearly. She gave me a little white paper bag full of chocolate balls and told me she was taking me home early, because there was a threatening sand storm on the way. The sky had taken on an odd dark red hue, but to me it was a beautiful afternoon as I went off happily clutching my sweetie bag in one hand and holding onto my mother with the other.

I was no longer a baby beauty. My hair was thick and yellow and Alan called me 'haystack head'. I had freckles on my face, which I tried for years to remove, but to no avail. I had to have braces on my teeth too. My lower teeth protruded over my top ones making me look as if I had been conceived by a bull dog! Even with all my defects, I always had many friends surrounding me. In spite of my inner sadness, I had a tremendous sense of humour and loved entertaining everyone. I worked hard to prove myself in school and sports. I wanted to win the admiration of the teachers and the trainers. Perhaps I was trying to prove that even though I had a broken family and a working mother, we were still respectable.

My Aunt Mary had married a Salvation Army man and when my uncle would sing with the Salvos in the local square on Saturday, I would be sent to listen to them. When I was about ten years old, I must have done something really bad that made my mother think that going to Sunday school wasn't enough for me. As my punishment, I was sent to the Salvation Army Hall every Sunday afternoon with my cousin Shirley for one year. My Sundays became a mass of conflicting religious ideas. As usual I adapted, but looking back it was very confusing. I could never really sing, but at the annual meeting of the Salvation Army, I was put on the stage, bellowing out, *Suffer Little Children to Come Unto Me*. The Salvos were good people. They were always ready to help when there were floods or bushfires. They didn't care if I wore a

Jennie and Peggy.

hat or not and they always had a kind word for people. I have to admit though that I did giggle on the day when my cousin received her first bonnet and tambourine.

Since I was much younger than my siblings, they grew up and left home when I was still quite young. While my sisters were still around, life was good. I felt protected and secure. Then suddenly it seemed to me that one day my sisters just weren't there anymore. They disappeared just like my note to Father Christmas had in the hollyhock bush. I'm sure their departure wasn't so drastic, but for me it seemed so. Joan and Peggy occasionally came home for holidays, but it wasn't the same. Around this time, I turned into a sour-faced brat around the house and hung onto my brother out of the fear I would lose him as well. Alan had to leave school at the age of 14, because my mother didn't have the money to let him continue. He started doing odd jobs such as delivering papers and groceries. As he got older Alan took on the role of father and head of the house. He was very respectable, good looking and a prime example of a polite young man. He won the hearts of everyone in town and fortunately for me, he also cared very much for his little sister.

Joan married in **1949** when I was ten. She went to live in Adelaide with her husband, Les. I adored Les, but somehow I seemed to terrorise him whenever I went to stay with them on school holidays. He was a fanatic around the house and I was a young bubblegum-popping, school girl. He would

Max, Mom, Peggy, Les and Jo in front.

been easy, but back then I just lashed out at her.

I realise now what a strong woman my mother had been. She brought up four children on her own and all of them turned out to be good, respectable people in their own way. I was the only one who didn't really get my act together. The only unstable one of the litter. I suppose that was due to my being born too late when the happy united family had broken up. My poor mum was forever dragging me to her lawyer's office, trying to get Mr Favola to locate my father in hopes of getting some money from him to help his children. She didn't succeed and eventually gave up. I still remember that lawyer's name, because the name came up again in my life many years later.

Our closest relatives were my mother's sister Mary and her husband, the Salvation Army man. Their eldest daughter, Shirley, was about the same age as me and we spent quite a bit of time together. She was a real giggler and I've always loved people who giggle, but the poor dear suffered from asthma. I would do anything to make her laugh until she became blue in the face. My mother and aunt were always telling me not to have her running up the street or playing softball because she would lose her breath, but we did anyway. Her father had bought a fruit block in a new settlement on the Murray River in Mildura. The house he built seemed to be made of Hessian bags and each year another room would be added on. The lavatory, which we call the *dunny* in Australian bush language, was built about fifty yards from the house in the middle of nowhere. I remember sitting there with the Hessian walls flapping in the wind, praying it wasn't emptying day! I enjoyed my visits with them. We would swim in the river or lie on the river bank chewing on a gum leaf. However, I didn't like having to look for snakes under the bed

follow me around their spotless house wearing an apron and sporting a dustpan and brush, so he could clean up any messes I made. He was always very nice to me in spite of having to deal with my messes. He loved tennis and was always happy to take me with him to make up a double on the courts. A little while later Peggy married Max Lowery. Peggy was always creative, artistic, amusing and clever. Her talent could have taken her a long way if she had chosen to follow that path. I am sure she is happy and never regretted not having fame and fortune.

Around that time, I also began to make an enemy of my mother. I was constantly criticising her way of life. She started bringing men around the house, all of whom I considered awful. I would be a brat to them and to her. If any of them showed up when she wasn't home, I would just throw them out. Joan heard about my behaviour and tried to get me to be nicer to our mum. Once she asked me why I always fought with our mother and my answer was quite revealing. I said it was because I wanted a normal mother like all the other kids in school. Perhaps I was petrified of losing Mum as well. I must have made her life hell for sometime. I can understand now that her life couldn't have before going to sleep. All the blocks around them seemed to flourish, but not theirs. As their neighbours were building bigger and better houses and driving the latest cars, my uncle just kept adding a new piece of Hessian to their *dunny* wall.

One day when I was 14, I came home from school in a filthy mood and with blood on my knickers. I knew what it was all about from things I had heard from my friends. My mother never talked to me about it herself. Such things were never spoken about in our house. When I told my mother, she just handed me this hand-made 'thing', told me I was sick and that I would be sick for a few days every month for many years. That was that. What a great entrance into womanhood.

Mildura was hot—very hot. It seemed to be hot for nine months of the year. Most of my friends loved swimming either in the river or at the local pool. Many of my friends were fair-headed like me and we were forever sporting green hair from the chlorine in the pools. One of my best friends, Barbara Lear, was the only girl who had a small swimming pool in her back garden. The pool was an oversized galvanised-iron tank situated under a weeping willow tree. We loved swimming in it. Getting tangled up in the branches of the stately old tree was like swimming in a forest.

Barbara was very beautiful and had the smallest waist I had ever seen. She took ballet lessons and was a wonderful classical ballet dancer. How I envied her. I wanted to dance. I wanted to dance so badly that I was in a frenzy for years. I went from toe shoes to tap shoes, but only in my dreams. A classical ballet school had opened up in Mildura and some of my friends were attending the classes. The teacher was Hungarian and his beautiful wife played the piano during the lessons. He was a good teacher and I thought he gave Mildura a touch of class. My family couldn't afford to pay, so I would just sit in on the classes and then go home and practice on my own or Barbara would come over and teach me what she had learned. I was desperate to join the class. I begged my mother, but she said, 'You'll never be able to make a living walking around on your toes.' I understood money was scarce, but my mother was making me take piano lessons, even though I wasn't interested. Why couldn't the money she spent on my piano

Florence Maude Hanlon.

teacher go towards ballet lessons instead? I could tell I was fighting a losing battle with my mother, so I just continued to daydream about dancing.

I heard of another school of dance. It wasn't really a school. It was a class run by a large cheerful lady, who lived on the next street over from me. Her living room was her studio, which was tricky, because there was always a fear of bumping into tables and knocking statues off her sideboard. However for me, it was finally an opportunity to attend dance classes. The classes cost only two shillings and six pence. My brother gave me five shillings a week to make his bed, so I was covered for two lessons a week. The woman taught a mixture of classical, tap and show dance—none of which she had mastered very well. That didn't stop her from ambitiously planning a recital at the Town Hall called *A Night at the Ballet*. I can't quite remember which ballet we did, but I was chosen to play the prince. A prince in toe shoes, black knee-length tight pants and a white satin shirt. The hall was full of curious onlookers including the Hungarian maestro and his wife. The princess was Myrna Cherry, a giggly friend of mine. I suppose with a name like that, she couldn't help

Peggy and Alan.

but giggle. She giggled every time I picked her up by the waist.

After the performance, the Hungarian teacher wanted to know who the girl who played the boy in toe shoes was and why wasn't she attending his classes. When he met me, he offered to give me lessons at a less expensive rate. However even that didn't budge my mother to let me attend his classes. The money I got from making my brother's bed wasn't enough for me to pay for the classes on my own. I needed help, but who could I turn to? From the time I could write, I had kept up a correspondence with my father. I figured I had nothing to lose by asking him to help, even though no one in our family had ever gotten anything from him since he left, including my mother. I didn't ask him for much, but just enough to pay for a couple of terms of ballet school until I could get a part-time job and pay for the school myself. I was so pleased and surprised when he sent me the money! The next time I danced at the Town Hall, I had the Hungarian maestro as my partner. That time I had a comedy role in the show and it was great fun. I continued to study with the maestro for a few years until his school folded.

Our family had a big break just before I started high school. My mother was able to get a government commission house at 6 Hunter Street, which was quite near to my high school. The house wasn't huge, but after all those years on Magnolia Avenue, this house seemed like a mansion to me. It was a corner house with front and back gardens and it was brand new! There would be no more standing in front of someone else's house pretending it was ours. Now, I could show everyone we lived in a mansion. I could finally put my past behind me: the shabby house, the broken fence, the muddy street and the ghosts of my childhood. I did have more lawn to mow and a larger garden to weed, but that was just fine to me.

I still didn't have my own bedroom. There were only two bedrooms in our new house, so I had to share a room with my mother as I had before. Mum gave me a free hand in decorating the house. The first thing I did was get rid of her beaded, antique lampshades and anything else which looked old. On the walls I hung up sets of plaster of Paris birds and cheap prints of ballet dancers. In the fireplace I put a huge plaster of Paris elephant. I even convinced her to sell the piano. I had hoped we could get a radiogram instead, but we never did. My mother stood firm about keeping my father's art work. Even after he left, we always had many traces of my father around our house. He was a talented artist and woodcarver. Now his tables and carved objects, seemed out of place next to my new ballerinas and birds. It would take me years to begin to appreciate the beauty of older things.

My mother and I were getting along a bit better by this time. She had little oddities, which I really got off on. She told me never to say the word 'HATE'; to her it was the worst word in the world. She always kissed me whenever I left the house, just in case anything happened to me. Torn underwear or safety pins in your knickers were forbidden. 'What if you had an accident and had to be taken to hospital?' One nostril was to be blown at a time, otherwise you could burst an eardrum. All this useful information was handed down from mother to daughter. She often gave me boxes of handkerchiefs as presents, but at the same time she told me that they meant tears, so I shouldn't give them to people I wanted to see again. That made them a rather confusing gift to receive from my mother. She told me 'Never aim higher than your own level.' I never agreed with her on that point. Honestly, I didn't know what our level was. Mum never missed the Sunday morning hillbilly show on the radio and she adored Elvis Presley, whilst I was listening to classical music such as *Swan Lake* because of my love of ballet. She was always saying, things I thought were hilarious, but she said them in a very serious way. To this day I'm not sure if she was being funny or not. The walls in our loo, which was on the back porch in our new house, were filled with cut out pictures from women's magazines and she had posted a carefully hand-written sign, which said: 'Our aim is to keep this clean—Your aim will help.'

Jennie, second from right, dancing in Mildura.

That was a very positive year for me. A new house and a new school. The four years I spent at the Mildura High School were some of the happiest years of my life. I loved wearing the grey tunics, blazers and berets in the winter and the green cotton summer dresses. High school opened new horizons for me. I didn't feel the odd one out anymore. I could feel I was becoming very strong inside.

My grades were excellent and I always managed to be in the top three places when it was time for exams. I made the basketball and softball teams and travelled all over the country competing against other schools. I won the Etherington Cup for athletics when I was 15. I had my circle of friends and we were considered to be one of the 'important' groups. Not only did we excel at sports, but we were also the brains of the school. We tormented some of the teachers, but they couldn't do much about it, because our pranks were so well thought out and they couldn't really get too angry at us since we were all getting good grades. The only negative remarks I would get

on my report card were for talking too much in class or disturbing other students. I always loved making people laugh, especially when I knew they shouldn't be laughing and I could usually do it without batting an eyelid, which often kept me from getting caught.

As a teenager, going to church became more interesting. My friends and I no longer attended the Sunday morning church school, instead we went to church on Sunday evenings. My evening sessions were with a great group of fun-loving people. I felt privileged, because all the boys my age happened to belong to the Church of England, which meant when our friends split up on Sunday evenings, I got to go to the church with all the boys. I had a crush on Ivan, but there was a problem. I was taller than him, but I was also clever. I managed to cultivate a way of walking with bent knees so Ivan and I were on the same level. Then when I sat in the pew next to him I would slink down to make myself seem shorter.

The service for the Church of England was over before the Catholic one, which was held across the

Jennie with high school friends.

street. As soon as our service was done, I couldn't wait to dash across the road and into the church where my Catholic friends were. At that time I wanted to be Catholic. The Church of England was becoming a little boring. The Salvation Army was good, but modest, but I thought the Catholic Church was the utmost in religion, holiness and sanctimony. I would tip-toe in and see the marble bird bath. I longed to dip my fingers in it and make the sign of the cross, but I knew I shouldn't since I didn't belong there. I would stand and stare, transfixed as people were rising and falling to their knees, kissing their rosary beads and chanting in a strange language. I never knew if their faces held expressions of pain, terror or just fatigue from all that getting up and down. I longed to go with my friends and talk to the unknown figure hidden in the black box in the corner of the church. I wanted to tell him everything, knowing he couldn't repeat what he knew about me. Back at home I tried practising the sign of the cross in front of my bathroom mirror, but that wasn't enough to make

me really a part of the exotic world of the Catholic Church.

Over time, my desire to become Catholic eventually passed and it was replaced by a desire to become Jewish. I had a friend named Phyllis and one day she invited me to dinner with her family. When I arrived at her house, I entered another world. Again, I heard a strange language. Candles were lit and her father was sitting at the head of the table wearing a little cap on his head. After a few visits to her house I decided I wanted to be like them, so I had a chat with Phyllis about my intentions. 'Phyl, I love coming to your house to eat. Not only because your mother cooks such strange, interesting foods, which I like, but because meals with you are like a ceremony or party and your dad's always wearing that little cap. What's it all about?' She told me it wasn't a party. It was just their religion. They were Jewish. I asked how I could go about joining up myself, but she told me you had to be born into it. Well, so much for that.

I continued on with the Church of England, but I stopped praying at night. The priest told me he was convinced I only showed up in church before one of my sporting competitions to pray for my team to win. Perhaps he was right. By then I had stopped asking questions and listening to the sermons. Instead I found myself counting the mosaics on the wall or the number of pieces it took to put together one of the stained glass windows.

I was less interested in church, because I was too busy being a teenager: going to birthday parties, playing Spin the Bottle or Postman's Knock, having crushes on the senior boys and the prefects, giggling in the locker room about who was in love with whom. There were many parties amongst my friends and we would always invite the senior boys. It was the only way we could get them away from the senior girls. I especially remember Marianne Lind's 15th birthday party. I wore a beige corduroy velvet skirt with a lilac angora sweater, which my sister Joan had knitted for me. I had a crush on a senior named John and that night he walked me four doors down the street from her house to mine and he kissed me on the lips.

Marianne Lind was a very close friend of mine and she was one of the brains of our school.

Marianne seemed to know everything. She was the first amongst us to have the courage to use a tampax, whilst still a virgin. That was something we had been told was taboo. She was smart with her dates as well. If she didn't like a boy she was going out with, she would eat cloves of garlic before she met him. That boy would never ask her out again. She was also the one who taught me to strike a match if someone farted. One afternoon I went over to her house and found her in a frenzy striking match after match and screaming, 'Jennifer, help me light a few more matches. Tom is on his way over now. I really like him and I've been farting all day!' I had thought she had been trying to burn the house down so she could be rescued by him.

Marianne was my partner in crime the time we played hooky from school and went to the Ozone Cinema to see *Rock Around the Clock*. It was actually rare for me to skip school. School was my haven, but there were a few times I did skip. My most exciting day of playing hooky was when Queen Elizabeth and Prince Phillip came to Mildura. The students in our school lined up in Henderson Park—the park my father had designed—to greet the royal couple. When the Queen left, we were all to be herded back into school, but a few of us silently slipped out of the ranks. We got our bicycles and rode out toward the airport following the royal car. As their car passed us on a deserted road, we gave our final wave to our English sovereigns in private. The queen actually waved back! When we went back to school, we were caught and taken to the headmaster. We didn't get into trouble. When we explained that we had skipped school to get one more glimpse of the Queen, what could he say?

We always needed pocket money, so Marianne and I got part-time jobs at Woolworths on Saturday mornings. That wasn't always enough, so once or twice we wrote false notes to the school saying we were ill. We signed them respectively, 'Mrs Hanlon' and 'Mrs Lind'. Then, we would go work extra hours at Woolworths. During school hours we were safe. However, after school we spent most of our time on our hands and knees behind the counter trying to avoid any teachers or students.

I was on reasonably good terms with my mother throughout my high school years. I suppose my life was so full and exciting, I didn't have much time to get into myself. I was such a Miss Pringle in those days: anti-alcohol, anti-smoking, anti-anything which wasn't straight on the line.

Then when I was 16 and nearing the end of my fourth year of high school, my mother told me my school days would be over at the end of that year. It was time for me to a get a full-time job. At that time, my mother was working in the co-op packing sheds, filling little cartons with dried fruits. She said there were some decent young girls working in the factory who were making eight pounds a week. I screamed at her that I would sooner die than put raisins into packets! I begged and pleaded with her, but to no avail; she said I had to leave school. The dreaded day arrived. The school met in the assembly hall, so the teachers could wish all the students who were leaving good luck for the future. I was totally broken. I sobbed during the ceremony without a trace of modesty. My friends, who were going on to the fifth form to do their matriculation, were saying, 'Half your luck Jen. I wish I was getting out of this dump.' It didn't seem fair to me. I wasn't able to continue with my studies, when I desperately wanted to, whilst the kids who could afford to stay were only doing so to fill up the next couple of years. My life was shattered.

Although I couldn't change my mother's mind about staying in school, I stood firm about not going into the factory. I wasn't about to throw away four years of high school just to be a fruit packer. I had excellent references and knew typing and shorthand. I decided to use that to my advantage. I began to search for a job. The first advertisement I saw in the local paper said: 'New Zealand Insurance Company opening offices in Mildura—Wanted a Jnr Secretary.' I applied and got it! I was still bitter about having to leave school and I dreaded seeing my friends riding their bikes home everyday. I was very sad knowing that before long my life would not be connected to school anymore. At least on the weekends I would still see my friends when we got together in our basketball and softball teams. That was a little thread which still held us together.

Jennie and friends in Mildura.

It didn't take me long to get into my new life at the insurance company. Our office was affiliated with an adjoining office and I soon made friends with the girls who worked there. One of my class-mates also had gotten a job in the same office, so things weren't so bad. I had no other choice, so I tried to make the most of the situation. I discovered typing renewal notices for insurance gave me a lot of time to think. I would fantasise and daydream and before I knew it the clock showed 5.30 pm and it was time to leave. Insurance wasn't really up my alley. I never took much interest in what I was doing. However, I did my job well and that's all they expected from me. In spite of working full-time, my purse always seemed to be empty. I had to pay money for board to my mother and I had instalments on a Vespa motor scooter I had bought. My Vespa was my freedom. I couldn't wait to get on it and go soaring off down the street. In the summer I would ride for miles and miles, going nowhere.

I now had a new group of girlfriends and they were all quite crazy. Other people found us

entertaining. When I was younger I just wanted to be normal, now I enjoyed being considered rather odd. The more people spoke about us, the crazier we became. We didn't do odd things just for show, but for our own private entertain-ment. We all seemed to be naturally high. One of my new friends was Lorraine McWilliam, who everyone called Snooks. In **1957** Snooks and I began wearing mini skirts, which we had made ourselves. No one had ever seen skirts that short before and they set the tongues wagging in town whenever we walked down the street.

Mildura is situated on the Murray River across a bridge from New South Wales. The river was our haven and it was where we spent our weekends. Weeping willows and gum trees flanked the river-banks and the sandbars enabled us to walk a great distance across the massive stretch of water. As far as I was concerned, nowhere in the world could come close to that little paradise on the Murray River. Sunday was 'our' day. We would pack our picnic baskets and head to the river for eight hours of sun, swimming, eating and chatting. We didn't need drugs or alcohol. We just needed the sun, the fresh water of the Murray and our great friends. Boys weren't invited, although sometimes they crashed our picnics. By sunset our bodies would be frizzled. When the cool breeze of the evening began to set in, we knew another sacred Sunday was over, so we would prepare ourselves for our entrance back into town. We would create exotic hairstyles using gum leaves, twigs and wild flowers. Our towels would be turned into togas and with a final dab of lippy on the mouth, we were ready—ready to face our public. On our way home, we had certain places we would visit before we arrived at our respective homes. There was an Italian restaurant, oddly called The Mary Elizabeth. The Italians loved us and couldn't wait for our arrival on Sundays. Sometimes we would catch them making illegal grappa in the kitchen, but they trusted us not to talk about it. They would teach us a few Italian swear words, which we would use when we passed by the Italian fruit and veggie vendor, just to see the expression on his face. Our Sunday procession through the streets became sort of a local event. One time when I arrived home my mother seemed quite distressed. She said, 'Jennifer, I've been told you and your pack of girlfriends have been pushing old ladies into the gutter.' I assured her that wasn't at all true, 'No Mum, we only do that to old men and cripples.' We acted outrageous, but we were really all sweet and kind. We didn't bother anyone. We were always laughing and life seemed great to us.

Eventually most of my friends had Vespa motor scooters and those who didn't rode on the back of others. Our summer evenings were often spent at the local drive-in cinema. This event entailed preparation as well. Blankets and cushions had to be packed. The scooters would be parked by the side of the speakers, the blankets spread out and the cushions puffed up. It was a rather dangerous thing we did. More than once a car nearly ran over us as they tried to pull up to a place where they thought there wasn't a car. Even that made us laugh. We imagined the headlines in the local paper, 'Six Young Local Girls Flattened Out Like Pancakes at the Drive-in Cinema Last Night!' Before Mildura had a drive-in, the closest one was in Berry about 80 miles away. If we wanted to go

there, we needed the boys, since none of us girls had cars. We wouldn't think anything of driving all that way and back on a Saturday night just to see a movie.

When I was about to turn 17, I had to prepare to make my debut at the Church of England's Coming Out Ball. Once we had made our debut, we would be allowed to go out to the dance halls. There was no way any of us were allowed to go dancing before that. For the ball, we had to wear long white dresses and long white gloves. It was complete debutant style!

The most exciting thing about making your debut was choosing your partner. You could choose anyone you wanted and you just hoped you wouldn't be turned down. I knew lots of boys and there were also my brother's friends, who would have been happy to accompany me. Actually my brother's friends could have covered my entire group of girl friends, if the boys we really wanted had refused us. A long list was made with comments noted by each name. Just for fun, I put down Barry Kilpatrick, one of the most popular boys in town. Barry was a few years older than me and he had been the head prefect when I was in the second form of high school. His younger brother John had been the one who kissed me after Marianne's party. I had seen Barry every day in school and I suppose he had seen me, but that was it. Soon the idea of going with Barry became an obsession. I thought he would most likely refuse, but I knew that if he did he would be very polite about it and give me some believable excuse. I didn't have the courage to ask him myself. When I discussed my outrageous idea with my friend Betty Lewis, she offered to call him and ask him pretending she was me. I thought that could work. After all, Barry had never spoken to either of us, so he wouldn't know our voices. I was shocked when I heard he accepted 'my' invitation! I never understood why. Perhaps he was too polite to refuse or maybe he also found the idea amusing.

Not only did Barry agree to be my date, but even before the ball we started a relationship together, which lasted for five years. He was my first steady boyfriend and I was very much in love, as a 17 year old should be. When I was presented to the Archbishop of St. Arnaud, I was sporting two

Barry and Jennie at the Coming Out Ball.

in Queensland one Christmas. I was so excited and my mother was even more so. Dad wanted to know what sort of food I liked and what I would like to see whilst I was there. I travelled to Brisbane and went to a hotel where I was to stay until Dad could come pick me up the next day. But then he telephoned me at the hotel. He told me he wasn't coming to get me. He apologised and said he couldn't have me as his guest for personal reasons. I was torn to pieces. When I got back home I told my mother *I* had decided *I* didn't want to see him. She was so angry with me, but I had too much pride to tell her the truth.

Over all the years since my father had left, my mother had never said a bad word about him. In fact she never really spoke of my father at all. I think it would have been better for me if she had told me what had happened between them, so I had a clearer view of the truth. Instead, she said nothing and just left a photograph of him in his army uniform on the mantelpiece. I always treasured Dad's letters and considered him a sort of mentor for me. In my mind, my mum was the wrong doer, but years later I found out I had it all back to front.

black love bites on my neck, which my *décolleté* neckline didn't cover. As I was getting out of the bath tub before the ball, my mother asked me, 'What on earth are those marks on your neck?' I casually said, 'Oh nothing, Mum. I've probably been bitten by some insect. There're lots of them around ya know...' My mother adored Barry and my brother said I had made a good choice. Everyone in my family was happy and so was I.

Over all the years, I continued to correspond with my father. I often sent him photographs of myself growing up. He always answered in such a poetic and wise way that it made me put him up on a pedestal. There was only one time I ever got close to seeing him when I was a teenager. He had invited me to visit with his new family

Seventeen was a glorious year for me. I had a wonderful loving boyfriend, caring girlfriends and many activities to keep me busy. I swam in the swimming club, played competitive basketball and softball and I marched with the Rowing Club marching team, which won the Victorian Championship Cup one year. I also sang in the Gilbert and Sullivan theatre group with my crazy girlfriends.

Meanwhile my brother, Alan, had reached the height of respectability in our town. He was vice-president of the Rowing Club, a Mason, played the trumpet in the local brass band and was much sought after by the young women. He was good looking, sportive and a little shy. His sense of humour was as dry as a riverbed after a drought. Alan and I shared that same sense of humour—poker faced. My mother fell for everything he said. 'Hey Mum, you know Jen got a job in the kissing booth at the Rowing Club Regatta next week? She can make a bit of extra cash that way.' I would immediately pick up on what he was doing and join in with, 'Don't worry Mum, men over 60 aren't allowed in.' Mum would scream and yell thinking we were serious. She didn't find it amusing at all. Alan was also my best friend. If I ever had trouble with Barry, he would wait around the dance hall and take me out for a late supper at the Rendezvous Café to cheer me up. He would also let me swap my Vespa for his car whenever I needed it. My brother was wonderful and I often found myself surrounded by adoring women, who used me to try to get through to Alan. His friends all looked after me as much as he did. They were my personal security guards and they made me feel very safe during those years.

Towards the end of my 17th year, something strange happened to me. Something inside me began going amok, for what reason I will never know. I was having a problem at the office keeping my eyes open. As soon as lunch time came around, I would go to the back of the office and fall into a deep sleep. After work, I hurried home and refused to go out again. I was anxious to just get into bed. My sleep was tormented and when I awoke I felt as though all the nerves in my body were having a tug of war. I began to fear the days and dread the nights. I didn't discuss my fears with anyone, because I didn't know what to tell them. Eventually I decided to see a doctor. The doctor sat me down and began firing questions at me about my life and my family. He told me I was having a nervous breakdown. He wasn't sure why and I couldn't figure out what would be causing it either. I begged the doctor not to tell my mother or anyone else that I had seen him. When I presented my prescription at the chemist, he was quite amazed that the medicine was being prescribed for me. Fortunately the medicine seemed to work. It calmed my days and let me sleep at night.

I had been with Barry long enough that everyone was waiting for us to put a mortgage on a

Jennie's father's photo on the mantel.

house and start setting the date. That was the usual procedure then, to have the house half paid off before you got married. Personally, I hadn't really thought much about it myself. Then Barry told me he and his father were going to go opal digging. He promised to bring me back the biggest opal he could find. He went away for a few months. He wrote to me regularly and I thought I missed him. After all, we had been together for quite some time. Finally, he came back. He was the same sweet Barry, but he had grown a moustache. Nothing else had changed, except for the moustache. God knows why, but I took one look at him and instantly realised it was over between us. The moustache must have been an excuse in my head, because the next day he had shaved it off and I still felt the same. He showed me the opal he wanted to have set in gold as an engagement ring. When he said that, I felt a little hidden devil come to life in me. I told him if he wanted to give me a present, that was fine, but I didn't want it if there were conditions attached. Something had broken

Jennie on the basketball team and on the Rowing Club marching team.

The Gilbert and Sullivan theatre group.

for me, I just knew nothing he could say would bring my feeling back for him. It was very difficult for me to explain, because there was no explanation. It was nothing he had done, it was just as if a door had closed. I didn't feel sad or sorry. I didn't feel anything at all.

No one could understand what happened. My mother was furious and refused to let me go out. My brother was disappointed. He was very fond of Barry, but as usual Alan respected my decision. Barry was a dear, sweet person. I had really loved him, but maybe I just wasn't ready to settle down. Perhaps my secret breakdown had something to do with my decision to break with Barry. I feared that terrible feeling might come back. I began to think the only solution would be for me to go away from my roots, however I wasn't quite ready to leave just yet. When my mother finally cooled

down and let me go out again, I went on with my life as usual. Mildura was a small town so I saw Barry frequently, but I now saw him simply the way I saw all of my other friends.

The Rowing Club became the centre of my social life. I was on their marching team and on Sunday evenings they held a dance in their Club House on the river. Mildura was beginning to change. It seemed to be filling up with city folks. Teachers were coming in to teach at the local schools, nurses from afar were working in the hospital. Even Alan had begun dating a young woman from the city whose name was Barbara. I kept coming into contact with so many new and interesting people. All these city people were different. They dressed differently, danced differently and talked differently—and I found I liked their differences.

21

Barry and Jennie.

asked again, 'Jen, you don't think you have hepatitis or something, do you? You've gone a weird yellow colour.' Oh dear, I guess I must have put on too much tanning lotion! Fortunately by the next day it had toned down a bit to more of an orange colour, so I didn't look sick for the ceremony. Alan had made it in many ways and this was his big day. I was so happy for him, but I was also a bit sad. All my life Alan had been my brother, my father, my advisor, and my protector and now he was leaving home to start the next phase of his life with Barbara.

Soon Alan and Barbara became engaged and Alan set out building their house, so it would be ready for them when they got married. Since he had left school at 14, Alan had gone from job to job. He had never learnt a profession, so finding a good job wasn't easy for him. Around the time he became engaged, good luck came his way. Alan answered an ad in the local paper looking for a representative for a large city company, which was opening an office in Mildura. He got the job and the owner of the company immediately took a liking to him. Within a short time Alan became one of the directors of the office. He also became like a second son for the owner. I was so happy for him. As far as I was concerned, Alan deserved every good thing that came to him.

When I was 18 years old, Alan and Barbara were married. They had asked me to be one of their bridesmaids. Their wedding was in July, which is the middle of winter in Australia and I had decided that since my dress was white and lemon satin it would look better if I had some sort of a tan. The night before the wedding, I applied a tanning lotion to my face and body. That night Alan took me to a Chinese restaurant for dinner for his last night as a single man. He kept staring at me during our meal and finally he asked me if I felt alright. I told him I felt just fine and was looking forward to the big event the next day. He

Around this time, I had met a young school teacher named Keith, who had became my steady escort. He was from the city, spoke quietly, wore crewneck sweaters, desert boots and a kerchief around his neck. He was polite and interesting and he was filling my head with city lights. Keith and I always had a good time together when we went out, but there was never any necking in the car or petting by the river late at night. That didn't really bother me. I figured he must be too sophisticated for that. Maybe city people didn't use cars and river banks for such things. I was 18 years old and still a virgin. Most of my friends were too. Times were different then and virgins were plentiful in my group. Barry had tried desperately to 'take it' and nearly did on many occasions. He never insisted too much, since he thought we would be getting married in the near future. I enjoyed what Barry and I did when we were alone, especially down by the river at night, however I didn't have the courage to take the big leap. Alan seemed rather agitated about my new romance with Keith. One day he approached me and told me I should either go back to Barry or get myself another boyfriend. He didn't think Keith was right for me. What he was trying to tell me in a roundabout way, was that Keith was gay. Apparently I had just met my first homosexual man and hadn't realised it.

Mildura friends.

I began to think more about moving out of Mildura. That nervous breakdown had triggered something in me, which made me feel the only way to clear my head was to go a long way from home. Even during good times, I was still very closed, although everyone always had the impression I was the most open, easy going person around. I was the one my friends all came to when they had secrets to tell or needed someone to listen to their problems. They thought I didn't have any of my own, but I did have secrets, cobwebs and ghosts in my head. I had many—probably too many to cope with.

When I was 19, I decided to apply for a transfer to Melbourne to the head office of the insurance company and was accepted. The whole town knew I was making plans to leave for the city before my mother did. I didn't have the courage to tell her. She was broken when she heard the news from other people. I know it was rotten of me not to tell her myself, but I always had a problem telling her anything. I just hoped she would understand. After all, Melbourne wasn't so far away and I would be coming home for weekends and holidays.

I loved Mildura. It was an easy going town where I had wonderful friends, a good steady job, and my mother and brother were there. In going to Melbourne I wasn't running away from my town or the people in it. I was leaving because of the dark fragments of my past, which still tormented me. I knew I would be anonymous in a big city. I hoped that if I cut all ties for the time being, maybe I could get rid of my ghosts forever. Wendy, a friend of mine from school, was planning to move to Melbourne with me. There were many farewell parties for us and many tears shed. We were all growing up and things were bound to change. I cried for weeks, which wasn't hard for me. Crying has always come easy to me, whether from happiness or sadness. Before I got on the train, heading off to my new unknown future, Alan stuffed a few pounds into my purse and said, 'Keep smiling Jen. Keep smiling.' I think I cried all the way to Melbourne.

Getting Rid of the Hayseeds From My Hair

Our parents had arranged for Wendy and I to stay in a hostel for decent young ladies when we first arrived in Melbourne. We immediately named it 'The Virgins' Retreat'. The girls who stayed there came from all different places and backgrounds. Most were wholesome young girls whose parents didn't want them out on their own in the big city. The hostel had a curfew of 11.00 pm. We had to sign an 'Out and In' book telling where we were going whenever we left and no boys were allowed. I loved the hostel. It was the closest experience I ever had to living in a college dormitory. I knew it would take time to get adjusted to my new city life. I had a lot to learn and I planned to learn as much as I could to broaden my outlook.

My big city lessons began about an hour after our arrival at the hostel. I was allotted a room to share with a girl named Marty. Marty had freckles and a temper to go with her fiery red hair. She was not quite like anyone I had ever met in Mildura. At times, she could be rather sweet, but then she would explode into foul language. She was what my friends back home would have called 'sort of sluttish'. In the wee hours of the morning, after she had climbed up the drain pipe to our bedroom window, she would give me her never-ending descriptions of what she did with the American sailors who were in port that night. Her stories went well past even my most vivid imagination. I would lie in the dark as she told me all the sordid details, while I would grunt in response, not really wanting to hear anymore. I was always terrified she would ask me about my own sexual experiences. What could I say? I could never own up to her that I was still a virgin.

I really didn't mind having Marty as my room-mate. I found her very amusing. Whatever she did in her private life had nothing to do with me. I just took it all in as part of my new schooling. One evening when I came home from the office, I entered our room and found Marty there and she seemed to be talking to the ceiling. I looked up and saw a girl on top of our wardrobe. Marty was telling her to jump. She gave me a side glance and said, 'I've just given the silly bitch a bottle of gin to drink and I stuck her in a hot bath, but nothin' happened. Now I'm trying to get her to jump off the wardrobe to see if that will shake the baby out of her.' 'Oh, I see...' I answered casually as I proceeded to go about my regular chores, as if what was happening in the room was absolutely normal. Back in Mildura, the word abortion had never been mentioned and I certainly had never met a person who had had one, but I didn't want to tell Marty that I was that naive.

I led a very quiet life for the first few months I was in Melbourne. I didn't want those little monsters popping out in my head again, so I thought lots of sleep and a healthy lifestyle were the answer for the time being. It didn't take long for me to gather a new group of friends around me at the hostel. As usual, they were all wonderfully mad in their own ways. Tiffany Forward from Adelaide became a very close friend. She was from a wealthy family and was very spoilt. She could be quite difficult at times. I'm sure her family had sent her to Melbourne to get her out of their hair. Tiffany was a bit deaf and wore a hearing aid. She would turn it off when she was in a bad mood just to make us all crazy. I loved Tiffany, she was another giggler. A few times she took me to Adelaide to stay with her family on weekends and to meet her 'posh, pissy friends' as she called them.

Kitty was another favourite of all the girls. Kitty was my alarm clock in the mornings. She would awaken me at 6.30 am on the dot, without fail. Kitty was deaf and mute and by the time I left the hostel, I had learnt to talk fluently with my hands because of her. She took me into a world of silence and showed me how full the lives of deaf mutes can be. Kitty's boyfriend would pick us up in his car and take us to parties with all their deaf friends. I was always a bit nervous on the way since I knew he couldn't hear any car horns or sirens as he drove. All their friends seemed to love dancing. They would turn up the volume until the music was blaring and then they would dance in rhythm to the vibrations. Then, their conversations would begin. There would be silence as many topics were discussed and opinions exchanged. Sometimes when they got excited over a subject, strange noises would come out of their throats. I tried to

Jennie with friends in Melbourne.

keep up with their hands to follow the conversations. Kitty was part of our special group of friends and we didn't leave her out of anything, so we all began talking with our hands whenever she was present. It actually turned out to be quite useful at times. We were never caught by the matron whenever we had an all-night pyjama party, because we never made any noise. After a short time in the hostel, I felt I was cured. I had locked away those horrid, little monsters forever.

The first day in my new office was quite nerve racking. In Mildura, I had worked with only three other people. Now in Melbourne, I was confronted with 200 new faces. I was given a tour of the building by a kind man, who introduced me as, 'the young lady who had come all the way from Mildura to join them.' I was greeted by a sea of very kind faces and warm welcoming words, even though I knew they could all see the hayseeds sticking out of my hair.

Amongst the sea of new faces we came to a sandy-coloured crewcut. I was introduced to Vern Lambert, who was dressed in the chicest, well-tailored, tiny-chequered suit with a pair of black patent-leather, pointed-toed shoes. My meeting with Vern felt almost electric. I thought he seemed like such a kind and elegant young man. What he saw in me with my country clothes and rotten shoes, I will never know. Yet some sort

of chemistry passed between us. It only took a couple of days before I was assigned to be Vern's secretary whenever he needed help. Apparently he had worked quickly telling his boss that he had masses of letters to be written every day and the new arrival would be a big help to him.

When he needed help, Vern would call for me in a very businesslike manner, stating there was work to be done in his office. The first day I was called to his tiny office, which was the size of a broom cupboard, Vern immediately locked the door behind me. He told me the letters would take no more than five minutes, but we had to pretend there was enough work to keep us busy for the entire morning. I wasn't nervous about being locked in the room with Vern. I didn't feel any sexual vibes from him. We would write a few lines to a client and then we would get to the real work he had in mind for me. He wanted to teach me about life: the city, art, fashion and music. My relationship with Vern was the fastest and closest friendship I have ever encountered in my whole life. I had arrived in Melbourne thinking I knew a bit about life, but I quickly discovered I knew next to nothing. As my new school began, Vern would take me out to museums, bars, restaurants and concerts. All the places he thought would get rid of those hayseeds from my hair. He was teaching me so much, not only about culture, but how to

Jennie and Vern in Melbourne.

act. I was learning to walk into places I had never been and not feel out of place. Vern must have seen me as the perfect student: innocent, curious and progressing further as each day passed.

Our fellow workers who had known Vern for a long time would often ask me if I had gone out with Vern the night before. They knew he was now my regular date. They wanted to know where we had gone and what we did. The last question they asked me was always the same. 'And what did you do after...?' I would tell them the truth. 'He escorted me home, of course. Then I presume he went home too.' I never knew what they were trying to get out of me. I just enjoyed Vern's company.

Back in Mildura, Alan's wife, Barbara, had given birth to twins, Julie and Peter. When they were about eight months old, Alan called me and asked if I could come to Mildura for a couple of weeks and look after the children. He was desperate. Barbara was exhausted and needed to

get away for a rest. I never had any real experience with small babies, especially two of them at once, but I agreed to help them out. I got through the two weeks, but just barely. The twins had just started crawling. They seemed to crawl all over the place in completely opposite directions at the same time. Instead of one baby crying, there were two. I would run from one to the other, pampering each one in turn. So much went wrong while I was there. I nearly poisoned my brother and lost an arm during those two weeks. I was trying to do all I could to help out, so I prepared dinner for Alan each night. I decided I could cut my work down if I made a big pot of stew, which would last for a few days. I left it in the same saucepan and reheated it each evening. After about three days, it went bad. I didn't know and when Alan ate the poisoned stew, he ended up rolling around with poison pains. Meanwhile, I was also helping with the laundry. They had an electric wringer to wring out the excess water from the clothes after they were washed. I must have been exhausted whilst I was using it, because I didn't notice when my hand and then my arm disappeared with clothes under the wringer! It was like a cartoon, where Jerry gets flattened out by some heavy object Tom dropped on him. I let out a piercing scream and Alan had to come dashing in and turn off the power. I think by the end of my two weeks with him, Alan had had about enough of all my 'help' around the house.

In addition to writing Vern's letters, I also worked in the back of a large room typing renewal notices again. I didn't mind. I knew the system and I knew it would give me plenty of time to daydream. I was seated next to the Duggen sisters, who I had met back in the Gilbert and Sullivan group in Mildura. They were in Melbourne to study opera singing. As they typed their renewal notices, they were dreaming about La Scala in Milan. I didn't know what La Scala was, but as usual, I nodded in approval. I spent many years nodding when people told me something I didn't know. I didn't want to own up to being ignorant about what was being talked about. The two large-breasted sisters were gigglers, so working with them was fun. We were so far at the back of the room, we could chat away to our hearts content. They decided they would give me singing lessons as we worked. The lessons started with nasal exercises, which make a sound like a nasal hum. It made my nose tingle. It took the manager of the department weeks to figure out where that weird noise was coming from. When he found out it came from the 'bush trio' in the back of the room, my singing lessons were abruptly stopped.

I was never promoted, but that was fine with me. I knew insurance policies and renewal notices were not my future. Once I was given a new job on the central telephone exchange. I lasted about 15 minutes in that position. It was too complicated and dangerous for me. All the lines seemed to ring at the same time. I pulled out the line nearest to me, but then didn't have a clue where to plug it in to make the connection. I tried to think and stay calm, but I couldn't. I had a pencil in my hand. I began chewing on the end of it, but I quickly realised it wasn't the pencil. It was the telephone plug and it gave me a slight electric shock! I screamed so loud half the staff came running to my assistance. That was it. I refused to ever do that job again.

For my 21st birthday my mother wanted to give me a big party at the Mildura Rowing Club. I invited all of my old school friends along with my new friends from the office. Vern was the first to accept. We all took a train from Melbourne together filling up more than one entire compartment. It was an overnight journey, so the girls put their hair up in rollers to be ready for their arrival. My brother met us at the station. He told me our mum had sent him ahead to check out the party guests. Not long before, I had gone home for a weekend wearing a duffle coat, with my hair teased up in a beehive hairdo and my eyes heavily

Jennie with her mom and Alan and Barbara's twins.

Jennie's 21st birthday.

made up with black kohl. That was the style in the beatnik era, but my mother didn't approve. Mum was terrified my new friends would be a bunch of freaks, so she had sent Alan to give her a report on what to expect. She was pleased to learn my new friends were not as crazy as she had feared.

Back in Melbourne, I continued my education with Vern. He often talked about a trip he had once taken to Europe. His dream was to go back there in the near future and he tried to convince me that I should follow him. He thought it was necessary to further my education. Then one day Vern was gone—destination, London. The office just wasn't the same without him, so I decided it was time for a change. I found a new job as secretary to Steven Komloshy, a Hungarian who worked in a textile office. Now instead of being in a large office filled with people, I spent most of my days alone answering a telephone and typing. When my boss came in, he would quickly dictate a few letters and then proceed to tell me about Hungary, the homeland he had fled from back in **1956**. Tears would come to his eyes as he brought back his past. I promised him that when I went to Europe I would visit Budapest just for him.

My school friend Snooks had also moved to Melbourne. She was training to be a nurse at Queen Victoria Hospital, which was right across

from my office. When she was in the operating theatre, she would telephone Mr Komloshy and we would hang out our window and wave across the street to her.

By this time I had left the hostel and was living in a small house on Punt Road, South Yarra, along with Wendy and Jan, a new friend of ours who was studying at the university. I began taking dance classes at the Rex Reid School of Dance, which was one of the best dance schools in Melbourne. I took lessons in classical, character and modern dance four evenings a week and two other evenings I attended a gym. The modern classes were new to me and they were wonderful. I soon realised that was what I should have been studying for years.

Taking six classes a week didn't stop my social life. I fell in with a group of Asian students who were fun loving and fast living. I called this my Asian Period. My big love was Joey Wong. Joey was probably the most despicable, nasty little Chinese boy in the whole city, but he had a tremendous charm in a weird way. He would appear at parties dressed in a white linen suit and a white Panama hat. He would be sure he was always the last to arrive and then he would walk in and announce himself saying, 'Joey's here, gang!' as he pulled himself up to his full 5 feet 4 inches. Joey wanted to marry me just so he could stay in Australia after he had finished his studies. I adored him, but not enough to marry him. I had almost considered letting him take my virginity, but I still had the idea it was for a special occasion and for a very special person. I still wanted to fall in love forever and ever, Amen. My mother was beside herself when I told her about my escapades. She quickly wrote a note pleading for me to come to my senses:

Dear Jennifer, Can't you find yourself a nice Australian boy or at least someone whose eyes aren't slanting upwards!
Love, Mum

Joey was very pompous and he hated when anyone made fun of him. He considered himself a 'Lady Killer' and thought he could get any woman he wanted. I decided I would show him. I got the telephone number of the Melbourne Zoo and one evening when Joey arrived, I told him a friend of mine had just arrived in Melbourne from Europe. I said my friend, Miss Lion, was a very beautiful model who needed an escort for the night and I thought he would be the perfect man. When I gave him her number, Joey swelled up like a peacock. He must have thought I was the greatest girl a man could have. The idea that I would lend my boyfriend out to some other woman made me very special in his eyes. He dialled the number and in his best English asked to speak to Miss Lion. 'This is Joey Wong here. I want to speak to Miss Lion, please.' *Pause* 'LION… L-I-O-N.' *Pause.* 'What do you mean calling me a bloody loony? I want to speak to Miss Lion.' *Pause.* 'What did you say? I'm speaking to the zoo? Miss Lion has already been put in her friggin' cage for the night!?' Joey slammed down the receiver. He didn't find my sense of humour so funny that evening…

I went through my surfing period around that same time. I spent many weekends at the beach in Ocean Grove with my friends and the surf boys. At first, I found the surf boys a bit on the fast side for me, but when I got to know them better, they treated me well and with respect. The strongest

Jennie and Snooks.

language I had ever heard up until then was 'bloody bugger' and 'bastard'. Then one night at a barbecue on the beach one of the boys got up and shouted 'Fuck!' It made the hair on my arms stand up. I was grateful it was dark, so no one could see the blood rise to my face.

Most of the boys I knew were about the same age as myself. Then I met David, who was 27 years old—to me he seemed like a real man. He lived around the corner from our house in a flat which he shared with a man named Bob. Their life style was more grown up and I started to grow a little more when I was with them, or at least it felt that way to me. I occasionally began to have a glass of wine or a Pimms No. 1, which was the Australian drink for beginners. I loved riding around the

Jennie at Ocean Grove.

town in David's red MG or having dinner with David, Bob and Snooks in their apartment.

During my relationship with David, I heard a new word—'cunt'. I asked Snooks what it meant, but she didn't know either, so we decided to ask our friend Dennis Payne, who was a policeman. We had always been taught, when in trouble, go to the police for help. When we asked him, he told us to forget it and never mention that word in public again. Now we were more curious than ever to find out what it meant. It had to be worse than the F word. David and Bob were giving a big open house party at their apartment and Snooks and I got there early to give them a hand. We mentioned the word to them and asked them to tell us what it meant. When they giggled and told us to forget it, we threatened to get up on the table and call out 'Cunt, Cunt, Cunt' as each guest arrived. They knew we were serious, so David finally gave us a

confusing definition of the word. He said it was 'a vagina full of boiled snow.' That didn't really help us understand what it meant, but we decided to let the subject drop since he was the only one who had at least tried to explain it to us.

I decided to take David to Mildura to meet my mother. She had wanted me to find a nice man and settle down and she adored David. However something happened on that trip. The moment we arrived in Mildura, something clicked and I lost interest in him. Once again I felt a door close and I wanted out. David didn't want to give me opals like Barry, but he did come home one day with a baby kangaroo he had found in the bush. I took one look at the little joey and told him to take it back where he had found it. David seemed to be different in Mildura, although it was more likely that I was the one who was different. He wanted to get married, but I wasn't interested. I wasn't interested in him as a husband or even as a boyfriend anymore. There have been quite a few men over the years who I thought I was in love with, but then one word or one action, could make me change my mind in a matter of seconds. I suppose that meant it was never really love in the first place.

Since he had left for London, Vern kept writing me amazing letters. His stories were incredibly colourful and exciting and at times quite bizarre. I could sense he was going through some massive changes.

Darlink, I just can't tell you what a ball we're having, so I'll jot down a few little phrases and hope you can make sense of it all.

Went to a party run by an Australian model, Pauline O'Dwyer, heavily sloshed lots of cha-cha… Bought the most fabulous Italian suit. All the wenches are wearing leather to death. LEATHER coats, hats, slacks, vests and they never get out of black stockings… too much for a white man from Melb. …Bought the most fabulous blazer, the full 1920s number, mad stripes etc. in black and brown & a big matching umbrella, look the full dapper.

Last Saturday just for shrieks we went to a Rock Show at the Albert Hall and sat in a marvellous box. Of course I was furious that I didn't wear my leather jacket and by the time I arrived they had sold out of chewing gum, I didn't tell them what I thought of them... Keith Richards sang with The Shadows and everyone thought he was marvellous although they couldn't hear him, cause they had such a lot of screaming to do... I got an almighty headache and really enjoyed myself immensely.

I've conned the most fabulous job as a waiter in the jazziest restaurant. It's only a tiny restaurant with lots of carpets, candles, antiques and brass. The maddest mixture of old and contemporary imaginable. Cliental consists of rich American tourists and wealthy Englishmen, Peerage, Actors, Film Producers. I jazz around in a hounds tooth checked shirt and black cotton daks as tight as possible (almost obscene) and a big white apron... Vivien Leigh arrived at the Restaurant last night and I had the pleasure of waiting on her. She was in a marvellous mood and just so jazz, also had her fiancee with her - that made my evening, even though I didn't get home until 3.00 am and am feeling the effects now. As I mentioned before the restaurant has black carpet and is dimly lit. Some woman arrived with a black poodle last night, which could not be distinguished in the gloom. Vern comes sweeping through with plates of goodies and puts his little footsy right into the doggies's stomach - the resulting chaos was hysterical as you can imagine. ...we have had Joan Collins & James Darren in twice... Bing Crosby & wife. Lionel Bart (who wrote the musical 'Oliver') Duke of Bedford & a few Continental Counts and Royalty... business is booming and Vern's pocket is benefiting accordingly.

Lover when are you coming over to iron my shirts... with your talent and beauty you shouldn't be wasting away in the Colonies. Darlinks I must swirl as we are tottering off to a rather jazzbo coffee-bar (Cafe des Artisit') which is mentally beat and madly jazz, but blasted with the music, like...
Love, darlinks, heavy cha-cha. Vern XXXX

The place Vern was working was Parks restaurant in Beauchamp Place. It was a favourite of the in-crowd and Vern met so many famous people there. Once he wrote to say Rudolf Nureyev had given him a Russian fur hat as a present. Other times he saw Princess Margaret who came there for a 'casual' night out. Vern was so popular at the restaurant that they had Vernon dishes and Vernon cocktails on the menu. He promised me that when he went to Amsterdam he would send me a Dutch cap. Apparently you didn't put them on your head. Dutch caps were what they called condoms in Holland. He also told me about a friend of his in London who went into a drug store and asked for Durex with Mickey Mouse on it. Durex in Australia is scotch tape and in England it was a brand name for condoms. I loved Vern's letters, but they did make me feel unsettled. I wanted to be in Europe experiencing it all with him, but it seemed so far away and my bank account was so empty.

Sister Hanlon in Tasmania

Snooks left her job at the hospital in Melbourne. She was now in Tasmania where she was working as a private nurse for an old lady. One day she called and told me the family she was working for was in need of more help and she asked if I thought I could pretend to be a qualified nurse. Snooks said the salary was good, there were no expenses and the place was beautiful. I thought, *Why not?* Pretending to be a nurse may sound a bit crazy, but I think I inherited my father's knack for taking on all sorts of jobs without having any previous qualifying experience. Throughout my life I often told people I could do a job and then would just improvise until I figured out my way. Somehow that always seemed to work for me.

I had spent four very happy years in Melbourne, but it felt like it was time to move on, so I accepted the position. When my ticket arrived, I said a tearful goodbye to my Hungarian boss promising him again that one day I would send him a postcard from Budapest. As I flew over the Bass Strait to Tasmania, I hoped that after one year of working as a 'qualified nurse', Snooks and I would have enough money to go to Europe together.

The job was in New Norfolk, a small village outside of Hobart. The enormous family estate, which was named 'Valley Fields', consisted of a manor house and 14 small cottages where their workers lived with their families. The farm grew hops for beer and it had the biggest kiln for drying hops in Tasmania. I soon learnt it wasn't unusual to see a load of tourists streaming down the tree-lined entrance of the farm to look at the kiln.

Nellie Maude Warner was our patient. She must have been in her mid-80s, although no one was really sure. The family couldn't find her documents. She had suffered from Parkinson's disease for many years. A number of nurses had previously been employed by Nellie, but she could be a very difficult patient, so most of them only lasted a short time. We had been warned that if Nellie didn't like us we should just pack our bags and get

out. Her eldest son ran the estate. Actually, that was not quite true. Nellie Maude ran the estate from her bed and her son did what he was told. Mentally she was very alert and nothing could be done on the property without consulting her first. Her son was known to the locals as the Lord of the Manor. He and his wife, Mary, had two children who were attending The Hutchins School. The same boarding school Errol Flynn had attended in his youth.

I was now Sister Hanlon and I knew from the start I was going to be gloriously happy in my new beautiful surroundings. Snooks and I shared a charming bedroom in the attic. Which ever of us was on night duty would sleep in the adjoining room to Nellie Maude, so we could hear if she cried out or needed help during the night. She was completely paralysed, so we had to do everything for her. We would have to turn her over in bed, lift her into her wheelchair and slide her into the bath tub each morning.

The house was quite isolated. We were completely cut off from the world with no social life and no friends. It was just Nellie Maude, her son, his wife and Snooks and I at the house. Laughter was the only pastime we had. Mary Warner was a super lady. She was also a laugher, so the three of us got on incredibly well together. Her husband was charming, but quite reserved. He never understood what we had to laugh about all the time, so he would excuse himself after dinner, leaving the three of us alone to have fun together.

Nellie liked Snooks and me and her family was relieved to have finally found two nurses she could get along with. We entertained Nellie in ways she had never known before and we got her to laugh along with us. One of her favourite pastimes was to have us make her up. We would pull out her makeup and put bright red lipstick on her lips, paint her nails and then put a little rouge on her white powdered cheeks. To finish her off, we would pull up her wispy, white hair and fix it at the back with a large, black Spanish comb. She loved it. She would giggle so much her little body would practically go into spasms.

Bath days were a joy for Nellie, at least the way we did them. Snooks and I would soap up the head of the tub, sit her on the edge and then carefully let her slide into the water. She would giggle and ask for another ride before we began the serious work of washing her up.

We kept a very orderly daily routine. It began with giving Nellie breakfast in bed. After washing and dressing her, we would take her out into the garden in her wheelchair. Then we had an hour of being serious as the daily paper was read from top to bottom and front to back. Nellie listened to us attentively, never missing a word. I remember the day we heard John Kennedy's speech about the Bay of Pigs. Snooks and I were worried it might affect our trip to Europe. Then a while later, we read of Marilyn Monroe's death. We all shed a few tears as we discussed Marilyn's life, her films and her beauty. After our intellectual hour was over, it was time for games. We would wheel Nellie over to the tennis court and leave her near the fence out of harm's way, while Snooks and I played. She enjoyed watching us, but would threaten to throw us both out if we hit her with a ball. We would give her lunch and then put on her favourite, black felt hat and take her for a drive around the country-side in the old Vauxhall car we had at our disposal. Her supper was served in bed and then the three of us would settle down to watch the telly.

During my stay in Valley Fields, I decided to get my driving licence. I figured it would be easy in such a small town. Before this, I had only driven when my brother had swapped his little green Mini Minor for my Vespa scooter. I was under age back then, so I had to keep it a secret from my mother. I knew how to drive. I just needed to learn the rules of the road to pass the test. On the morning of my test, I felt very confident. The examiner had me drive all around the country roads. I never passed or even saw one other car. Parking was easy since we were in the middle of nowhere. As we were heading back to the police station, the man said everything had gone fine and I would have no trouble passing the exam. That

Jennie and Snooks.

33

made me so excited that instead of stopping the car in front of the police station, I put my foot on the gas and went straight into the building itself! All the policemen inside came running out. They must have thought a bomb had been thrown at the building. Not surprisingly, I was told I didn't pass the test, but they did let me come back the following week. I was better behaved the second time and was given my licence.

Nellie's mind was still very alert, but there were little things she couldn't quite put together. When it was time for her to sleep she would say, 'Girls, please turn off the telly. I don't want all those strange people watching me when I am on the commode.' Over time, Nellie's mind began to wander more and more. She would get very confused and forget things. Once we had read her an article about the Japanese waifs the Australian soldiers had left behind in Japan after the war. Later as I walked into her bedroom, she asked Snooks, 'Sister, when did that Japanese girl arrive?' Instead of trying to explain that the Japanese girl was me, Snooks and I made a theatre out of it and played the parts with me shuffling around the room, bowing and mumbling to Nellie in my made up Japanese language.

The truth finally came out about me not being a qualified nurse when Nellie developed a large wart-like growth on her hand. They called in Dr Sweetie (that was his real name, believe it or not) who decided the growth had to be removed. That entailed a small operation, which was to be done in the house. Snooks and I were to assist Dr Sweetie. As he began to cut into Nellie's hand and blood started gushing out, Snooks suddenly felt ill and had to leave the room. I was left alone as his assistant. The doctor handed me a pair of scissors and told me to cut after he sewed. I followed his instructions, *snip, snip, snip...* and thought to myself that being a nurse wasn't so difficult. During the procedure, the doctor chattered on about modern medicine and new drugs. When he began asking my opinion on certain matters concerning the medical world, I was silent. I didn't know what to say. When he didn't get any response, he asked, 'You are a nurse, aren't you?' I knew I had to admit the truth. I wasn't a nurse. I was a secretary. Fortunately when the family heard

the news, they didn't mind one bit. By then, they were used to Sister Jennie and they knew Nellie was happy with my care.

Nellie Maude was beginning her slow decline—physically and mentally. No more slippery dips in the tub. No more tennis matches or rides in the old Vauxhall. However, she still ruled the property from her bed. She began to get fixated on certain things. Once she insisted on looking at her jewellery, which she hadn't worn for many years. The bedroom had to be turned upside down to search for all of it. Drawers had to be taken out and emptied in front of her. Then, as suddenly as her fixation appeared, the subject was forgotten. Their house was huge, so the family decided to put 'Cry Babies' in several of the rooms, so we could hear Nellie when she needed us. What a mistake! Nellie had us running to her room every minute of the day. When we went to see what she needed, she would always tell us the same thing, 'I was just testing to see if the machine works.' Dr Sweetie visited Nellie regularly and she trusted him more than anyone else. Actually, she was beginning not to trust any of us anymore. We knew that because when Dr Sweetie would come, Mary, Snooks and I would turn on the machine in another room and listen in on their conversations. She would tell the doctor, 'I'm having trouble with the nurses. They're very rough with me and are trying to starve me to death so they can have my jewellery.' She would even make up tales about problems between her son and his wife, which were also untrue.

Around that time, I saw snow for the first time in my life. There was a mountainous area a short drive away and when we heard it had recently snowed, Snooks and I took off in the old car to see it for ourselves. The trip home wasn't easy and we ended up returning to Valley Fields very late. When we came in the house, we heard that Nellie had been very worried about our safety. It was then we realised just how much the old lady actually cared for us.

One night about six months after I arrived at Valley Fields, I was on night duty and I heard Nellie making a sniffling sound. She was having some sort of a spasm. I wasn't sure how to cope with it, so I woke Snooks. By the time she came down from the attic, Nellie was very, *very* still. I called Dr Sweetie and told him Nellie had died. The doctor didn't seem surprised. Apparently he had been expecting it for quite some time. We were so sad that she was gone. We looked at Nellie again and then suddenly noticed something. She had started breathing again—very gently. She wasn't dead! I called the doctor back with the news. He came to the house as quickly as he could, wearing his striped pyjamas under his trench coat. He knew she wouldn't last much longer. We woke up the family, but they didn't want to be around for Nellie's curtain call. They left it to us. As I tried to make her comfortable, she looked me straight in the eyes and said, 'Sister, please straighten my cushions.' I did and then she counted to four and died. Her son and Mary, were in pieces. I'm sure it was a mixture of sadness and relief. Ever since they had gotten married, they had lived with Nellie's sickness and her nurses. Finally after all these years, they could begin to have a life together.

That was the first time I had ever seen a dead person. The doctor suggested it would be better if I left the room, but I decided to stay and help Snooks lay her out. I thought since I had gotten to this point, I should go through to the end. Only that morning we had played dress up games with Nellie. We hadn't had time to clean her up before she had fallen asleep that evening. Now there she was with her bright red fingernails, white powder on her face and the Spanish comb in her hair. That was how she was put into her coffin. The undertaker was called in. He was a dapper little man in a suit and tie. I thought he seemed slightly odd as he stood there rubbing his hands together and saying, 'Well girls, where is she?' Nellie's two other sons flew in from the mainland for the funeral. The night of the funeral finished with a real Irish wake. Snooks and I lay in bed in our attic room listening to all the drunken laughter, the stories from the past and the tears.

The day after the funeral, Mary asked us to help pack up all of Nellie's belongings. There was nothing of value left nor anything personal to keep. Mary said, 'The past is the past.' She wanted everything dumped off somewhere in the country-side. We loaded the station wagon up and off we went at night, so no locals would see us. A few days later, their lawyer telephoned and told Mary that Nellie had left a safe deposit box at the bank with instructions that it was to be opened after her death. He said the key was in a small black box in Nellie's bedroom. Oh God, that meant the key was now somewhere in the countryside amongst a load of garbage! We couldn't tell Mary's husband what we had done, so late that night the three of us went back to find our dumping ground. After several hours of snooping around with our torches, we found the black box and fortunately the key was still safely inside of it! There was so much excitement and suspense the day they went to open the box. Well, it turned out that Nellie Maude had the last laugh. The box was completely empty!

Nellie's death was a bit premature for us. I had only been there six months and I needed a full year's work to have enough money for my trip to Europe. To our surprise, the family didn't want us to leave right away. They had become used to us being there and they needed a little time to adjust to being alone. Snooks was able to get a job at the local hospital. I knew I couldn't pull that one off again, so I was happy when Mr Warner asked me if I would help him get his office and files together. A couple of years earlier, a flood had swept through New Norfolk. There was a river running along side the Warner property and it had flooded into Mr Warner's office. They told me that during the flood Nellie had to be taken out of an upstairs window, put into a boat and rowed to safety. The office had never been cleaned since then, so Mr Warner gave me six months to wipe the mud and slush off of all his files.

When our time was finally up at Valley Fields, Snooks and I left with heavy hearts. I could never explain why I was so happy and at peace with the world during that year, but I was. We flew back to the mainland on a small plane with just the two of us on it. We were already sporting our small-pox, cholera and yellow fever vaccinations in preparation for our next big leap into the unknown. I was finally ready and Europe was waiting for me.

János

A One-Way Ticket to England

I had saved enough money to pay for a one-way ticket by ship to England and had transferred 95 Australian pounds into Barclay's Bank in London. I felt rich for the first time in my life. In fact, I have never felt richer. I made plans to leave along with Snooks, Aileen, a hairdresser I had met at The Virgin's Retreat, and Pattie, a friend from school. My mother had given me a few of her frocks, which I packed in my new green cardboard cases, along with my trip book and diaries. I was worried my mother would be upset or worried about me leaving, but she was actually proud that I was one of the few young people from Mildura, going abroad. I hoped to come back with wonderful tales to tell and souvenirs for everyone back home. We planned to travel through Europe for 18 months, however deep down I had the feeling I would be gone much longer—if not forever.

I was 23 years old when I said goodbye to my mother and brother at the train station in

Mildura. There were many tears. As I was about to board the train to Melbourne to meet the ship, my brother once again slipped a few pounds into my pocket and said, 'Have fun, Jen and come back soon.' We boarded the T.S. *Flavia* and sailed from the port of Melbourne on **Friday, 25 January 1963 at 6.20**. At the dock, there were more fond farewells and oceans of tears as we promised to behave ourselves. We hung on to streamers until distance finally broke them. I was too scared to let mine fly in the wind, as I felt that little strip of coloured paper was my last link to home.

The four of us all settled into cabin No. T.73 and we were off to travel 11,000 miles over the next six weeks. Our first port of call was Sydney, then back to Melbourne and then on to Adelaide, where my two sisters and my niece Maxine came on board to say farewell. From there we sailed to Fremantle. By then we had been travelling for a week and yet we were still in our homeland! I started to wonder when we would finally get away from Australia and hit the open seas. The trip along the Australian coast was rough; it was actually the roughest part of the trip. I wasn't a good sailor and the thought of another five weeks on board the ship wasn't very encouraging. We sailed up to Perth and from there we finally headed off from Australia.

The ship was filled with young adventurous Australians. Everyone was leaving home to seek fame, fortune and adventure. We wanted the same things. I wasn't sure exactly what it was I was seeking. Maybe deep down, I imagined myself returning to Mildura in the not so far distant

Jennie, Aileen and Pattie on board the Flavia.

future with the mayor welcoming me home, the brass band playing *Waltzing Matilda* and the streets lined with people cheering out, 'Good on ya, Jen. Ya made it!' I had no idea in what way I expected to have made it. I didn't have a profession, I wasn't talented in any way and my face was not my fortune. I imagined I would somehow make loads of money and send it home to my mother, so she could give up her job at the factory, buy herself a beautiful house and live in luxury for the rest of her days. I was dreaming with my head in the clouds, whilst still desperately clutching onto what was left of my coloured streamer.

We had weeks at sea ahead of us with nothing but water between Perth and our first Egyptian port. The Indian Ocean was like a mirror. I immediately settled into my new life on board and I loved every minute of it. It was a large ship with a pool, deck tennis and bingo. Our days were busy and we were excited to be be meeting so many new people. Shipboard life is similar to that in a large hotel. It was fun to be on an extended holiday at sea, but one can only play so much deck tennis and bingo or read books and write letters, before one's mind turns to ideas about the opposite sex. It doesn't take much to imagine what happens on board a ship full of young, healthy girls and handsome men.

The *Flavia* was an Italian ship and most of the crew were Italian. Back home I had met many Italian immigrants who had come through Mildura. During the grape harvest season, scores of them would come into town to work. Most of them were from southern Italy. They were short and very poor. At night they would change out of their grape picking clothes and put on suits with tight trousers and pointed-toe, patent-leather shoes to wander through our town. They were really quite harmless, but because they often travelled around in large groups, our mothers all seemed to think their daughters were about to have their bottoms pinched. My image of the Italian race had been based on those grape pickers, but now I was meeting the crew on the ship. Some of them were tall with blue eyes and fair hair. My thoughts about Italians quickly began to change!

Two of the rules of ship board life were that no officer could dance more than once a night with the same girl and no officers could take passengers to their cabins or vice versa. We learned all these rules would be forgotten once the captain had found a woman for himself, so the officers tried to set him up as soon as possible. By the time we had reached Fremantle, my friends and I had already gotten friendly with some of the officers.

Giorgio Di Palma

We had even managed to have three of them put into the ship's prison for a week when they were caught walking with us in a park on our stopover in Perth. Throughout our journey they would regularly sneak little love notes to us.

There seemed to be scores of beautiful blonde girls on board and they all had their eyes on the same man, Giorgio Di Palma. He played double bass and sang in a band that played on the ship. I liked him too and I decided to concentrate my energy in his direction as well. I became a music fan like the rest of them and went to all of his shows. Somehow out of all of the girls, I ended up winning him and I spent the rest of the voyage madly in love. Giorgio and I spent all our free time together. I was so in love that I missed seeing the pyramids in Egypt. When the ship stopped in Suez, all of the passengers travelled by bus to Cairo. They

visited the pyramids and rode camels, but I wanted to be with Giorgio instead, so I stayed on board. I was probably the only passenger to go through the Suez Canal and it was because I was in love.

Our next stop was Port Said. The ship was too big for the harbour, so we were ferried in by small boats. On the little boat, I was approached by a large, charming Arab dressed in a suit. He was to be our guide for the night. He politely asked me to carry a very large envelope in my bag for him. He instructed me not to talk to anyone and not to stay close to him at all. He said he would make contact with me when we reached shore. I was happy to help him carry his excess baggage to the shore. I may have been naive back then, but I was also very curious. When I had a chance, I squeezed into a dark corner on the boat and discretely opened my bag. When I silently opened the envelope I saw thousands of dollars! There was more than enough in there for my mother to buy a big house in Mildura. Oh dear, there I was with just 95 pounds to my name. For a second I thought, *What if I just pulled out a few bills and stuffed them into my pocket?* No, I decided. I couldn't do that. It would be dishonest, so I just closed the envelope.

The boat landed and the second I stepped off I heard a hiss in my ear, 'The envelope, quickly.' I obediently handed the money over to the man. In the port, I wandered through the market stalls and bought a couple of stuffed leather camels and a few junky bracelets. I tried to focus on what I'd been taught when I was younger. 'Honesty is the best policy.' However when I told my friends about what had happened, they said I was bloody nuts. They said he wouldn't have missed a few notes and we could have seen Europe in real style.

Port Said was quite exciting. We went to a nightclub which looked like a sheik's tent after a sand storm. While we were there, someone slipped a mickey into Snooks' drink, making her fall across the table into a deep sleep. The next day we boarded another small boat to go back to our ship. This boat was driven by three large Arabs. I was with my cabin mates, the boys from Giorgio's band and a male and female ballet dancer, who were hoping to make it into the Royal Ballet Company in London. Our ship was to leave at sunrise. We had been warned that neither our embassies nor the ship's owners would take responsibility if something happened to us in Port Said. As we left shore, I realised we were headed in the opposite direction from our ship. The Italian musicians didn't seem terribly worried. They were laughing and talking, but I was scared that we were going to be sold in an Egyptian slave market. I had already done a big money smuggling job for an Arab and now this! I was starting to wish I had never left the bush. They stopped the boat in the middle of nowhere. One of them pointed his finger towards the female dancer and said 'We want her.' Then in nearly the same breath, he looked towards the male dancer and said, 'If not, we will take him.' They didn't seem particularly fussy as to which one they got. The girl was very quick to react. She must have seen her dreams of dancing with the Royal Ballet about to be replaced with her ending up as a belly dancer in a harem. She was smart and offered to take the men to her cabin if they agreed to take us all back to the ship. The Arabs agreed, but as soon as we arrived at our ship they were thrown into the arms of the Egyptian police instead.

We continued on our journey. I found all the Egyptian ports exciting, everyone was selling their goods from little rafts, magicians were pulling live chickens out from under their shirts, there was strange music and blazing colours everywhere. When crossing the equator we had spaghetti rubbed into our hair and then were washed down with water hoses. Afterwards I was presented with a certificate which stated I was a 'Swordfish'.

Our next port of call was Naples. We arrived at sunrise on **21 February 1963**. Instantly, I decided this was the most beautiful part of Europe—the Naples port! There was excitement everywhere. We were told we only would have five hours on shore. What does one do at 5.00 in the morning in Naples? We found out there was much to do. There were fantastic nightclubs close to the port for all the sailors. Today, just the thought of being in that area with sailors from all over the world in some sleazy night club sends shivers down my spine. I wouldn't have the courage to go there

anymore. However innocence is an amazing weapon. It never entered my head back then that the Naples port could be dangerous. I thought we were really living!

Diary — 21-02.63 — Naples, Italy
Very quaint city with cobbled streets. Many night clubs, which were open at strange hours like 5.00 am. I went to three of them with Giorgio. Walked around Naples in the rain and he bought me some flowers. I bought shoes and boots. Clothes fairly expensive. The most wonderful night of the trip so far.

Genoa was our last port of call. Apparently the engines on the ship were playing up, so the company decided to put all the passengers onto a train and send them off to London. On the ship I had met two girls from Melbourne named Jan and Robin. They were travelling to Cannes to buy a car to drive to London and they invited me to go along with them. My cabin mates decided to take the train, but I loved the idea of going by car. Jan and Robin planned to stay in Genoa until our ship left the port, since they had ship board romances too. That meant I could spend more time with Giorgio. I told my friends I would meet up with them in London.

Before the others left on the train we had a night in Genoa. We booked rooms at the Pensione Urania. It was there I saw my first bidet. Snooks and I looked in the bathroom. We saw a bath, a wash basin and a strange looking object rather like a bowl on legs. There was nothing that looked like any toilet we knew, so I told Snooks that the bowl on legs must be it.

**Bathroom Scene –
Pensione Urania, Genoa, Italy**

Snooks: What's that thing?

Jennie: It must be the lavatory.

Snooks: Funny looking one though. It's got a plug in it.

Jennie: Look here Snooks, we're not in Australia. We've got to adapt to new things.

Snooks: Okay, if that's what it is. I'll use it first.

Jennie retires to the bedroom and soon hears screams coming from the bathroom.

Snooks: Jen, come quickly! I can't get it to go down! There's no lavatory chain, no button to push. What can I do?

Jennie: Just stuff it down the best you can. Find a stick or something. I hope you haven't broken the loo. Just get rid of it before we get thrown out of the hotel.

When the owner eventually came to help, he called us something like 'dirty foreigners!'

Jan, Robin and I spent the next ten days enjoying the Italian Riviera with our boyfriends while they waited for the ship to be repaired. Giorgio and I scratched our names on a tree in a park in Sestri Levante near Portofino.

Diary — 8-03.63 — Genoa, Italy
The Flavia left Genoa at 11.45 am on 8 March 1963 on its return voyage to Australia and it took our hearts with it. We all knew when it returns to Europe again, there will be another three Australian girls doing the same things, seeing the same spots, with the same boys we had been with. What did we really care? It was fun and now we were off to Cannes and then to our new home in London. Very sad, but many wonderful memories. I loved Genoa, however I am glad to be leaving for Cannes tomorrow morning, as there is nothing here for me.

I'm sure my mother was happy when she heard my Italian boyfriend had sailed away. She had written to tell me she didn't want me dating Italians:

*Dear Jennifer, please could you find yourself a nice English boy called Charles, Michael or some such, instead of all these Giorgios, Benitos, Robertos etc., You know I really don't approve of Italians. Don't you remember? I don't even like Dean Martin.
Lots of love, Mum.*

Just Another Young Australian in London

Jan and Robin bought a car in Cannes. We drove to Calais, France, took the ferry to Dover, England and then drove on to London. When we finally arrived, we had to find our new home, a flat Snooks, Aileen and Pattie had rented in Rosary Gardens, South Kensington. It was a damp, dark basement flat, but when we first saw it, it seemed beautiful to us. It was so exciting to be in London, even the laundrettes were exciting. That was where everyone met and chattered whilst the soap powder went to work. There were many times I was so distracted chatting to someone that I accidentally put a half crown into someone else's machine instead of my own. The poor person who had been on their last spin would have to wait for the machine to go through the whole cycle again. London was much larger than any city I had lived in before, but apart from its size, it didn't feel much different than Mildura. It was a matter of getting used to the Tube and buses rather than pedalling around on a bicycle or tooting around on my Vespa motor scooter.

I called Vern as soon as I had settled in to tell him I had arrived in London. He was living in the same area and within a few minutes he was ringing my doorbell. When I opened the door, I saw a new Vern. He was wearing pale blue jeans and black leather boots which came to the knee. He no longer sported a crew cut. Now he had long reddish curls, which fell to his shoulders. Everything seemed to have changed about him. Even the pitch of his voice and the way he expressed himself seemed so different. Seeing these changes in Vern gave me a wonderful sensation. If he had changed so much, what were the possibilities for a new life for me? Everything seemed so exciting. It felt as though something new was being born.

Our 'beautiful' apartment in Rosary Gardens only lasted one month. The damp got damper and the dark got darker and the flat quickly lost its charm. I suggested that we leave whilst we still could. We found a bright, airy flat around the corner on Edith Road. We stayed there for only two months. I'm not sure what the reason was for the next move, but it was probably due to me again, as I was always telling everyone what to do. I'm sure there was something about the apartment that didn't suit me, so we all had to move again.

It was early **1963**, and I was just another young Australian in London. I didn't really have plans other than to find any job which would allow me to take off time every now and then to visit all the countries in Europe I had read about. I needed a job, so I signed up with the Alfred Marks Employment Agency. That was the place to find short term work. I hadn't gone to Europe to find a good permanent job. I had that in Australia. The idea of nothing being permanent in London was very exciting to me. With Alfred Marks I could

Jennie and Jan in Cannes.

just go from post to post and collect my salary from the agency at the end of the week. Even the boring jobs suited me fine, because I could always see the end of the road in sight.

My first job was probably the worst. I was stuck in a pokey little room folding pamphlets and putting them into envelopes for the famous chef Egon Ronay. I had to seal the envelopes with my tongue. I could hardly swallow by the end of the day. I could only stand it for a week. Next, I ended up at the University College Hospital, not for a swollen tongue, but in the accounts department. They were all very kind and tried to convince me to stay on permanently. However after three weeks of drinking about 15 cups of tea a day with elderly English ladies and gentlemen whilst discussing the sicknesses of celebrities and how much their accounts came to for the hospital, I got the feeling that if I didn't find something more interesting, I may as well leave London and go back home.

Then I had a job in the typing pool at Thomas Cooke's Travel Agency. It was boring, but at least I could dream away, since typing was very automatic for me. One day, a young co-worker from Liverpool turned to me and said, 'Ya heard about the Beatles?' I sort of cringed. It sounded like some plague or horticultural infection. 'No I haven't', I said. 'What on earth is it?' She replied, 'Ya don't know them? Crikey man! They're four young lads

from Liverpool who play smashing music. Saw 'em wit me own eyes at the Cavern in Liverpool.' I just nodded and that was the end of the conversation.

One night after everyone in our flat had settled down to sleep in their fluffy Australian nighties and with rollers in their hair, I smelt something burning. I've always had a paranoia about fire, but back then it was to a ridiculous extreme. At first I wondered if I should wake everyone up or just ignore it, but then my imagination started to go wild. I decided I had to get everyone out of bed and make them pull the flat apart looking for the fire. I was so worked up, I called the London Fire Brigade. I knew I had to be careful and not to exaggerate. After all, I hadn't actually seen anything in flames. I told them I only suspected something may be aflame. By this time my friends told me I was off my head. They were tired and headed back to sleep. It seemed to me that the smell had gone by then, so I had stopped trembling and started to relax. Within minutes I heard sirens. *Oh no!,* I thought. *What have I done now?* It wasn't just one fire truck that arrived, but three of them. Ladders were being put up against the walls of the building. Then what seemed to be an army of firemen came bursting into the apartment carrying axes and fire hoses. Talk about the efficiency of the London Fire Brigade! The other tenants in the building were running down the staircase in

Pattie, Jennie, Eleanor, Snooks, and Aileen at The Madison Room.

their nightwear with their hair tucked tightly into hairnets, clutching anything they wanted to save before the fire ripped through their apartment. I quietly tried to explain I had reported that I had only *suspected* the smell of burning and I thought it was my duty to have it checked out. Before they left, the head of the Brigade cornered me in the room and said to me, 'Miss, don't you realise that at the end of this street there is a steam train which passes each night? I presume that was what you smelt.' Oh my, I suppose he was right!

I continued moving from job to job and was happy to just be living day to day. I enjoyed being anonymous in the big city. My social life was more or less nonexistent. I was content meeting new people in the various offices I worked in. I was also happy to see my bank account grow, which meant I would soon be able to leave and go abroad in the not so distant future. Then after a

while, the agency jobs began to become a bore. It was nothing but typing pools and 'clock-in' cards. I didn't have a profession, but always had a lot of initiative and drive. Finally, the day arrived when I saw an advertisement in a newspaper which I felt was just meant for the four us. The ad read: 'Waitresses wanted in a Swinging London Club in South Kensington'. I was sure they couldn't refuse us even though we didn't have any experience as waitresses. We went to apply and they agreed to take us all on. So began a new and very different phase of my life. The club was a high class casino called The Madison Room. The club was so high class I knew as soon as I entered it that I was well out of my depth. I prayed I could fake it until I had the chance to actually become a good waitress.

I was still rather green back then. When some clients at the casino asked me why a nice, young lady such as myself was working in a joint like

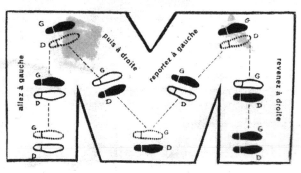

THE MADISON ROOM

The Madison Room is one of the most attractive places in London with a decor second to none. It comprises a Restaurant Bar and exellent Dancing facilities. The first club in London with the accent on the Madison. Twist and Bassanova. Many celebrities visit the Club. we can assure you of First Class Entertained.

this. I would go into a long monologue about it being a respectable club with respectable clients. What a dolt I was then! Most people working in these clubs were pretty shady, from the owners down to the dishwashers. I was so naive that when clients would give me a big tip, I would insist it was too much and give half of it back!

There was a line dance called 'The Madison' which was popular at that time. Since our casino was called the Madison Room, we all had to learn the dance. We would all get in a line in our black uniforms and give a little performance for the clients.

At the Madison Room I met Don and Terry, the O'Callaghan brothers. They were professional Irish gamblers. Terry idolised his big brother and would copy everything Don did. The way he dressed, the way he held his cigarette and the way he talked. They always looked sharp in expensive suits, especially Terry who always wore a flower in his lapel. They frequented the club and all the women fell in love with Don. The brothers seemed to take a liking to the four fresh Australian girls and we all became good friends. They would often take us to other gambling places after work and we would watch them play until the sun came up. I didn't drink or take pills, so I often found it difficult to stay awake that long.

Unfortunately our time at the Madison Room lasted only two months. One evening when we went to work, we were told all four of us were fired. There was no reason. We did nothing wrong. We were just fired. We stormed into the office and demanded to know the whys and the wherefores, but we were never given a real reason.

By this time we were living in Turton House in Earl's Court. I cannot quite remember the place, but I do remember us re-naming it 'The Virgin's Retreat No 2', due to the fact that no visitors were allowed. There were so many Australians around Earl's Court that it was called 'Kangaroo Valley'. We didn't like living there and we only stayed about a week. We hadn't come all the way from Australia just to hang out with other Australians.

London scenes.

Jennie and Don O'Callaghan.

Snooks and I decided to go back to Alfred Marks Agency. We both landed a job together at Paultons furniture shop on the King's Road. We were excited to be working in such a posh area, until we realised the shop was on the wrong end of King's Road. The furniture was dark, drab and ugly. No one even bothered to look at it, so there wasn't much to do. The front of the store was glass and faced a bus stop. Snooks and I spent our first day entertaining the crowds as they waited for their buses. We used the furniture for props. When the owner came in, he found us sitting on a ratty, old divan in his front window acting out *The Tramp In The Park* as the crowd outside was pushing to get closer to the shop window to see our show! He immediately told us to leave and not to return! That was the end of that job. Snooks and I laughed all the way home.

Next I had a call from a London clinic. Someone was needed to tour schools outside of London to give psychological tests to the children. I took the job and began to travel around to classrooms with my briefcase full of forms. The children were, more often than not, little brats. They would start jumping on their desks, whistling, shouting and throwing paper darts at me. Meanwhile, the teachers wanted to know what the tests were about and what they would be used for. What could I tell them? I honestly didn't know, myself. At tea break they would talk to me as if I were a child

psychologist. I wouldn't really answer. How could I? I would just be very nonchalant and pray they would stop asking me questions.

I had been dating Don O'Callaghan for a while and I eventually moved into his apartment in Swiss Cottage. He was still gambling until the wee hours of the morning, so I saw little of him. Usually I would be leaving for work right around when he was coming home. He would often return completely exhausted, either from his 'keep awake' pills, alcohol or from losing hundreds of pounds at the gambling table. I would have to take off his shoes and jacket before he collapsed on the bed. I knew whenever he had an unsuccessful night, when I saws his pockets full of I.O.U notes from the biggest clubs in London. I was never involved in gambling and didn't understand how dangerous that world could be, especially when you owed thousands to the clubs and couldn't pay up. All I knew was Don was wonderful to me. He was really very kind and charming. I felt so happy to be living in his house with him. We spent wonderful times together—he even took my virginity.

Then gradually I began to wake up to what was happening with Don. Early one morning the doorbell rang. Don instantly rolled off the bed and then right under it. He whispered to me in a painful tone, 'Say I'm not home to *anyone…*' I went to open the door and could already see by the shadow through the peep hole, that this was not a normal-sized man. He was more like a giant. He looked as though he could have been Al Capone's body guard. My hands began to tremble. The Irish gambler was under the bed and this character was at the door. I opened the door only a tiny bit and suddenly a big, black leather shoe wedged it open. 'Mr Callaghan at home?', he spat at me. 'No', I said. 'he's already left to spend a couple of days in the country.' The man left with a warning, 'Just tell 'im miss, that Jo sent me and I ain't coming 'ere again for nothing.' I told him I would pass on his message and then very quickly shut the door.

When we were out on the street, Don often quickly dragged me into shops, around corners, down alleyways or shoved me behind flower sellers or fruit vendors. He would whisper questions in my ear as his grip left bruises on my arms, 'Did you get a look at the guy who was driving that white Jaguar? Was he wearing sunglasses? Where did he turn off?' Our life was starting to feel like a James Bond movie.

Meanwhile, Snooks had been working as a nanny for a family in London. She had recently been offered a job to be the nanny for the children of a famous actress in Rome. She decided to take it, so her position in London would be open. She convinced me to take her current position, saying the money was good, their life was luxurious and the children were quite manageable.

[*To preserve the family's privacy, I will refer to the husband and wife as Charlie and Sophie. I should also have a name for the wife's lover, whom I will call Mr Browning.*]

Snooks' final words to me as she left for Italy were, 'The wife will tell you she is an Austrian princess, but she's really a first class hooker who's being kept by a very influential London businessman on the side. Her lover thinks her husband is dead, so that means the husband has to disappear whenever Mr Browning appears at the house. Oh, and if the husband occasionally tries to commit suicide, don't worry, most likely it will only be an overdose of baby aspirin… If it all gets too much for you, just call me in Italy and I'll get you a job there. Best of luck, bye!'

Snooks was right on all counts. It wasn't long before Sophie took off her princess mask. She kept very weird hours working with her 'clients' and her husband kept disappearing whenever Mr Browning appeared at their house. My job was supposed to be taking care of their two young children. However it wasn't long before I realised I would be spending more time taking care of the parents. Money seemed to be no object for them. I would learn that Mr Browning was the source of

all their money. Whenever I took the children on an outing, a chauffeur-driven Austin Princess car would be called for us and off we would go. It was pure luxury. Whenever the parents needed me more than usual, they would send their children for a stay at a small elite boarding school to get them out of the way.

I don't think Charlie was happy. He loved the money they had, but not his wife's job nor her lover. He spent most of his days and nights in the nearest pub. On evenings when he was sure Mr Browning wouldn't be popping in, Charlie would drag all the bums, which he called his 'arty' friends, home from the pub. He would insist I put the children to bed and then I was to serve his friends drinks. I would have to spend the whole next morning cleaning up broken glass and scrubbing beer stains out of their white carpets, whilst Sophie slept in after wherever she had been the night before.

Charlie and Sophie would fight often. Whenever I heard them start up, I would take the children out somewhere—usually leaving in a great haste, half dressed and dirty faced. Sometimes I would lock the three of us up in my little bedroom in the attic and play a game I made up for them called, 'Who speaks the loudest, gets the prize.' I hoped that would drown out the fighting below.

Sophie wasn't the healthiest young woman. There were frequent visits from the doctor or she would disappear into hospital for a few days. I never asked questions. That wasn't a part of my job. I was glad she never discussed her personal problems with me. That was a blessing, as she must have had many of them. She was actually a very sweet person and I liked her very much.

I suppose my year of playing 'nurse' in Tasmania helped me during the seven months I spent in this household. After the first month or so, all their craziness began to seem normal to me. One night Charlie rudely awakened me, dragging me out of bed yelling, 'Call the doctor immediately! My wife is fuckin' bleeding to death.' When I got to Sophie's room I saw blood oozing its way under the door and slowly trickling down the white-carpeted staircase! I called the doctor. When he arrived, the doctor didn't seem very concerned about the blood bath. He just proceeded to take what appeared to be a huge pair of fire tongs out of his black bag. Then turning to me he said, 'Now young lady, when I insert this into Madam's vagina, I want you to take them in both of your hands and slowly open them. I have to see what's happening in there. I can't do both jobs, so I need you to help. Off you go now, slowly… or you could do her some damage.' There I was, a nanny taking care of two young children. It was 3.00 in the morning and I was sitting on a bed, bathed in blood, with a giant pair of tongs, stuck up a 'princess's' vagina, with this doctor telling me I could do some damage! Later, after the ambulance took her away, I spent the next few hours trying to clean up the evidence before the children came down for breakfast.

There came a time, when Sophie must have felt she couldn't cope anymore and she decided to put an end to everything. Once again Charlie dragged me out of bed. This time he was saying, 'Quick, get up! My wife has taken a fuckin' overdose and we have to wake her up!' Sure enough there was Sophie lying in bed looking whiter than the sheets she lay on, eyes rolling from right to left, her mouth was hanging loosely open, but at least she was still breathing. When I told Charlie we should call the doctor immediately, I couldn't believe his response. 'What do you mean call the fuckin' doctor? You crazy? Ya want me to go to prison or something? There's no fuckin' doctor or no fuckin' police coming into this house.' With that, I was sent to the kitchen to make a large quantity of black coffee, which we poured down Sophie's throat. I was doing the pouring, whilst Charlie had a hold of her by her hair as he repeatedly slapped her across the face. Every time he let go she would flop back amongst the pillows. After what seemed like hours of slapping and pouring, she began to blubber some words about how she couldn't sleep, so she took a pill and then still couldn't sleep, so took another one and so on and so on…. Once Charlie heard her utter her first words, he said he was going back to bed, but he ordered me to keep her awake at all costs.

The ambulance was often pulling up in front of our house. Even the neighbours didn't peek through their curtains anymore at the flashing lights. Anytime Charlie wanted to be the centre of attention, he would pretend to take his own life,

which was a bit confusing, since to Mr Browning at least, Charlie was supposed to be dead… He didn't actually intend to die, so each time he would take an overdose it would be of baby aspirin and just enough to put him into a semi-coma, but never enough to go the whole way. I got quite used to calling the nearest hospital and saying that Charlie has taken all the kids pills again and needed a stomach pump. They would take him away and a couple of days later he would be back again.

Charlie was always drinking and it was becoming difficult for all of us to deal with his behaviour. His wife decided he needed a dry-out cure. She booked him into a beautiful 'hotel' where he would be well looked after and hopefully cured. Unknown to him (or to me), she had signed him into a mental home in the countryside. She signed him in and only she could sign him out again. After he was admitted, there were frantic telephone calls every day from him begging her to let him be released. Finally, Sophie broke down and told me I had to go to the clinic and speak with him. I called him beforehand and he pleaded with me: 'Jennie *please* come see me immediately. This ain't no hotel. This is a fuckin' nut house. That bitch *has* to get me out of here.' I made a promise that I would come see him, but told him he had to promise not to be violent when he came home.

The chauffeur was called and the Austin Princess car came for me. We headed off on a very foggy London afternoon to visit Charlie. We finally arrived at an enormous establishment in the countryside, surrounded by high walls and acres of parkland. From the outside, it looked very impressive. However as soon as I stepped inside the dining room, I realised it wasn't the place for anyone who wasn't totally crazy. Long wooden tables filled the dining room and seated around them were numerous patients all banging their tin mugs on the tables and screaming something that I think might have meant 'tea'. I felt very uncomfortable standing around looking for Charlie whilst all the inmates were screaming. At last I saw him sitting alone at a table in a corner. His collar was turned up and his face was hidden behind a large pair of sunglasses. I went over to him and asked why on earth he was wearing those dreadful glasses. He said, 'Ya don't think I want to be recognised by anyone in this nut house, do you? Please Jennie, she has to let me out of here before I truly go nuts.' I agreed wholeheartedly with him and promised I would convince Sophie to sign him out.

By the time I left, it was nearly dark and the fog had become very dense. The chauffeur had trouble finding his way out again. It felt like a horror film. The only person we could find to ask for directions was an inmate who was sawing down an old oak tree with a finger nail file. He said he couldn't help us as he was too busy. Another patient didn't even acknowledge us when we tried to speak to him. By trial and error we eventually found our way out and returned to London.

Sophie did agree to let Charlie be released, but she didn't give up trying to find a cure for his drinking problem. She booked him into an incredibly expensive health farm called Tring, which was the sort of place the wealthy go to dry out for a month or so each year. Just for the books, Tring was used in one of the James Bond films. When I visited Charlie at Tring, our Austin Princess looked like a Fiat amongst all the Rolls Royces and Bentleys parked outside. When Charlie's one month stay was over, he returned home. He threw his cases in the hallway and told me to unpack his belongings. He had met so many well-known people at Tring that he spent the next week or so name dropping every one, until the novelty wore off and no one wanted to hear it any more.

It was soon obvious that Tring hadn't solved his problem either, so he agreed to join the AA organisation. That seemed to do the trick for a while at least, until one night when he felt he was weakening. I suggested he call one of his 'brothers' and ask them over to the house to support him. I had read that in one of his AA papers, 'If in trouble, call your brothers to help you.' Charlie thought that was a fine idea. He couldn't wait to have company. He telephoned as many 'brothers' as he could find. They all came over, but rather than having the brothers talk him out of drinking, the situation reversed itself. By midnight we had a house full of drunken men. They were all shouting, 'Bullshit to the Establishment. Drinking is more fun!'

I don't think I ever had time to ask myself what I was doing in such a crazy household. I was rather out of touch with the outside world during the time I was with them. I suppose everything going on around me in that house simply became my normal way of life. To me, they were just a little different from other families I had known in the past—nothing else. It's rather crazy to say, but I was really quite happy with them. I loved the children, and there was certainly never a dull moment in that household.

Life went on as usual, up until the day Mr O'Callaghan put his foot in their door. I had told Don about Sophie and Charlie and he asked me to invite him to the house for a drink so he could meet them. I thought that was very sweet of him to want to see where I lived and to make sure they were treating me well. It never occurred to me that my ex-boyfriend was planning to make a pass at my employer, because he had so many gambling debts and he knew she was rich. It also never occurred to me that my employer would fall in love with my ex-boyfriend.

It wasn't until a day or so after their second encounter that the penny dropped. Sophie called me into her room for a private chat. I thought she wanted to talk about where she wanted to send Charlie next. Maybe into the cemetery! It was nothing as simple as that. She asked if I thought Mr O'Callaghan would pay her back if she lent him some money. I burst out, 'Sophie, are you crazy? Of course he wouldn't pay you back! I mean he couldn't give it back to you. He has no money.' As she heard my response, the little blood she had in her body seemed to drain away. She burst out, 'Oh no, I already did! I gave him a cheque for umpteen thousand pounds this morning and it's left my account with only £500 in it!'

As I gave Sophie a brandy to calm her nerves, I realised it may be time to call Snooks in Italy regarding a job I would be needing in the very near future. I sent an express letter to Rome and I secretly began organising my belongings whilst waiting for the axe to fall. Part of me thought they would sort it out together. After all, I'd seen so many dramas between them before, one more wouldn't make much difference. However, this time felt different. This concerned money, which was what their lives seemed to be all about. I was already feeling very sad for the children. I had become quite fond of

Don O'Callaghan

them both and I knew I would be sad to have to leave them.

A few days later, Sophie appeared at breakfast with the children. I knew something was wrong. She had never done that before. I realised the day of reckoning had arrived by the look on her face. 'Jennie…', she said. 'He wants to see my bank statement.' I began to tremble inside. I suggested we dress the children and go to the bank together. Maybe on the way we could think of something brilliant. I put their son in his pram and their daughter walked along side as the four of us set off towards the bank. Along the way, I had a brilliant idea. We could tell him the bank was on strike. It wasn't brilliant, but it did give us one day's grace. When we told Charlie the news, he just said, 'So, go again tomorrow.'

We did the same thing the next morning, but this time there was no miracle. There was nothing else to do but to present Charlie with the bank statement. I was frightened. I hurried the children up to my attic room. I locked the door and put a chest of drawers against it for further protection. I suggested we play a new game called 'Silence'. I wanted to be able to hear everything, so I could plan our next move. Outside the window of my room was a drain pipe. I knew I could get the three

of us down to the garden and from there we would make our escape like a scene in the movies. As we waited, there was silence… Not only was there silence in our game, there was a deathly silence downstairs. Maybe he fainted? Maybe he died of shock? A haunting silence fell over the whole house for what seemed like hours, although it was probably just a matter of minutes. The silence was finally was broken and then it seemed as if everything in the house was being broken at once. I told the kiddies their mummy and daddy were playing the game 'Who breaks the most gets the prize!'

When the noise finished, silence reigned again. Then I heard a *tap - tap - tap - tap* on my door. Charlie was begging me to open it, so he could talk to me. I had all these images of the headlines in the Mildura newspaper back home: 'Local Girl Slain by Alcoholic Ponce in Hooker's House in London.' I didn't actually think he would do such a thing, so I opened the door. I looked into his face and he looked pathetic with tears running down his cheeks. He pleaded with me, 'Please, Jennifer, *please* tell me it's not true. Please tell me that my wife didn't give all my money to that fuckin' Irish, gambler boyfriend of yours.' I realised then that Charlie was a broken man and would do no harm. I wasn't scared anymore and knew whatever Sophie had done wasn't my fault, so I replied, 'Well, if she said she did. She did!'

The next morning everything was back to normal. Well, normal for their particular family. Sophie was flitting around the house, humming to herself. Charlie was off to the pub and the children and I spent our day as usual. God knows what she had said to him, but whatever it was, it worked!

Not so long after that episode, I was told that the five of us were going for a short trip to Bexhill-on-Sea. It was the first time we had been out of London together. I was quite excited, as I had never been to that area before. The thought of being out of our routine and going to the seaside was very appealing. On the second day that we were in Bexhill-on-Sea, I was bringing the children back from the beach, when we saw Charlie racing down the street. As he ran, he had a small case in one hand and was doing up his trousers and pulling on his shoes. I tried to ask him what had happened, but he was in such a hurry I didn't get a reply. When we got back to our room, Sophie told me that Mr Browning was coming to spend a few days with us and was due in on the next train. Well, that explained why Charlie was running so fast! Personally, I was excited. I finally would have the opportunity to meet the man who paid for all our beautiful houses and chauffeur-driven cars. When he arrived, I could tell right away that Mr Browning was very different from Charlie. He was sophisticated and a real English gentleman.

The time had come when I decided to tell Charlie and Sophie I was leaving. I told them I wanted to see more of Europe before returning to Australia. The truth was I just had to get out. Enough was enough. I asked Snooks to help me find a job in Rome. I remember the morning I left. The whole family was in the front garden. Sophie was holding her son on her hip and had one arm around her daughter's shoulder. Charlie was hanging over the fence with tears running down his cheeks. As I left, he called out to me, 'If you aren't happy there, you can always come back to us.' I shed my own tears in the taxi. Most of them for the children, although I'm sure some were for Sophie and Charlie too. In spite of all

their craziness, I liked them and I was actually very happy and at peace with my life when I was with them. As the taxi turned the corner, I knew I would never see or hear from them again, and I never did.

An Australian 'Happening' in The Eternal City

It was time for me to leave London and head to Rome for the first time. As I was on the plane, I had many doubts about what I was doing: flying to another country, to another family situation and with new children to care for. Snooks had found me a position with an Italian family with two young boys. I would be paid 50,000 lire per month with a half a day off each week and no free nights. The boys only spoke Italian. I was to teach them English, feed them, dress them and amuse them seven days a week. Thank goodness Snooks was working nearby, in case of need.

When I touched down at the airport in Rome, I was greeted by a very pretty, short Italian lady. She was Simonetta, the mother of the two children. In her limited English, she told me we would be driving directly to Porto Santo Stefano, a small chic summer resort in the Argentario area north of Rome. During the trip, she told me about her sons Massimo and Valerio and explained what my duties would be.

Valerio was four years old. He had a problem with his eyesight and had to be watched very carefully. Massimo was eight and was quite spoilt and difficult. I was told never to slap the children. Only the parents could punish them physically. That rule only lasted a short time. Within the first hour of meeting Massimo, he kicked me in the shins and bit me on the arm. I retaliated by kicking and biting him back.

I soon discovered the parents had strange ideas about how to raise children. I realised if I was going to stay there, many things would have to change. I was expected to take the pips out of grapes before the children ate them. I still remember sitting at their table delicately removing each tiny pip and thinking to myself 'What in the hell am I doing? I came all the way to Europe and here I am de-seeding grapes, for a brat who just kicked and bit me?' I refused to do it after the first day. From then on, they either ate grapes with the seeds or they ate bananas instead.

My diary reminds me of how extremely unhappy I was when I first began working for them:

Diary — 17th August
Keep bursting into tears. Don't know whether I will enjoy it here.

Friday 21st August:
Another good cry.

Saturday 22nd August:
Still all very frustrating.

Sunday 23rd August:
Improvement today.

Eureka! Something must have turned the tables. I don't seem to have anymore crying episodes in my diary, so perhaps I began to settle into my new life. I adored little Valerio from the moment I met him and soon Massimo began to accept me as well. We all got on fine together. We saw very little of their parents, as they had a rather full social life. That was fine by me. I changed many of their crazy rules and the children were at ease. The children were picking up English so fast that I was amazed. Meanwhile, I was forbidden to speak Italian with the family, so I had little opportunity to begin learning the language myself.

During our time in Porto Santo Stefano, I saw Snooks and her two wards quite often. She was the nanny for the sons of a well-known Italian actress and her husband, who was a film director. After a while I began to get bored with boats, beaches, sand and sun. We seemed to stay forever in this little resort town, and I wanted to get to Rome to settle into my new life.

Finally I was told it was time for us to pack up and drive to Rome. When we arrived at their home, I was impressed. It was in a grand apartment block with a sweeping driveway, flanked on one side by a large swimming pool and on the other side by a tennis court. Living like this was something new to me. It was a rather interesting apartment block. Many Americans from the film business lived there, so I was able to meet lots of interesting people. I saw less and less of the parents since they were so busy all the time. I was becoming quite independent caring for the children on my own. I even convinced La Signora that I needed their second car more than she did and she agreed to let me use it.

Simonetta was from a wealthy Sicilian family. Her husband, although good looking and charming, didn't come from such wealth. His mother, Maria, was in her 70s and lived in a tiny apartment next to the prison in Trastevere. Nonna loved her little apartment, but she was often ordered to spend time with us doing any sewing and mending the family needed. That was fine with me. I adored her. I laughed for nearly two years with that old lady. I don't know how we communicated. She didn't speak a word of English and I only had a very limited vocabulary in Italian, yet somehow we talked, joked and laughed together. While language is important in a relationship, you can sometimes get away without it. I would often slip away and visit her and we would spend the afternoon giggling behind her chintzy curtains, watching the prisoners in the yard across the way in the Roman prison.

Many years later when my daughter was quite small, we were walking down the street where the granny had lived. I told my daughter about my time as a nanny in Rome and as we passed the entrance to the apartment, I suggested we tip-toe up the dark staircase and see who lived there now. Sixteen years had passed and Maria would have been in her late eighties, if she were still alive. I was amazed to read her name on the brass plate on the door. When I knocked, I heard the same voice I'd heard many times before saying, *'Chi è?* (Who is it?)' I was so taken aback that I didn't say my name, but instead just said, 'Maria?' I heard her

Jennie and Valerio in Ravenna.

say, *'Jennie, e tu!?* (Jennie, is it you!)?' Impossible! After all those years she actually recognised my voice. She invited us in and immediately began making coffee, just like in the old days. It was a wonderful experience.

I was now well organised with the family. I had arranged to have their car whenever I wanted it and had also insisted on having free time in the evenings and one full day off. After all, they wanted to keep the nanny happy. However it wasn't so easy for me to meet people. I wasn't the type to go off alone, especially in a city I didn't really know well. I needed to meet someone to take me out. I needed a boyfriend to take me to the cinema or to dinner. There were no single people my age living in the apartment block and the apartment was a long way out of the centre of the city. I wondered how I would be able to meet someone. The square

Jennie and Massimo in Venice.

in front of the apartment consisted of a cinema, a few shops, a small bar, a newspaper stand and a hairdressing salon. One day I was clutching Valerio's little hand and I pressed my nose up against the window of the salon to peer in. I found myself face to face with a tall, good looking young man, who smiled at me and motioned for me to enter. There was no turning back at that point, so in we went and I made an appointment to have my hair washed the following day. After that, I couldn't stay away. I kept going back. Within a week, I had had three different hairstyles and even more importantly, I had an invitation to go to the cinema with Nino, the owner of the salon. I was extremely pleased with myself. I wasn't the type men usually fell over at first glance. My sexual experiences up until then certainly wouldn't make a man turn cartwheels. Nevertheless, I always believed I had something going for myself, especially if the other person had a good sense of

humour. That is of course, if he spoke enough English and fortunately Nino did.

Nino called me nearly every day and we started spending more time together. I soon realised I needed to begin washing my hair at home again to save some money. I liked Nino, but as I spent more time with him I gradually discovered that he had some odd little habits, which put me off a bit. I didn't know Italian men very well in those days, except for ones I had met outside of Italy, so what I found odd in Nino was probably just normal for Italian men. For example, we would often go to the beach on my day off. He told me it was fine if I wore a bikini, but I was not to wriggle even my toes whilst lying down and taking the sun. He said other men might get the wrong idea. I would have to lie stiff as a mummy—not even daring to blink. Very quickly, beach days became sheer torture for me. Then sometimes when he would take me dancing and we would dance cheek to cheek to romantic Italian music Nino would suddenly get an erection. He would scoot off to the loo to relieve himself, leaving me standing alone in the middle of the dance floor! A few minutes later, he would return with a satisfied smile on his face and we would continue dancing as if nothing had interrupted us.

I saw or spoke to Nino every day for a very long time, but he lived with his mother and I lived with the family, so our outings together were just outings. He was a charming escort, but sexually he wasn't very stimulating. I was such a WASP myself that I wasn't about to pounce on him in the car. Then one day, he called and told me to bring my passport with me that night when he came to pick me up for the evening. I was so excited. I thought we must be going a long way for dinner and would have to pass some frontier! Then I began to wonder—what frontier? The nearest border to Rome would be Switzerland or Yugoslavia. I didn't think we could make it there for dinner and return the same night. It never occurred to me that he wanted my passport for sexual reasons.

He picked me up and drove us to a gloomy little hotel somewhere in the area of the Pantheon. Within seconds, he had us standing at a battered, old reception desk attended by an even more battered, old night porter. The man told Nino the price per hour for a double room. Nino paid in advance and then led me up a dark staircase to a room on the first floor. At this point, any romance or passion I may have felt towards Nino had flown away. I had a feeling of being led to the slaughterhouse. Nino opened the door to the room with such pride, as though he was giving me a tour of his father's castle. He switched on the light and I saw everything in the room was so tacky. I immediately wanted to flee. In the glare of the single bare light bulb hanging from the ceiling, every crack and stain showed on the walls. There was a double bed, one bedside table, a wardrobe with pale green peeling paint and a cracked washbasin with only a cold-water tap, which continually drip, drip, dripped. I slowly sat myself down on the bed, which creaked in utter despair.

Scene in the hotel:

Nino: Take your clothes off.

Jennie: You mean right now?

Nino: Of course. We only have two hours and then we have to leave the room free for other people.

Jennie: Well, I'm not too sure about all this…

Nino (now standing naked in the middle of the room): Don't keep me waiting any longer. Get your clothes off, *per favore!*

I took off my clothes in a flash and leapt between the sheets, mainly because it was so cold and damp in the room. I then assumed my beach position—completely rigid. Within seconds I decided I couldn't do it and I jumped out of the bed. I threw my clothes on and ran down the stairs. Nino followed, struggling to button up his trousers, with the rest of his clothes thrown over his arm.

It was really an awful thing for me to do, but the circumstances got the better of me. I apologised

profoundly and Nino told me not to get upset. He said the next time would be better… I think during our relationship he paid for four different hotel rooms and each time had the same result. I learnt to wear less clothing, so I could get dressed quicker each time I ran out. I continued to see Nino frequently for the two years I was in Rome, but gradually my life began changing and I came to see that Nino and his oddities didn't seem to be a good match for me anymore.

I did enjoy my time in Rome. Life was easy and I had a great relationship with the children I cared for. The younger boy became very attached to me, so much so that he didn't want to be with his mother. She admitted she was a bit jealous of my relationship with her children and didn't know what to do about it. I suggested she should try to spend more than just a few hours a week with them. Maybe then things would change.

The family had domestic help at home whom La Signora called 'the servants'. There were so many changes in the staff while I was there, I lost count. Simonetta was a very sweet woman, but when it came to the domestic help, she could be a bitch. The frequent changes of who was sleeping in the maid's room became a standing joke for the grandmother and me. It seemed like a monthly appointment for Nonna and I to be summoned to La Signora's bedroom to be told that a new servant would be arriving that day and would we please be on our best behaviour and not giggle when they were presented to us. When we met them, the granny was ordered to wear her pearls, the only jewellery the old dear ever had, and I had to look like a typical English nanny, complete with a pleated skirt and a twin set. We would sit on the divan in the living room holding our tea cups with our little fingers crooked in the proper position, while trying our best to stifle our giggles. Each time there was a new person, we made bets on how long they would last. Some of the people were so capable that their skills were wasted on our small family. However with some of the others, La Signora had good reason to send them away.

Alfonso was one I will never forget. He was tall, blonde, skinny and very feminine. He had a drinking problem and La Signora could never understand why all her liquor bottles were always

Nonna, Massimo and Simonetta.

evenings together. The man of the family was a lawyer for the film industry and he had helped Judy get work as an extra. She tried to convince me it was easy to get into the business. However she had everything going for her—long black wavy hair, flawless white skin, a pretty face and enormous breasts. I had long straight blonde hair and no breasts to speak of. I suppose everyone has their time in fashion. During the late sixties when big tits were no longer the style, Judy wanted to cut hers off!

Judy convinced me to give the film world a try. My first chance was a second-rate Spaghetti Western being shot in Cine-citta, the Rome film studios. La Signora agreed to let me go. She thought it would be fun for me and she wanted anything to keep me happy, so I wouldn't leave. Judy and I drove out to the studio at some outrageous hour early one morning. I prayed they wouldn't put me on a horse. Horses terrified me. When we got to the set, we were given gaudy, satin saloon dresses. I squeezed myself into an emerald green number, stuffed Kleenex tissues under my boobs and swayed out with the rest of the girls.

They told us we had to be ready to start work in two hours. I had to drive home to take Valerio to school. I figured if I went fast, I could drive there and back in two hours. I went speeding across Villa Borghese in my little Fiat van, fantasising about how this small part in the film could lead to bigger things… I was so absorbed in my grand future that I didn't hear the police sirens or see their motorcycles until they were abreast of me indicating I should pull over. I was speeding and didn't even realise it. I didn't have any documents on me, so the police escorted me home. I quickly toppled down from my pedestal with my dreams of the future broken into little fragments. After that, I owned up to myself that I was a nanny and not a movie star. The studio would have to find someone else for the emerald green dress.

I won't be mentioning anything about the treasures of Rome in this diary. Whilst living in Rome, I came to know most of them, but you can find

half empty. Maria and I knew, but we never told on the servants. Alfonso's stay came to an end on the evening of Massimo's First Holy Communion party. Alfonso was so drunk by the time the party was nearing its end that he fell onto the banquet table, breaking nearly every piece of crystal on it. 'Oh well,' he said as he left the house the next morning, 'at least it was crystal and not plain old glass.' I couldn't believe he was more concerned about being chic than losing his job! In two years I saw such a variety of people pass through that house: young and old, gays, whores and bums. Sometimes we ate burnt food for weeks until someone was told to leave. Other people left on their own accord, after half of the silver had departed out the door before them. It was a head-ache for La Signora, but for Nonna Maria and me, these people brightened our domestic life and were a great source of entertainment.

In those days, Rome felt like a huge film set. Many world-wide productions were being shot there and I met many people who were working in the film business. In the apartment next door to us, was an American couple with six children and an Australian nanny named Judy. She became a very close friend of mine and we spent many

Program for The Beatles concert at the Adriano Theatre. Rome, 28 June 1965.

them listed in any guidebook. I certainly enjoy and appreciate visiting such places. When I am there I can absorb them all and if I'm lucky I may be able to describe them a few hours later, but then they seem to fade for me. However if you ask me to describe the face of a flower seller near the Spanish Steps in Rome 50 years ago, I could do it as if it were yesterday. I suppose people and their lives are what make up the world for me. People and their words stay with me forever. I have always been this way. My memories are filled with people and more people.

The summer of **1965** was approaching. My friends in London were writing to me with stories of a new era filled with pop music, Mary Quant, Biba, the King's Road and Carnaby Street. I began to think it was time for a change. I was beginning to feel restless again…

When I told La Signora I was thinking of leaving, she was in despair. She asked me how could I leave the children. It would break their hearts. She suggested I take a month's holiday and then come back. What could I do? I didn't want to feel guilty for ruining the lives of her children, so I accepted her offer and made arrangements to go to Spain in the near future.

Around the same time, I heard some exciting news. The Beatles were coming to Rome! My thoughts went back to the typing pool at Thomas Cooke's Travel Agency. 'Ya heard about the Beatles? They make smashing music.' In the years since, these four young men had captured the world. This was to be their first big European tour. Everyone from grannies to toddlers loved John, Paul, George and Ringo. People were getting trampled just to get a glimpse of them. I was determined that now it was my time to see them. They would certainly go down in history and I wanted to be in on it. But how could I get the tickets? Kids would sell their own mothers to get Beatles tickets. I had become friends with another Australian in Rome named John Howard. He wrote gossip columns about movie stars for various magazines. Wherever you found a star or a starlet, you would find John. He would be hiding behind newspaper stands at the airport, or dressed in brown to blend into a tree trunk in front of some famous villa or sitting at a table in a cafe on the Via Veneto pretending to read a newspaper with two holes cut into the paper so he could peep through. He could worm his way into any situation if he thought there was a story about the stars in it for him. John was so

Front row at The Beatles concert, Rome.

well connected that I was sure he could get tickets to the Beatles concert for me. After one telephone call to John, he arrived at my house holding three front row tickets to the concert! He also told me we would be having a drink with some of the crew before the show.

The concert was on **28 June 1965** at the Adriano Theatre. I took along two Italian nannies, who were friends of mine. I knew how chuffed they would be to have front row seats at the Beatles concert. Before the show, we had drinks with the crew, just as John said. The concert was exciting, however I didn't get to hear any of the music or words of the songs even from my front row seat. The audience screamed from the moment The Beatles came on the stage until the performance was over. At one point, I even found myself screaming along with the rest of them! After the show, the three of us

tagged along to Club 84 with all of them. I chatted to their chauffeur, Alfie Bicknell, whilst the four super stars were off chattering to all the beautiful girls who had been lined up for them.

Alfie told me they were leaving Rome to do a one night stand in Barcelona. As it happened, I was about to leave on my month's holiday and had planned to make Barcelona my first stop. The concert in Barcelona was to be on the **3rd of July.** That was my 25th birthday! What a marvellous birthday present! Alfie told me I should meet them at their hotel, the Avenida Palace. I went with my Italian girlfriend Lisa, who was travelling with me for the month. As we went to the hotel, I hoped I was dressed right for the occasion. While in Rome, I had been following what was happening in the fashion world in London very closely. I knew the styles were getting more eccentric by the moment.

When we got to the Avenida Palace, Alfie greeted me like an old friend and he hurried us off to have a drink with the Beatles manager, Brian Epstein, and his secretary, Wendy Hanson. Brian was a lovely man and quite charming. When we were done, we were told there were five limousines parked at a side entrance of the hotel waiting to drive the Beatles and their crew to the Plaza Toros Monumental di Barcelona for the concert and that we could ride in one of them! We were shuffled down dark passages, through hidden doors and then into one of the cars. As I sat in the limo, it suddenly dawned on me where I was. Here I was, Miss Jennifer Nobody from the Australian bush sitting in a limousine in Barcelona with the Beatles in the car in front of me ready to be escorted to a bullfighting arena to watch their concert from a VIP position. Wow! What fun it was to be in Europe! The streets were completely full of people all trying to get a glimpse of the Beatles. The police were dragging people off our cars and pushing them out of the way so we could depart. The concert on that hot summer night was the most memorable one I have ever seen in my entire life. Seeing these four young men who had turned the music world upside down perform on a flood-lit stage in that huge bull fighting arena was amazing. I doubt if any matador had ever received a reception as great as those boys from Liverpool did on that night.

As we drove back to the hotel after the show, I wondered if I should remind Alf about a promise he had made that we could meet the boys. I didn't think the Beatles were interested in meeting us, but I was very interested in meeting them. Before I had a chance to ask, Alf came up and said we would be going to have something to eat with the boys in their room. I remember sitting in their hotel room having a few snacks and chatting a bit with George Harrison. He was wearing pale blue jeans spattered with white spots. I had

never seen jeans like that before and presumed it was the fashion. When I asked him how he got them, he replied in typical Beatles style, 'Just go to Greenland, take a left hand turn and then….' We made a little more small talk and then it was time for us to go.

The rest of my month in Spain wasn't anywhere near as memorable as that night. We visited Madrid, Granada, Malaga, Valencia and Costa Brava. Then we went to Tangiers for a few days before returning to Spain via Gibraltar. I was glad I was finally getting to see a bit more of Europe, however I was relieved when our trip was nearing an end. My friend Lisa was getting thinner and thinner by the day. All she wanted to eat was pasta. I tried to explain to her that Spaniards don't eat spaghetti and she needed to find something else to eat. I started to worry that if I didn't get some pasta into her, I would end up with a corpse on my hands. She literally gave up eating the last few days of our trip.

My month in Spain had been a good break for me. I felt ready to settle back into my job as a nanny again. The fact that 'London Fever' was filtering more and more into Rome helped ease my restlessness. I was excited when my friends in London sent me a mini dress from Mary Quant's shop, the Ginger Bread Group. Up until then, mini dresses hadn't been seen in Rome, but I didn't care. Now that I'd met the Beatles, I felt I could wear a mini too. Besides, back in Mildura Snooks and I used to wear mini skirts we had sewn ourselves. That was back in the **1950s** when no one had ever heard of mini skirts. Now, I just needed the perfect opportunity to show off my new Mary Quant dress.

59

Hitchhiking in Tangier.

his back as I got undressed. However as he began to sketch, there was something I found a bit odd about him. His apartment was not well heated and it was very chilly in the room, especially for me since I was naked. Yet, he continually perspired. He also seemed to have trouble keeping his hand steady and kept throwing drawings into the wastebasket. I was worried that maybe I was the wrong shape or I wasn't the right kind of model he was looking for. But no, at the end of our session he paid me and asked me to come back the following afternoon. That was great. I was already calculating how much extra money I could make a week just for lying around on fluffy cushions. I was hoping he had lots and lots of drawing to do!

I was much more at ease when I arrived at his studio the following day. I was so at ease that I was out of my clothes within minutes and in position on the cushions; so at ease that I didn't notice him leap from his position near the easel and suddenly land on top of me amongst the huge pink cushions. A chase of cat and mouse began with me holding one of the cushions in front of me as I ran. As he followed me, he tried to excuse his behaviour in his broken English. Eventually, he gave up. Trying to run and explain himself in English at the same time had exhausted him. He flopped down in the middle of the pink cushions. I took my chance to put on my clothes and I politely told him that I would not be working for him anymore. By the time I reached home, I was in tears. I told Simonetta what had happened and expected some sort of compassion from the her. After all, she was the one who had sent me to the painter. Instead, she burst into laughter and asked how far he had gotten with me! I was shocked at her reply, but La Signora simply said, 'You still have much to learn about Italian men, Jennie.'

I was invited to a party given by a marvellous Italian woman I knew. She was friends with many artists and I knew they would all be invited to her party as well. The night of the party, I sneaked out of the house wearing a long coat over my little dress. I wasn't sure if the family was ready for a nanny in a mini that barely covered my arse. At the party, I was introduced to the guests who included many up and coming young painters in Rome. I felt as though I'd stepped into a new world and it was a world I felt I wanted to know more about. Everyone at the party approved of my dress and they fully supported the liberation of the mini in Italy.

In spite of working full-time, it was difficult for me to put much away on what the family paid me. I decided I needed to make a little extra money. I suggested a raise, but La Signora had a better idea. A painter friend of theirs was looking for a model and La Signora told me she was willing to give me a few hours free each week so I could go work for him. They were such a respectable family that I was sure their friend would be the same. I hoped the artist would want to paint me swathed in chiffon or draped in silk, but I had no such luck. What he wanted was a classical model with big hips, little tits and he wanted her naked. Oh well, I thought, it was for the sake of art. My first session went quite well. The man was polite and kind and he turned

Rome continued to fill up more and more with mini skirts and pop music. The word 'marijuana' was being whispered amongst my friends. Three Australian girlfriends of mine opened up one of the first Op and Pop boutiques in Rome. They were selling all the latest styles that were being sold in London. They didn't seem to have many customers, probably due to the odd location of their shop on a little street in Trastevere. The shop may not have had many customers, but it was always full of their friends who would pop in to chat and hang around. We decided they needed publicity to bring in some paying customers and I agreed to help them with the campaign.

We needed a good photographer to do a series of photos for the top Italian fashion magazines. Once again our friend John Howard came to the rescue. He arranged everything and sent us the best photographer he could find. My friends had no funds to hire any models, so the three owners of the shop and myself decided we would be the models ourselves. We were all tall enough, had good bodies and were all sporting long straight hair which was the rage in London at the time. We found an American boy who had the look we wanted too. The photo shoot was done at night, so we wouldn't be disturbed by any of the non-buying 'customers'. After the photographer had taken reels of film of us dressed in every garment in the shop, he suggested we have a bit of fun just amongst ourselves while he took a few more photos. I'm sure that was John Howard's idea. We were promised we would be given all the photos and negatives from the 'fun' shoot, so we agreed. We decided to have a 'happening', which was the 'in' thing to do in London. My friends were just as naive as I was and we would do anything for a laugh. We painted our faces and the parts of our bodies which showed around our clothes. Then with the help of a few props we found in the shop, we came up with some weird and wonderful poses. For the final photograph, the photographer suggested I take off my tank top and dance in front of my painted friends, clad only in a mini skirt. He said, I didn't have to face the camera, so the photo would just show my bare back half covered by my long blonde hair. That seemed innocent enough to me, so I agreed. After all I had recently taken off all my clothes for that randy painter!

The fun shoot was over and the photographer left. We didn't hear from him, but then a week or so later I was in the piazza in front of our house. As I passed the newspaper kiosk where all the latest magazines and papers were displayed something caught my eye. I did a double turn and thought, *No! It can't be possible!* One entire wall of the kiosk was covered with *ABC* magazine, probably the trashiest magazine in Italy. Each magazine was opened to the same page with the headline: 'Happening at *prezzo fisso*' (Happening at a fixed price). Underneath the headline was an over-sized photograph of a half naked girl with long blonde hair cascading down her back, surrounded by four painted freaks! Oh no! I wanted to get rid of all the magazines. If there had been only a small number of copies I would have bought them all, torn them into little pieces and flushed them down the loo. I looked at the kiosk and there seemed to be hundreds of copies stacked up inside. I quickly bought one copy for my scrapbook and hurried home, desperately hoping my family hadn't been down to the piazza today. As I put the key into the lock, I heard the father's stern voice call out, 'Jennie, would you please come into the living room? We have something to discuss with you.' I ran to my room, slipped the copy of *ABC* under my bed and slunk out to face them. They screamed and yelled at me about the trauma they had been put through that morning after seeing a photograph of their nanny half naked on the newspaper stand down in the piazza. Fortunately, the well-known Italian actress Rossana Podestà, was visiting them. She was a very close friend of the family and she saved me that afternoon. Rossana had made many films where she would drop her negligee to the floor and stand with her naked back towards the camera. After the family finally stopped screaming at me, Rossana spoke up and said, 'Jennie, you looked just great. It was a wonderful photograph.' With that, the subject was dropped and never spoken of again.

I have to admit that until the next edition of *ABC* was on the stand, I wore my hair pulled back in a severe chignon and wore sunglasses whenever I crossed the piazza. I often wondered if Nino had seen the photo. His salon was only about ten meters away from the newspaper stand. However

"Happening" a prezzo fisso

SERVIZIO A PAG. 20

since he had never really had the opportunity to see my naked back, he probably wouldn't have even recognised me in that photo. I know John Howard had been behind all of this. He probably made a lot of money on the article. I bet he could have sold it in Australia, too—perhaps with the headline: Australian Happening in the Eternal City!

My friends who owned the shop decided to forget about the publicity campaign. They hoped the store would take off on its own. I often spent my free afternoons with them there. I always met new people and loved going through the new stock as it arrived from London. Then, one afternoon when I stopped by I noticed a big change. For a second I thought maybe they were redecorating. No, it looked too bad for that. The dressmaker's dummy was standing in the corner, naked. The clothes racks were there, but with nothing on them. The display window was completely empty. Even the artificial flowers were gone. My three friends were sitting on the customers' bench and they said in unison, 'We've been robbed.' Whoever had done it took everything, even the pins and the paper shopping bags.

We decided to find out who had robbed them. A few weeks ago we were models, now we became detectives. We spent that afternoon planning how to find the stock. The first thing to do was to go to the early morning markets. That was the usual procedure after a robbery in this area. The local gangs usually tried to get rid of the goods as soon as possible. We searched all the markets in the area thoroughly, but to no avail. Then a few nights later, an envelope was slipped under the door of the shop which read:

> We have your goods well hidden in a house near your shop. We are willing to give you the first option to buy them back.

The price they demanded to get the items back was much more than their actual value, so my

Jennie at the bar in Porto Santo Stefano.

friends didn't respond. That ended the little touch of London on the back street of Trastevere.

That summer I drove the children down to Porto Santo Stefano for our holiday. Little did I know I was about to meet some people who would bring an enormous change to my life. At least this summer wouldn't be as lonely as the last one had been. This year the family took an apartment in a hotel rather than renting a house. The parents were friends with an American family who had rented a large villa on the coast. We spent many days with their six children. Massimo and Valerio had plenty of company, while I enjoyed passing my time on the terrace chatting to the mother, Julie. I hadn't met the father. He had stayed behind in Switzerland where they lived. He owned a hotel in Zermatt and the Museum Club in Montreux.

One afternoon when the children were having their nap, I decided to sit at the bar and chat to the barman. I was approached by a blue-eyed, fair-haired, tall, handsome man dressed in jeans and a denim jacket. He came up to me and said, 'How's it going, Tiger? I hear you've been keeping my kids company.' So this was Karl Iverson, the daddy of the six children. He wasn't what I had expected at all. After a few minutes, I felt as though we had been friends for years. Charm oozed out of him

First view of Positano, 1966.

and he was very amusing. He offered me a drink, but I told him I couldn't drink alcohol, as I had to drive the children into the village that afternoon. 'Then, how about a margarita?', he suggested. 'There's no alcohol and it's very refreshing.' The name sounded fitting for a hot afternoon. I really wasn't into drinking in those days, so even if he'd have said it was a tequila margarita, I wouldn't have known what that was. I sat on the bar stool next to him and had five of those delicious little 'non alcoholic' drinks before I realised it was time for me to take the children into town. I was feeling just marvellous, at least until I tried to get down from the stool and my knees gave away. The last thing I remembered was being carried to my room. My excuse to the family was the strange smelling clams I had eaten for lunch! In time, Karl would become a very dear friend and an important person in my life.

Judy and I continued to spend many evenings together. We often discussed plans for a trip around Europe together. She was still doing crowd scenes in spaghetti westerns, but now only for the extra money, not with the idea of becoming a movie star. I always felt that with her pretty face and voluptuous body, she could have gone a long way in Rome at that time, but I think her Irish-Catholic upbringing wouldn't let her think in those terms. Next to her, I always felt like the ugly sister, but that didn't get in the way of our friendship. In many ways we were quite different, which sometimes was a good thing. Our tastes in the opposite sex were entirely different, which meant we got on just fine when we went out together. One thing we did have in common was our naivety.

In **November of 1965**, I had the urge to travel again. Judy and I asked for four days off. We rented a Fiat 500 and headed south to Capri. We knew there would be very few tourists on the island at that time of year. On our way back after visiting the island, I insisted we drive along the Amalfi coast towards Salerno before returning to Rome. As we drove along the coast, I thought it was the most beautiful coastline in the world. We came to a small village called Positano. The magic of the town called our car to a halt. I got out of the car to feel the magical vibration for myself. I remember saying to Judy, 'Look, it's all pink! I mustn't forget the name of this town—Positano. I want to come back here again one day.'

We returned to Rome and I worked eight more months as a nanny. Finally in **July 1966**, I left the family so I could tour Europe with Judy. She and I had planned to travel around by hitchhiking, but we weren't the usual sort of hikers. The way we were decked out, we looked as though we had a rail pass. Maybe it was our naivety that enabled us to hitchhike across Europe the way we did, wearing dainty shoes, pleated skirts and blouses and carrying proper suitcases instead of rucksacks! My family agreed to drop us off on the highway near Rimini. It was sad saying our good-byes. Two years with one family day and night is quite a long time and I was very fond of the children. Of course, I had a little cry as I waved to them as they drove away.

Judy and I put out our thumbs and found a ride up to Venice. From there we went to Verona and on to Bremen, Germany and Innsbruck. We stayed at youth hostels along the way, but in Innsbruck and Munich the youth hostels were full. A man who had given us a ride to Munich put us up for a few days in an apartment he shared with his girlfriend. I loved Munich. We moved on to Heidelberg, Frankfurt, Russelheim, and Cologne. Hamburg came next. It was there we saw a line of tourists going into a courtyard. We followed, although most of the tourists were men. Inside we saw ladies in little rooms facing the courtyard. I started taking photographs of the ladies, but was quickly stopped by a large blonde woman who screamed at us. We learnt we had stumbled into the Reeperbahn, the area famous for its prostitutes.

From Hamburg we headed to Copenhagen to see the Little Mermaid. We said goodbye to the mermaid and headed to Goteberg and then on to Oslo, where we had a look around and watched the shrimp boats come in. Next we travelled to Stockholm, which was the most expensive city I had ever seen. Fortunately we had an apartment lent to us by friends of a friend, so we were able to spend a month there, which allowed us to get to know the city well.

We headed back to Nyborg, Denmark and then to Germany again, where we visited Braunschweig and Berlin. Berlin was still separated by the wall and people were only allowed to visit the east side for the day. It felt strange on the east side. All the East Germans stared at us with sad curious faces, there were the piles of rubble left over from the war and broken down buildings everywhere.

We went on to Ingolstadt and then Munich again, followed by Vienna. After Austria came Hungary. I was finally able to keep my promise to Mr Komloshy, my former boss in Melbourne, and I visited Budapest for him. Budapest didn't seem to have any hostels or small hotels, so we were put in a private house with a very kind woman. I still remember the family portraits hanging on their walls. They had no more than four pieces of cutlery and four plates in the kitchen. We tried to get the woman to talk about the political situation, but it was impossible. Budapest seemed to be such a sad city with very sad people. It was difficult to get around because so few people spoke English. While we were there, we went to two pharmacies attempting to buy tampax or pads, but we

couldn't make ourselves understood and they threw us out. Who knows what they thought we were asking for! Finally, we found another pharmacy with a kind assistant who seemed to understand what we wanted. He started rolling off meters of some sort of bandage to sell to us— at least that was better than nothing.

In those days you could only get a 48 hour visa for Hungary. As our time was running out, we tried to get a ride out of the country, but the driver we found wasn't going that far. He left us in the middle of nowhere. There were very few cars on the road and we weren't sure how we would make our way out in time. I didn't like the idea of being put into a prison in Hungary just because they didn't have enough cars! Fortunately, a van with four young men from Manchester, England came by. They stopped, but didn't really want to give us a ride. Judy and I begged and pleaded until they eventually agreed to take us along with them.

We travelled on to Belgrade, Yugoslavia and looked for a place to stay. We met two young men, one Italian and one English, who took us to a bar for cakes and lemonade. That was what we would order in those days—cakes and lemonade! They helped us find a room in their friend's house. Their friend Momo was 51 years old and lived together with his elderly parents and a couple of young kids in a small house with only two bedrooms. It was a weird set up. Judy and I were given one bedroom and were told that to get to the bathroom we had to cross through the other bedroom. That night when we had to use the loo, we found Momo, his mother, his father and the children all squeezed up in one double bed. We realised then how much they must have needed the little money we paid them.

From Belgrade we got a ride with two men in a battered old American car. They were either Greek or Turkish. I got an uncomfortable feeling from them, so even though it was dark, I told them to stop at the next exit on the highway and let us out. They dumped us under an exit sign which read 'Kumanovo'. I had never heard of Kumanovo, but didn't really care. I was just glad we were out of that car. We started walking down a long, dark road with our luggage, with no idea where we were going. After some time, the road curved and I saw a sight I have never forgotten. There was a huge gypsy camp with fires burning. The people were dressed in colourful clothes and playing music as they gathered around brightly-painted caravans. We couldn't believe our eyes. It was like walking into a dream. It was amazing. No one from the camp approached us or tried to talk to us. They just looked at us and then went about their business as we passed by and continued walking down the road.

Soon we came to the village of Kumanovo. There was one dirty hotel with one available room with a single bed. Instead of running water to wash with, we were given two bottles of water. We met two men from the hotel and they invited us to a nightclub called Kumanovo Banja. It really wasn't much of a nightclub. I needed to use the toilet and asked where to find it. The toilet was a hole in the floor, which was fine. I had seen that before. The problem was that no one who had used it before me had hit the hole. The floor was a pool of *merda*—shit! I really had to go, so I used it anyway, somehow. I just kept saying to myself, 'I wanted to experience travel. Well, this is all part of the experience.'

We travelled on to Skopje and then spent a few scorching days in Athens. By this time we were exhausted, so we took a bus and two boats to reach the island of Moni, where we stayed for about twenty days. That was twenty days of bliss. There were only tents on the island— tents, peacocks and a few sheep. We rented a tent, which came with two mattresses and sheets. We settled in and began to get to know our new home. There was one small grocer shop, which had fresh wares brought in by boat each morning. There was only one restaurant built with fake Greek columns, which was open only for the few weekend tourists who would come by. After our first week, we asked if they had a job for us. They said sure, we could help setting up the tents. So we spent a couple of weeks setting up tents and preparing for any new arrivals in exchange for the rent on our

tent and our food. We were living for free. Our days were spent swimming in the crystal clear water and going for walks. At night everyone gathered around a bonfire on the beach, singing and dancing to the music of *Zorba*. I have great memories of that holiday. It was heaven. After all we had gone through earlier in our trip, it seemed like going though hell to get to paradise! After nearly three weeks on Moni, we finally headed back to Athens, boated our way to Brindisi and then returned to Rome.

I am not sure how much longer I stayed in Rome, but eventually I decided to go back to London. It was **1967** and a new era was well on its way in London. I felt I should be there to see what was going on and try it out myself. Everything I had read in the papers about the scene in London sounded so exciting. Hippy fever had taken over and it seemed like a fantasy land filled with music, fashion, Indian jackets, beads and bells. It all sounded so loving and peaceful. People were even giving flowers to policemen on the street. All we had to do was end the Vietnam War and we could live in peace forever!

Elegant, Weekend Hippies in London

When I returned to London, the first person I contacted was, of course, dear Vern. I let him know I was back and I was ready to attend 'school' with him again. I was sure he would catch me up on all I had missed out on during my time away. It was a quick crash course! Last time I was in London, Vern had been running a little stall selling antique porcelain in the Chelsea Antique Market on King's Road. I remember the kitchen in Vern's flat was always crammed with plates, dishes, teapots and anything else made from beautiful old porcelain or Wedgwood that he could sell in his stall. Every time I stopped by, his collection of antique porcelain seemed to grow larger and larger. Then one day he came across a beaded dress from the 1930s. He hung it up in his stall and it was snatched up immediately. So he bought more old dresses and then more and more. They all sold out as quickly as he could get them. Soon there were so many dresses, jackets and fringed shawls in his stall that the little teapots and Wedgwood cups began to disappear under all the sequins and fringe.

Vern now had a stall in the market selling vintage clothing. He ran it with Adrian Emmerton and they called it Emmerton & Lambert. Their customers were looking for the latest fashion. They included the famous pop stars, actors and people from all over the world who would fly to London just for the weekend to buy from the market. London seemed to be where one should be at that time and Vern's shop was the place to be in London. That made Emmerton & Lambert one of the most well known stores in the city.

When I arrived, Vern immediately offered me a job at the market. Wow, I thought. Now I'll be right in the middle of everything that's happening. The vibrations of the city back then are hard to describe. You had to be there to feel it. Whenever I talk to someone who was there or was connected with it I still feel an incredible rush, as if my blood is going to my head at a great speed. I was so lucky to have been in the right place at the right time and to have the right friends. All of London felt like a great big carnival—day and night. It was pure magic.

Adrian was Vern's business partner and they also shared a wonderful flat together in South Kensington. Vern offered to let me stay with them, so we all flatted together. Adrian was a lovely man, good-looking and tall. He was quiet and rather shy, especially compared with Vern who was always so full of life. Adrian was a very nice guy, but I don't think he could have made that business work on his own without Vern's input and personality.

Vern had another woman who worked for him, a Swedish beauty named Ulla Larson. Ulla and I got on immediately. She was lovely and seemed

Jennie Ulla, Adrian and Rudy.

Adrian, Ulla and Vern.

to know everyone. She called me 'Yennie', because she couldn't pronounce the letter 'J'. Together Ulla and I were in charge of the small shop upstairs and a small terrace that looked onto the King's Road. Before the terrace, there was a coffee bar run by Pearl and her husband, Bob. Pearl and Bob were always dressed in black, like bohemians from the beat era. We all loved their quiet and gentle manner, which was so different from most of the characters who frequented the market. Whenever the shop was quiet, we could always be found at their coffee bar.

Vern was always busy. Whenever someone's granny died in London or beyond, Vern would run off to see what he could find. He would buy up Victorian nightdresses, fur collars, beaded dresses, costume jewellery, fringed shawls and anything else he thought might be a good fit for his customers. Once he came back from a sale at one of the big auction houses with a waistcoat they claimed had belonged to Napoleon. That was a quick sale to one of the pop stars!

Vern kept an eye on me. I was still the 'girl from Mildura' to him, yet by now he was sure I could cope, or at least know how to cover up any gaffs I made and I did make a few. I didn't know all the famous people who came into our shop and I was

still learning the new language being created by the musicians and hippies.

One day Vern called me over to the door to tell me Jimi Hendrix was in our shop. He asked me to be very careful and treat him well. I went back inside and saw three people there. A stocky, middle-aged English man, a tall, thin woman, who looked as if she could have been an actress and a black dude (to use my new language) with dread locks. I wasn't sure which one Vern wanted me to treat well, but I put a bet on the white English guy. Then I saw Vern at the door making strange faces at me and pointing in the other direction towards the black dude. 'Oops.' It didn't take me long to learn who Jimi Hendrix was and why Vern wanted him to be treated well. The ceiling of the market was decorated with antique, fringed shawls. Jimi said he dug the way they looked and asked us to come decorate the entrance to his flat the same way.

My favourite faux pas in the shop was with a young boy who came in and told me he was going on a trip. He said he needed the right clothes to get him through the weekend. My immediate retort was, 'Where are you going? Abroad?' The boy smiled and gave me a hearty slap on the back as he said, 'Cool man. You're sooo cool!' I thought that was a strange response and I still didn't know where he was planning to travel. He started trying on velvet jackets and trousers, so I assumed it wasn't anywhere hot. Later when I told Vern about it, he explained that when someone said they were going for 'a trip', it meant an acid trip... LSD! I really didn't know anything about drugs, apart from smoking pot in Rome one time. There was still so much for me to learn.

There were times when Ulla and I both gaffed together. We had four young American boys in the shop one day. They seemed like the type of customers who would have a lot of money, so we started dressing them up in everything we could find, as fast as we could, thinking—money, money, money... Again, Vern's non-smiling face appeared at the door. I slipped out and he said, 'What the hell are you two doing with those guys? Those are The Monkeys and they've just arrived from America. Lay off them!' We stopped being so pushy and in the end Ulla even had her photo taken with them on the terrace. It was published in the paper the next day.

So many famous people came to the shop. Paul McCartney, Jane Asher, Roger Daltry and Georgie Fame's girlfriend, Carmen Jimenez. Twiggy came in when she had just started working as a model. Eric Clapton and Alice Ormsby-Gore used to stop in together all the time. They often dressed in our clothes. I remember one time when Alice came with her sister and brother. They were looking for something to wear to their mother's funeral after she had died in a car crash. Although Paul McCartney did come to our shop, the rest of the Beatles never came. Some famous musicians wouldn't come to us. Our shop was small and didn't have a back exit. They were afraid they might be caught inside if crowds of fans heard they were there. We never made a fuss over any of our famous customers. As far as I was concerned, all our customers were the same, just people looking for some unusual clothing.

There were several times when Vern and I arrived to open the shop at 10.00 am and we'd see the Rolling Stones waiting for us out front in their Rolls. Vern would say, 'Oh my God, here they are again...' One time Brian Jones came in with his chauffeur. Brian was tripping and he started slowly

Micky Dolenz and Ulla at the Chelsea Market.

going around touching all the black velvet clothes in the shop. He ended up buying everything he touched. The next day his manager called. He wanted to send all the clothes back saying, 'What the fuck did you do, letting him buy all this black velvet stuff?!' The Stones used to return things so often after tripping that Vern finally told me not to charge them anymore. He said I should just write down what they took and they would settle up later for the things they actually kept.

I was working full-time for Vern, but I still needed more money. I took a second job in the evenings as a waitress in a casino called the Victorian Sporting Club. The casino was a complete other world from the market. It was quite an adjustment every time I had to change into the grey uniform and pale pink apron we had to wear at the club. Only the permanent staff were allowed to work in the high-stake Chemine di Fer and Roulette rooms. Since I was only part-time, I had to waitress at the two and six pence Kalookie tables. The low-stake gambling tables meant my tips were lower too. I worked with two girls, Patti from New Zealand and Shirley from London. They taught me a few tricks of the trade, which helped make our hard work a bit more worthwhile. They told me if I ever saw a chip on the floor I shouldn't pick it up. Instead I should kick it to the side of the room and not retrieve it until the night was over and the customers had left.

The Victorian Sporting Club was a Jewish club. Most of the male customers there treated me well, but many of the women clients were not so nice. Some of them would call out to me with their false eyelashes flickering, 'Miss, Miss! Our sandwiches are late." In my memory they all wore vibrant coloured, mohair sweaters covered in sequins and appliqués. We knew some of the women were kosher, yet sometimes some of them would beckon one of us waitresses with a brightly painted fingernail and whisper, 'Miss, bring me a toasted bacon sandwich over near the entrance to the loo and don't let anyone see what you're bringing.' You would think doing a favour like that would get us a nice tip, but it didn't. I really didn't like most of those women. They came to the club every night and saw us all the time, yet they never called any of us by our names.

Another trick I learned from Patti and Shirley also gave us a little extra money to take home each night. When we put in our orders we had to pass a plump, grey-haired lady who worked at the cash desk. She would write the bill for the customers and record the order for the club. Then we would return to her with the money before delivering the order. Several times a night one of us would involve her in a deep conversation whilst another would slip by with her tray and place an unofficial order with the kitchen. We would always make it for smoked salmon sandwiches, which were the most expensive item on the menu. Each night we tried to make sure each of us pocketed the money for one or more of these orders. We were all

basically very honest young ladies, but with rude customers and lousy tips, this little extra we took home each night seemed justified to us.

I really needed the extra money from this job, but working two jobs was making me quite over tired. One evening on my break at the casino, I was in the kitchen drowsing over my coffee when a croupier from the high-stakes gambling room asked me what was wrong. I explained I was working two jobs, day and night. The work was exhausting, but so was the double life I was leading. At night I wore my grey uniform and had my long hair done up in a French pleat. The rest of the time I floated around in long robes, mini dresses, bathing suits from the 30s or whatever else we were trying to sell at the market that day. Leading two different lives at the same time was turning me into a schizophrenic. Mr Croupier listened and then took my hand and placed a small white pill in it. 'Try this and you'll find you can get through the night much better.' I thanked him, but tried to explain that I didn't have a headache. He said the pill wasn't for pain and I should just give it a try, so I did. Pretty soon I was flying around the tables, kicking fallen chips into corners, serving three people at the same time and not pausing even to breathe. I went home with more tips that night than ever before.

That was my first experience with speed. I tried it a few more nights before I decided it wasn't for me. My body is so full of natural adrenaline that any chemical addition turns me into a flying machine! I was still quite ignorant about drugs, even though I was in the middle of all of it. I was basically too straight to be bent and probably too practical and aware to be totally corrupted. Eventually I had to give up the night job at the club. It was all becoming too much for me.

I find it quite difficult to describe what I felt during that period in London, as it was so extraordinary and unreal. Everyone seemed completely happy and positive about life. Ulla and I became elegant, weekend hippies. Vern wanted us to be seen everywhere to show off the clothes. What Ulla and I were wearing wasn't the latest, we were way ahead of that. The clothes we wore were the *most* beautiful, the *most* extravagant and the *most* sensational. Before each event, we chose our outfits from the clothes at the shop. Then, the next day we would put them back on the racks. Most of the clothes were secondhand and old, so who cared if they got worn one more time before they were sold!

Vern heard that Jimi Hendrix was going to give a concert just outside of London. Of course we would be attending. The day before the show I had a small operation to remove a cyst from under my eyebrow and was sporting a few stitches. I told Vern maybe it wasn't a good idea for me to go. What if some of the fans got too excited and accidentally whacked me in the eye? For some reason I had a strange feeling I shouldn't go. Vern didn't agree. He convinced me it would be fine, so I went along. We had a long walk from where we parked the car to the concert hall and along the way we encountered groups of Mods. They were hanging around drinking cans of beer and making nasty remarks about all the hippies going to the show. The Mods and Rockers were always breaking up the beach establishments down around Brighton and Bexhill-on-Sea. They were into leather, studs, chains and motorcycles. They didn't like the hippies at all and would do anything for a fight. When we got to the door of the club, we saw it was mobbed with people trying to get in. Suddenly the body of a bloody Mod was thrown from the inside of the foyer, out the door, right over our heads and into the crowd. The screams, blood and noise were too much for us 'make love and not war' people, so we turned around and went home. I checked the newspaper first thing the next day to see who had been hurt in the Mods versus Hippy War, but there was only a notice describing the successful performance given by Jimi Hendrix. We later heard from our friends who had gone to the concert that nothing had happened inside and it had been a great show.

LSD was topping the drug scene, just like The Beatles and The Stones were topping the Top of the Pops. From what I had heard, LSD didn't seem to be a drug, but rather an experience to be done every now and then, almost like fasting once a month to cleanse your body. I hadn't tried it yet myself, but everyone seemed to be getting initiated. It wasn't just hippies either. Everyone was doing it, even bank tellers and insurance brokers.

One day I overheard a conversation on the metro train between two shop assistants coming home from work. One said, 'I've kept next Saturday free for my first trip, so I'll have Sunday to get over it. Would you like to trip with me?' The other said she couldn't, 'I have a wedding to go to this Saturday, but if you could change the date, I'll certainly go with you the week after.' It was like asking a friend to go bowling or to a movie. I was now used to seeing many clients come into the shop when they were tripping. I could always tell by the way they spent such a long time feeling the different fabrics and oohing and aahing over the colours and the beads. Ulla and I would giggle to ourselves thinking that we probably looked like two monsters to them. I knew my time was coming up and the 'girl from the bush' would have to take the plunge and join the others. I suppose in those days it was rather like losing your virginity. Even Vern had done a few trips, although generally he was more into liquid highs.

One day Vern approached me in his usual kind and gentle way and said, 'Babe, we think it's time you had your first little trip on Sunday. There is a Sit-In in Hyde Park, so the atmosphere will be perfect. It will be only a short ride, since it will be your first time. Then, the following weekend you can have the usual three-day ceremony at our house. Adrian will accompany you, because he hasn't been initiated yet either.' I completely trusted Vern to take care of everything, so I told him, 'Okay, if it's my time, I'll jot it down in my date book. What about my clothes? What should I wear?' He assured me he would have it all planned and under control. He added, 'There'll be no need for shoes Babe, since you'll be in the park on green soft grass, but I won't go into that now. You wouldn't understand.'

Sunday finally came around. In my room at Vern's, which was decorated in the Liberty Period style that Vern adored, I found laid out on my bed a long, white cotton Victorian nightgown trimmed with delicate old lace. I dressed very slowly and then brushed my long hair a hundred times. I felt like Alice going into Wonderland. I was sitting on the bed shoeless, when Vern came in with a bunch of the palest pink flowers. They were my initiation bouquet. He also gave me my little half-portion

of a pale pink pill and told me to swallow it. My followers were all waiting downstairs. Everyone had put on their best Sunday robes for the occasion and together we all started off to Hyde Park barefoot. It all seemed so solemn, which made me giggle inside, even before the effect had come on—or maybe it had… By the time we reached the green grass in the park, I was feeling wonderful. The grass became like a carpet, which had been rolled out just for me. Hundreds of Flower Power people were already sitting in the park and singing Beatle songs, although most of them didn't know the words or the melodies. Mounted police were everywhere. I suppose they were looking for drugs. That thought made me giggle all the more. I knew I had already put the drug where they could never find it!

Knowing Vern and his disciples were watching over me gave me a great feeling of protection. However, I also felt I didn't need anyone at all at the moment—too much was happening. The sun was shining and I was floating along in my own world. What got to me the most that day were the flowerbeds in the park. The mixture and intensity of the colours made my eyes burn. I knew most of the flowers by name, but I had never seen them so big before. They were gigantic and the way they were breathing and pulsating so heavily – in and out, in and out – put me into a quasi-trance. I'm not sure how long I was there watching the flowers breathe before I heard Vern's voice say, 'Okay, its time for Babe to go home. She's had her antipasti and must rest up for the main course next weekend.'

The next morning I thought about all that had happened the day before. Now I had done it. Now I was one of the Flower People. I wanted to go back to the park to see the flowers again, but Vern told me they wouldn't be that big today. I couldn't believe they could shrink so much over night.

My next trip was scheduled for the following Sunday. The day before was spent cleaning and polishing. We sorted the best books to be left on the coffee table and the perfect music to be played. Lists were made for the food to be bought, including many juicy honey melons, which we later cut into perfect slices and laid to rest on silver platters. Our clothes were carefully selected. They had to be made of the softest fabrics and in vibrant colours with no sequins or anything rough. The most important detail was that they be comfortable. Our preparation had the feeling of a family getting ready for an important cocktail party or a wedding. Everything had to be perfect. This time it wouldn't be just a gentle meander on the grass in the park.

On Sunday morning, Adrian and I were ready when the guests arrived. We both swallowed a pill. The trip started with a half hour of uncontrollable laughter. It was so exhausting and so liberating that it brought tears to my eyes. I knew I would have to have a lot of strength and courage to get through this, because even though I was surrounded by loving people who I knew would protect and guide me—I also knew that basically I was alone.

The horrors began very early. I was trying to crawl through a dark tunnel whilst pushing cobwebs out of my way and off my shoulders. Finally, I came to the light at the end. Whew! I tried to smash the record player in the room, because I didn't want to hear the particular song that was playing. I can't remember the song. It's one of the few things I don't remember about that trip. I just remember it really upset me. The singer was a woman and the words of the song really got to me. I just had to put a stop to it. I wished I could go back to the beginning of the trip and just laugh and laugh again.

Then, the last of the horrors came on full force. Our apartment was on the 4th floor and it had large windows overlooking a church. I was drawn to the window and became totally fixated on the door of the church as the congregation started coming out after Sunday service. The priest was there to say a few words to his flock as they left. Next to him was a high wooden stand with an open Bible leaning on the top ledge. I was looking down from the window to this very small book near the door of the church. I felt lost. My breath was so strong I had to continually wipe the windows which kept steaming up. I could hear the low whispers of my friends saying, 'Stay close to her. She probably won't jump, but let's not risk anything.' I knew what they were saying and thinking. In fact I could hear and see more than I had ever had before. I thought

Illustration by János Zigmond.

75

János

how wonderful it would be to open the windows and fly away, but I had no intention of doing so. I couldn't take my eyes off that Bible. The more I stared, the larger the letters became. The words started to come towards the window, as if they were floating in the air. Just as I began to put the words together, they would disappear back into the pages. I knew there was a message for me in that book. I was frantically wiping the window and crying hysterically. The frustration of not understanding the message was too much for me. Then the priest said his goodbyes to the last of his congregation. He took the stand inside and closed the door. I was devastated and screamed, 'They've locked me out! I can't get in! They won't let me read the message!' Who knows what it all meant. I felt as though I had been tripping for years, not just a matter of hours.

After a while, everything became serene and beautiful. I decided I didn't want to come back down. Much later in the evening some more friends dropped by. Everyone was whispering very quietly, but I could hear that they were saying, 'Don't tell her yet and spoil her first trip.' 'Don't tell me what?' I screamed. 'I want to know everything!' Apparently Brian Epstein, the Beatles manager, had just been found dead in his apartment. Because of that, I will always remember **27 August 1967** as the date of my first real trip. Brian Epstein was only 32 years old. He had died while The Beatles were in Bangor, Wales to attend a seminar given by Maharishi Mahesh Yogi. I was sad. He had seemed like such a nice man when I had met him.

Eventually, I was getting ready to land, although I didn't want to come down towards the runway. I would have loved to circle the city for a few more hours. However I was low on fuel and exhaustion would have taken over. —That was how everyone seemed to speak in those days.

We spent the next day cleaning up the mess. The mess in the house and the mess in our heads.

Sorting out the whys and the wherefores. Trying to analyse what we had been through. Listening to the same music, touching what had been around us, looking at the same things and trying to sort out what they meant to each of us while we had been away. There were more trips to follow. Our trips were always well planned and organised. It wasn't like kids going to discos and dropping a tab for fun.

Scene at the Kitchen Table

Vern: Do you feel like a trip this evening or would you prefer to go to the cinema?

Jennie: Why not, I haven't made any plans.

Vern: Don't bother putting on a special frock. We'll just be with the boys in their apartment. Remember the Dutch painter you met? It will be a sort of family evening, but instead of playing bridge or chess, we'll take a little trip.

Vern had two friends who had a super mews house. In it the painter had hung a large painting of a nude man in front of a window. The title of the painting was *He came in through the bathroom window*. They had set up an amazing tripping room on the top floor full of colourful toys, divans, soft pillows, books, kaleidoscopes and music. They also had a black and white Dalmatian running about. Whilst we were waiting for the train to pull out, we were watching *Lost Horizon,* an old black and white film about Shangri-la. It was very mystical. It was a perfect choice for us while we were waiting for the trip to come on. Everything was going fine until Vern burst into tears. He seemed to be very angry with me. The Dalmatian was at his side and even the dog was giving me disapproving looks. Through his continual sobbing, Vern managed to explain to me what was wrong. He said he had been sent by God to pass on a message and I had been sent with him as his assistant, but all I was doing was laughing. Of course, that made me laugh more, but I had to control myself. Vern was really upset. Even the dog seemed to be snarling at me. The episode eventually passed and Vern became tranquil once more.

Half the young and not so young people in London seemed to be tripping around. They were people from all walks of life, including people you would never suspect. It all seemed so normal. We would often find ourselves roaming around the city early in the morning after tripping at a concert or a party dressed in our flowing robes. Covent Garden was one of our favourite spots. The fruit and veg market began setting up at 5.00 in the morning. The stands were as colourful as our clothes and the fresh fruit was great for breakfast. The people were fresh too—sometimes too fresh. Some of the vendors would yell out to us in their cockney accents, 'Lock em up in a bloody cage or send them to Vietnam.' We would giggle and keep on walking. 'Make love and not war!' was our motto!

It may sound as if I spent my entire period in London tripping, but that wasn't so. Emmerton & Lambert was one of the most popular stores in town, which meant we always had a lot of work to do. In addition to selling clothes, I was also tinting Victorian nightdresses and altering them into mini dresses. I shortened some of the beautiful sequinned numbers Vern found from the 1930s as well. None of the glittering leftover material would be thrown away. We sewed it into little headscarves or some such. Marianne Faithful once had me on my knees pinning up an old dress she wanted to turn into a mini. We were the first to take Indian bedspreads and make them into the Indian style jackets that were such a symbol of the 60s. There was even a photo in the paper of Paul McCartney wearing one of our jackets as he was coming into the market with Jane Asher. Vern bought old pairs of trousers from the Navy, both summer and winter weight, and we shaped them into elephant style: tight around the thighs and large at the bottom. He must have bought thousands of them. The antique clothes were always in, but these new styles were what was really selling by the hundreds.

Around this time I had written to my mum and mentioned that I was now living with Vern and Adrian. I don't know why I was forever writing

Emmerton & Lambert at the Chelsea Antique Market.

and telling her all the intimate details of my life. We had never had that sort of relationship when I was living at home, but now for some reason, I kept pouring my heart out to her. Soon after my letter to my mum, I received this reply:

Dear Jennifer, I just received your last letter, which upset me very much to say the least. I have never met any of these people in my life. I don't think I have to actually write the word down, as you know whom I am referring to. I have read about them and I am sure that they are basically nice people. Have you ever thought what the neighbours might think when they see you leaving that apartment? Please think about it and try to find yourself a nice, normal roommate.
Love, Mum

When we weren't working, we were out at clubs. I met Jenny Kee, an Australian Chinese woman, who was working at a club called the Speakeasy

Ulla and Jenny Kee outside the Chelsea Antique Market.

at 48 Margaret Street, just north of Oxford Circus. The club was owned by a Persian man, named David Shamoon. All my friends frequented the Speakeasy. It had a big curved bar, where Jenny worked. There was a little stage with seats in front of it. We saw some of the biggest groups play there including Eric Clapton and Cream, Jimi Hendricks and many more. I remember when we went to see Eric Clapton there, just after one of Cream's albums had come out. I was sitting on the floor near the stage with Ulla, because she wanted to be closer to the musicians. They were playing all the music from their new album and Ulla shouted out, 'Come on Eric, play something we know.' Clapton yelled right back at her, telling her to keep her voice down. That surprised me a little. Whenever I had seen Eric at the market he was always such a gentle person. One evening Jenny and I were staying over in someone's apartment, which happened often after our late nights out. We were laying in bed together and she whispered to me. 'Jen, I slept with John Lennon.' *Wow!*, I thought. Many years later I read a statement printed about Jenny, which said she had paved the way for Yoko, since Jenny is half Chinese and John had never slept with an Asian girl before Jenny. Years later, on one of my trips back home, Jenny showed me the hotel where she had met John. I remember she told me she had been wearing a Scottish kilt the evening they slept together.

The UFO was another big club at that time. It was located in the basement of 31 Tottenham Court Road. Hundreds of people would cram into it. We rarely went there; it wasn't really our scene. To get to the bar, you had to step over bodies in the dark, because people were lying down either stoned or tripping. We felt we were too chic for that sort of atmosphere. However one night, Vern said there was a new group playing at UFO, so we should go and check them out. We had dinner in a restaurant and then entered the dark dungeons of the club. The minute we arrived I didn't feel well. It wasn't from the scene at the club, by then I could cope with pretty much anything, so it must have been something I had eaten for dinner.

They had strobe lighting, which had just come in and was being used everywhere, but I hadn't seen it until that night. Then the band came onto the stage and began to play. It was Pink Floyd! I heard the first few chords. Then I looked at the swirling coloured lights and had to run to the loo, where I lost my dinner. I spent that whole evening that way. Throwing up in the loo, returning to Vern, the music and the lights and then back to the loo again. It wasn't the greatest night for me, but I did get to see (at least parts of) one of the first performances of Pink Floyd and I've loved them thereafter.

There was a small casino on Queens Gate Road, which Ulla used to go to most nights. It was quite rare for Vern and me to go there. We always lost all our money, which meant we would have to walk home—

JULIE DRISCOLL

BRIAN AUGER & THE TRINITY

and it was a long walk home! One night when we were there we saw a group called Julie Driscoll, Brian Auger and the Trinity performing and we loved them. They began to visit the market and we all became friends. In fact, they became very close friends of mine over the next few years.

Ulla was the only one of our group who hadn't been initiated into the world of 'Fantasyland'. I really didn't think Ulla would be interested in tripping around London in her spare time. She often spent her nights at the casino, always looking her beautiful and elegant self. There was one morning when she didn't turn up at the market for work, but we presumed she had a late night and had lost her money on the gambling tables, so we weren't worried. Then about midday, she appeared at the door wearing a long blue skirt and a Hungarian-style, loose blouse. She had a slice of half eaten pineapple in her hand, which was dripping down her already stained clothes. I took one look at her and knew where she was at, particularly because she couldn't stop laughing. Vern and Adrian more or less hid behind a row of Indian shirts and whispered to me, 'Take her upstairs and look after her.' I took her up to the coffee bar near our shop and proceeded to give her some water to drink. I turned my back on her for half a second and turned back to find her trying to get over the rail of the balcony onto the King's Road. She was yelling, 'How beautiful the green hills are. I just want to jump down and walk on the grass.' Oh no! There wasn't any grass around for miles. Only a very busy road filled with moving cars and pedestrians! I managed to grab onto her just in time before she flew away!

That afternoon, I had an appointment with a man from Mexico, who wanted to show us his wares. I told Ulla that if she would agree to sit down and not open her mouth while the man was there, then afterwards I would take her on a magical mystery tour. The Mexican arrived and began pulling brightly coloured dresses and trinkets from his bag. Each time he showed us something new, Ulla would point at it and start rolling around the floor in laughter. That poor man had no idea what was happening. I apologised for her behaviour and told him it would be better if he came back another day. I thought I should get Ulla out of the shop. After about 24 hours of walking her around London, I eventually got her home and into bed. I found out that it was much more exhausting going along with someone else on their trip than it was taking one yourself!

A couple of doors down from the market, there was an Australian doctor who had opened up a drug rehabilitation centre. I heard he had opened it due to his guilty conscience. In the past he had dealt out too many pills to his young patients and some of them had become hooked. Heroin addicts would go to the clinic to get their legal dose of methadone, but then often their next stop would be the market where they would try to sell the methadone. Then they would come and try on all our clothes over their sweaty bodies. We were very aware of what was going on and wanted to help them. Vern particularly was kind to some of them. I remember one young boy from the clinic who would stop by the shop nearly every day. He seemed to be from a good background and was well educated. Vern wanted to help him. At the time, we had started selling hand-painted tennis shoes as something new. Vern had the idea to give this boy a few pairs of tennis shoes to paint for us. He would get paid, have a job and maybe kick his habit. Vern gave him some money to buy paint, but the boy went off and we never saw him again.

One morning, I was in the shop organising some clothes on hangers when I heard footsteps coming up the stairs. I turned around and saw a beautiful young woman with long blonde hair wearing a mini skirt and a suede fringed jacket. She was quite extraordinary. Ulla greeted her with a big kiss and a hug and they began to chat. Ulla introduced us and told me this was her friend Amanda Lear. They had lived together in Berlin years ago. I would end up crossing paths with Amanda again years later in Paris.

I was feeling doubtful about the future of the scene in London and our lives there. It began to feel as though something was coming to an end and I didn't want to be around for the funeral. I needed a break, so I decided to go on holiday for a couple of weeks. Around that time, Vern had told us about a program he had seen on the telly about an old lady who was a psychic. A group of our close friends decided to ask her to come to Vern's apartment to read our futures. It felt like a good time to do something like this. We all excitedly awaited the arrival of this woman who would point each of us in the right direction.

We gathered in Vern's living room on the day of her visit. She arrived and sat her tiny frame down in the centre of us. She would begin talking about something and then turn to the person it involved. It was really spooky. She seemed to know so much about us. She started talking to me at one point, but I think she made a mistake. What she was saying seemed to be a better fit for Vern. Maybe our vibes were so close that she mixed us up. Finally, she turned to me and said a clear, short statement: 'You will be soon going to a land full of churches and at some point you will pass the place where Saint Francis lived. You will have one child, a daughter. She will be the most important person in your life.' As I listened, I had no idea just how accurate her prediction would be…

I went on my short holiday, but I never came back. I hadn't planned that. It just happened. That pattern followed me for many years—never planning my path, but rather just going with the tide. I travelled to Italy and visited the family I had worked for in Rome. While I was there, I had a telephone call. When I answered, I heard, 'Is that you Tiger?' It was Karl Iverson, the father of the children I had met a few years earlier in Porto Santa Stefano. The man with the 'non alcoholic' margaritas. He and his wife, Julie, were in Rome and he asked if I could meet them at the Hilton that evening. He said they had a proposal for me.

Their eldest daughter was going to study at the French School in Rome. She was only 16 and they didn't want her to live by herself. That's where I came in. They wanted me to live in an apartment with her, drive her to school and make sure she studied and stayed out of trouble. I had been thinking it might be time for a change, so I agreed to stay with her for the next year.

I was terribly sad when I realised I would be leaving London. When I went back to collect the rest of my things, I told Vern my plans. He was sad too, but as usual he understood. He told me he had a feeling this would happen. Adrian and Vern drove me to the airport in their old Rolls Royce, 'Take care and be happy,' were his parting words to me.

I spent the next year in Rome and when my job watching Karl's daughter was over, he asked me to go to Switzerland and work for him there. He had some grand ideas for his business, which included opening a boutique at the Hotel Post, his place in Zermatt. He asked me to run the boutique for him, which sounded very interesting.

The Hotel Post was not the chicest hotel, but it was well known for its two famous discotheques. I convinced Karl to bring Vern and Adrian to Zermatt to help me create a Chelsea Antique Market in the Alps. The season before, the famous Biba shop had been in the space we were to use for the boutique. The walls were still covered in Biba's iconic black and gold wallpaper. I also invited Julie Driscoll, Brian Auger and the Trinity, who were very well known by then, to come play at the discotheque. As **1967** was nearing an end, I was busy painting the upstairs attic bedrooms for my friends to use while they were staying in Zermatt. Soon, crates of clothes arrived from London, followed by all my London friends. I was so excited for us to be together again. Karl liked my friends, although he did have to call me into his office soon after they came saying, 'Your freaky friends seem to be a great bunch of people Tiger, but please tell them not to leave their roaches around the hotel.' I promised him, 'Yes Karl, no roaches.'

Zermatt

My friends helped me set up the new market and it was a great success. We spent Christmas together while Brian, Julie and the Trinity played music. It felt as though the King's Road had been transported to Zermatt. I was very happy living in Switzerland. My memories of that time are filled with piles of snow, colourful clothes and loads of fun. I was continually taking off on short trips to London, Paris and Rome. So much so that my friends called me the 'Swiss Connection.' I found Karl was a super person to work with. His ideas were so far ahead of his time.

Often when I went back to visit London I would stay with Brian Auger and his Italian girlfriend, Ella. Ella and I would have such fun. We would smoke a joint in the morning and then go shopping. I stayed with them when she was pregnant with her first child. They were trying to decide on a name for the baby. I remember Brian wanted to call their child Hammond Auger, like Hammond organ. After all, Brian is one of the greatest organists ever.

I used to travel around Europe to see them play whenever I could. I had seen them in Rome and had flown to Paris to see them in concert at the Olympic Theatre. Karl never wanted me to miss anything that was happening. At some point during these few jumbled years, I joined the band on their tour in France.

We had a close friend named Jean Claude who had opened up a club called Open One on Rue du Vieux Colombier in Saint-Germain-des-Prés in Paris. I stayed in Paris for a short time and while there I was often at his club. Open One was quite different from other clubs. It was a long narrow room with a small stage for dancing at one end. No alcohol was served there, only tea which was brought to you by attractive young Vietnamese boys, with long black hair. They carried silver trays holding ornate silver teapots and small silver dishes laden with wonderful biscuits and cakes. There were no tables or chairs, just beautiful coloured velvet cushions of all sizes. You could have a cushion for eight people, four people and so on. Bridget Bardot's sister Mijanou had made the cushions for him. I remember visiting Mijanou and her husband, Patrick Batchau, a couple of times while I was in Paris.

Open One was very famous and it attracted an impressive clientele, including Ari and Jackie Onassis, and the French singer Johnny Hallyday. One night, Brian and I went to the club. We saw Ari Onassis there along with a well known female French singer, a few other friends of Ari's and his Greek body guard. When the club closed, Jean Claude asked Brian and I to come around to his apartment for a drink or a smoke, whichever one suited us. There were about six of us at his place sitting around a low table smoking a joint when the telephone rang. It was Ari Onassis. He said he was on his way over with the singer and his bodyguard. By this time, we were all floating along and we just nodded our approval. Ari arrived with a bottle of whisky. The joint was offered to him, but he refused saying he didn't touch the stuff. However, he was happy to roll our joints for us! Later, when the phone rang again Ari said, 'Oh no, that must be Jackie. She's always calling around to try to find out where I am.' All night long the Greek bodyguard seemed to be coming on to Brian. It was making Brian very nervous. He wasn't at all into men touching his knee. The next morning Brian flew off to London. He called me when he arrived to say he had fallen asleep on the plane and was woken up just before landing by a large man looming over him. It was the bodyguard who said he just wanted to say goodbye!

I don't completely remember how I ended up staying outside of Paris in a wonderful little house. I was there with Antonia, a well-known Dutch model whose face had once been on the cover of Vogue, and Robin, a delightful young Canadian girl. I believe Antonia had been the girlfriend of Jean Claude. My bedroom was in the basement of the house, right next door to the panther's cage. Yes, a big black panther whose cage extended out into the back garden where it spent its days in the open air. Apparently, when the panther was smaller Antonia would go into the cage and play with him. She showed me photographs of when they had been playmates. As it grew bigger, his play became rougher. In one photo Antonia's leather jacket was torn to pieces. After that, the vet told her it was time she stopped being his playmate. It was obvious the panther loved her, but he was too strong now. She had his nails cut down, but

she was warned that he was still dangerous. I liked the panther, but it really stank in my bedroom and the cat would growl at night, making it difficult for me to get a good night's sleep. There was also a monkey, a Boizoid hound and a German Alsatian who lived there. It was like being in a zoo, but it was so much fun.

Jean Claude decided to put on a rock concert in Rhuon, the home of Joan of Arc. He called it the Open One Circus and it was held in an enormous tent. The circus included a few clowns and a lion with his trainer, but the main events were well-known pops stars. Antonia, Robin and I decided to drive to the circus to see Brian and Julie perform. Rhuon is quite a long way out of Paris. We left Paris, got lost and drove for hours before we finally got to the circus. When we arrived we discovered we had come one day early! Confused and disappointed, we returned home giggling all the way. We made the same trip the next day. This time we were greeted with bright lights and circus music floating across the fields. Brian and Julie played followed by James Brown. It was quite a show, but what got to me most was the lion and his trainer. The cage was in the middle of the arena with the big lion gazing out into the crowd with a blank look. The lion trainer appeared, dressed with only a small piece of cloth around his middle and what looked like a fur piece thrown across one shoulder and tied at his waist. He used a whip as he tried to get the animal to perform. He tried to put his head into the lion's mouth. He pushed and shoved and tried to pull the poor animal's mouth open, but to no avail. He really couldn't make Mr Lion move in any way. I think he had given the animal too many sedatives; the poor lion just wanted to sleep. After a while, the trainer just gave him a scruff on the head and said something in French which I'm guessing was, 'Fuck you, you stupid lion!' That was the laugh of the night.

I continued to fly all over the place. My home was in Switzerland, but I was forever at the airport in Geneva meeting with all the jet setters I knew from Zermatt, Geneva and Paris. Some were quite well known, either they were married or dating some European royalty, or just rich or famous on their own. Some of them had no idea what my

Florence in a Peruvian poncho.

name was or who I was, but each time I saw them they all greeted me as though I was one of them. They just knew I seemed to be around all the time. 'Where are you off to this time?', they would ask. 'Just flying over to Paris for a concert', I'd reply. A few more goodbyes and I would be off.

In **1969**, I was running the shop in Zermatt along with a girl named Florence Cannon. We needed to get stock for the shop, so Florence flew to Peru to buy Peruvian ponchos, hats and shawls. Meanwhile, I decided to head to Tunis and check out what I could find there. My first stop was Rome. I often seemed to be spending a few days in Rome. I had a good friend named Audrey Rose, who lived in an amazing apartment in Via del Corso. She had also come to Europe from Australia. She met Jack Rose, the Hollywood director, and they had been married for a while. Audrey was always great fun, so when I arrived in Rome I asked if she would like to take a trip with me to Tunisia to buy clothes for the shop. Audrey loved the idea and so off we went.

Even though this was many years ago, I still remember this business trip like it was yesterday. I call it my giggling trip. We laughed from the time we got on the plane until we returned a week later. It all started when we boarded the plane. Both of us were nervous about flying, so when we saw the first class section wasn't full we decided to up-grade ourselves so we could be more comfortable. As we settled ourselves into our new seats, the hostess came and told us we needed to go back to our own seats. We tried to reason with her. These seats were empty. We didn't see the point in not using them. She insisted and said the plane should have taken off already, but we were holding it up. We refused to budge. She called the pilot, but he couldn't get us to move either. Eventually they just gave up. We kept our up-graded seats and were even served champagne and chicken sandwiches! As we started to come down for our landing, we looked out the window and all we could see was water and more water. There didn't seem to be any land for the plane to land on. We started getting hysterical and the other passengers began to panic just from listening to us. When the wheels finally touched the runway we both started laughing and laughing with relief.

In Tunis, we booked a cheap hotel and early the next morning we headed for the souks. The market was enormous and colourful. We found so much to buy—clothes with bright vibrant colours, junky jewellery and little caps. I knew all these colourful items would sell quickly in Zermatt. After a couple of days at the market, the owners of the stalls began to hide behind their wares whenever they saw us coming. They must have thought of us as the two blonde witches. We were driving them crazy with our bargaining.

We had only been in Tunis a day or so when we were approached by a distinguished man. We had a long conversation and he said he had a proposal to discuss with us. He convinced us to meet him and a friend for a drink one evening. We didn't think he seemed the type to be scared of, so we agreed. When we met them, he told us we would be going out of the city and into the desert for the evening. That sounded a bit spooky, but it was okay with us. We were strong and were probably carrying some sort of spray in our bags for an emergency. We headed out and seemed to travel for miles in the desert before we came to a coffee shop that looked like a Bedouin tent. Our new friend explained why we had to travel so far to meet. He was married and he told us that in his country a wife could put her husband into prison if she found he had been seen with another woman. He would only be released if she gave her permission. That could have been an excuse. Who knows? However I believed it, since there was no funny business going on.

Winter in Zermatt.

We learned that he was the cousin of a very well known politician. He explained there was a law restricting the amount of money a person could take out of Tunis. He wanted to travel in Europe and needed a way to get some money out. That's where we came in. He said he could come along on our buying trips at the markets and he would be sure we would get the best prices possible. That sounded good to me. I had the feeling the merchants in the market didn't want to deal with us anymore. His plan was this: he would shop with us and pay for everything himself. Then when we took the boat to Palermo, he and his friend would be waiting for us so we could hand over the money I owed to them there. It all sounded so exciting, Palermo, secret deals, handing over money in dark alleys… Of course, we agreed to the plan.

We continued our daily shopping trips to the market, only now we went with our new friend. In one stall we came across some long brown coats with hoods. They looked like monks robes. I thought they would be super in Switzerland. What fun it would be to see all the skiers coming down the slopes dressed like monks from a monastery! I bought many of them. Later that evening Audrey and I were sitting in a restaurant looking out onto the street, when I saw what looked like a dwarf walking by who was balancing a towering pile of something dark on his shoulders. I asked Audrey what he was carrying. She said, 'Those are your

coats. You did buy a lot of them, didn't you?' Sure enough she was right. That huge pile of coats were mine! That was a big pile for me to get back to Switzerland.

After any of my shopping expeditions, I always booked a wagon-lit compartment on the train all to myself for my return trip. That way I could fit everything I bought inside. Then as soon as I settled into my compartment, I would put a 'Do Not Disturb' sign on the door, get into bed and close the light. That way the customs agents or ticket collectors never bothered me.

The day before Audrey and I took the boat to Palermo, I developed a big boil on my lower cheek. It grew so quickly that soon my whole face was swollen up. It was so bad I called a doctor to come to the hotel. There was nothing he could do at such a short notice, other than give me some ointment. He advised me to put a scarf around my head until I got back to Italy to conceal it. I was petrified that I might be put in quarantine and not allowed out of the country. I wrapped my face with a scarf, so you could only see my eyes, and I walked with my head down. Audrey and I even giggled about this! It was dark when we arrived in the port of Palermo. The plan was for us to look for a car close to where we disembarked. We were told we would know it, because the driver would be blinking its lights. We were to follow the person who got out of the car. We did as we were

Michael Dunkley

Dunkley and that he loved music. When I mentioned I was on the look out for a DJ to work in Zermatt for the winter season, he immediately offered to take the job himself. He seemed polite and intelligent, so I was happy to let him work at the hotel. I told him he had to be ready to leave in two days. He couldn't wait to go home and pack his belongings for the trip. Now that I had found a DJ, my list of things to do before I left London was complete.

Michael and I arrived at the port in Dover along with my huge bags full of coats. Suddenly I had a nervous feeling. I asked Michael if he was carrying any dope on him. He looked like a clean, English boy just out of school, but I didn't want anything that might make the customs officers take extra notice of us. It was bad enough that I had bags of smelly Afghan coats, which I had to pretend were for my own private use, without the trouble of dealing with someone who was carrying drugs. He assured me he didn't have any of that stuff. When we passed through customs, the agent asked to see my bag. I felt offended and a bit worried. I glanced at Michael and saw a weird look on his face. He looked scared. Then he bent down and seemed to tie his shoelace. They searched his bag next. I was very relieved when they didn't find anything and we were told to go on. Once we were clear, I turned and asked Michael if he had been carrying something and if so, what did he do with it? He looked at me and said, 'I had some hash and I ate it.' Then, he sort of slipped into a coma—for the entire trip. I had a hard time trying to wake him when we arrived in Switzerland so he could help me get the bags off the train.

In addition to the new English pop group and the English DJ, we also had a young English hairdresser with us. It felt like London in the Swiss Alps. Brian Auger and his wife, Ella, came over as guests, along with Vern and Ulla. Audrey came from Rome as well. Such fun! We had photos taken of us which were published in *Vogue* magazine in **November of 1969**, with the title of 'The Snow Gypsies'. I suppose that was what we were.

told and ended up in a dark alley. We counted out the money we owed, handed it over and bade the man a happy holiday. The whole scene felt like a spy film.

There was a lot to do organising the shop for the next season. Karl took a group of us to London to shop for clothes and to find a pop group and DJ to bring back to his club. There were six of us from the hotel who boarded a plane in Geneva and flew to London. We found a group called Ashton, Gardner and Dyke, which was Tony Ashton, Kim Gardner and Roy Dyke. They agreed to come perform at the club. We shopped for clothes and in general had a good time. Karl and the other employees returned to Zermatt, leaving me alone to finish the buying and to arrange my return trip by boat and train with all of the clothes, including a large number of Afghan coats and jackets. I also still had to hire a DJ.

I was having a coffee in the market at the coffee bar next to Vern's shop when I saw a handsome young fair-haired boy sitting at a table. We got to talking and he told me his name was Michael

It was quite a scene. No one was taking acid trips there, but there was a supply of mescaline, which made all the snow look pink. It rather felt like acid, but the corners were smoother. Someone told me that they had to trek over a few hills in the snow to get hold of it. Oh well, that was the sixties!

In addition to working and partying with the crowd from London, I joined three different ski schools. I had been very athletic when I was younger, but by the time I started my skiing lessons, I had either forgotten what it was to be sporty or skiing just wasn't for me. Zermatt wasn't the easiest place to learn to ski. There was only a small area for beginners and it was up high on the mountain with a long way down to the bottom again. It scared me. The teachers grew tired of watching me hang onto trees or shuffle down the mountain on my knees. That's why I had to go to several schools… Karl heard I was trying to learn, so he took me up to a very high spot one afternoon and said that he would help teach me. I thought that was so nice of him, but when we got to the top he just turned and said, 'Now Tiger, you know the way down. See you back in the hotel.' That time I literally went down holding on tree by tree, sliding down on my knees and moving in any position that wasn't standing up on my skis. I moved so slowly it began to get dark

Top: Taking a break during the Vogue photo shoot.
Bottom: Skiing during Carnival.

87

while I was still way up high on the path. Finally, the rescue team had to be called to bring me safely to the bottom.

We celebrated Carnival by skiing from Zermatt to Cervinia, Italy, all dressed in wonderful costumes. It was such fun skiing in a group filled with monks, furry animals and clowns. Skiing seemed so easy for me that day, even with a mask on my face. I'm sure all the hot wine we drank at lunch before heading back to Zermatt must have helped.

I went back to London again for a short time, via Paris. We took a train from Geneva and I still remember it as the most wonderful train journey I have ever had. This time my group consisted of Vern, Ulla and Ashton, Gardner and Dyke. We were going to stay at Florence's brother's house in Paris to have a bit more fun before we all went our separate ways again. It was winter and we were dressed in long fur coats and hats. It looked as if we had come out of a scene from the film *Doctor Zhivago*. As soon as the train took off, we began to decorate the compartment with our antique shawls and scarves. We turned off the lights and lit candles and incense burners. We played music and then drifted off into a world of fantasy. The whole scene was unreal. There was beautiful snow falling outside, making everything more romantic. When the ticket collector came by, he opened the door to ask for our tickets. He took one look at us and thought better of it. He closed the door and left us alone for the rest of the trip. In the middle of this extraordinary train ride, Vern told me something that completely shocked me. He said he would like to be the father of my children. I was speechless. I didn't believe what I had just heard. Vern was my best friend, my mentor, my everything, but I never thought about having his children. What he was saying just didn't fit together. We actually stopped talking for quite a while after that. It took me a long time to get over his proposal and it wasn't until years later that we really resumed a good relationship again.

Paris as always was exciting and Open One was still very popular. One night Ulla and I went there with Ashton Gardner and Dyke all dressed in our finery. At one point we noticed a casually dressed, young girl staring at us with a little smile on her face. She disappeared out the door, only to re-appear half an hour later, dressed in a tight, black sequinned dress. She had on full makeup and she held a long cigarette holder between her fingers. She was extremely pretty, rather like Marlene Dietrich as a young girl. She made straight for us. Ulla and I, who were continually giggling about everything, stopped our laughter and wondered why this stunning woman chose us. She introduced herself as Marie France and started a conversation with us in perfect English. We ended up spending the rest of the night together at the club. At Open One they served breakfast at 7.00 in the morning to any of their late night customers. As we began our breakfast, Marie France told us she had to leave and said goodbye to us. Later someone at the club informed us that the beautiful girl we had been talking to was a boy. Ulla and I thought we knew so much about everything, but I guess we really didn't. I became intrigued with Marie France. We learned she was a well-known star in the Alcazar Club in Paris where she often performed an act impersonating Marilyn Monroe perfectly.

Ulla's friend Amanda Lear happened to be in Paris when we were there. Amanda had met Salvador Dali a while back and they had become very close. You could say that Amanda was Dali's muse. When Amanda heard we were in Paris, she invited us to meet Salvador and his wife, Gala. We were to have afternoon tea with them at the George V hotel, where they were staying. Someone had lent me a long fur coat and off we went, giggling as usual. Dali himself met us at the door of the hotel room. I seem to recall that Dali had been teaching Amanda Spanish poetry that day. Gala was there talking to a young French boy. There was another boy there with them, a young dark boy dressed in a long white robe. The hotel room was scattered with many objects which Dali had bought to take back to his castle in Spain—gold taps and fittings and many other treasures. He started showing us some large sheets of white paper with what seemed to be scribbles on them. He asked if we could decipher what they were. Of course not! They were just scribbles. Then he put a large mirror on the floor and held up one of the pieces of paper to it. When I looked into

Amanda Lear

paintings which had taken 25 years to put together. Of course we had to go. By this time, Marie France had become a good friend of mine, so I wanted to take her along. Ulla wasn't so sure Marie France should come, but finally she agreed. Perhaps, I should have listened to Ulla. When we met Marie France, she looked as though she had just left Open One. She had on a long, tight evening dress, long gloves and a feather boa. The minute we entered the gallery and started moving around various rooms looking at the paintings, we noticed everyone else in the gallery began to move with us. Every time we left one room, they followed us. We started going faster and faster and the crowd stayed right with us. We soon realised they were more interested in Marie France than in the exhibit. We decided it would be better if we left so everyone else could look at all Monet's paintings properly without distraction.

Marie France invited me to her apartment in San Germain for afternoon tea. I was so excited to see where she lived. My friend Antonia told me I should be very careful about going around with *those* sort of people, but I didn't see anything wrong with it. I was curious to know about all sorts of people. I arrived at the address she had given me and walked up a narrow staircase to the top floor where she was waiting with a group of her 'girl' friends. Her little studio apartment was dark, even though it was daytime. I looked up and saw a blue sky painted on the ceiling with little silver stars fixed to it. I found her friends to be very sweet and I loved their stories. Marie France had made an appointment for us to have lunch together at the famous restaurant La Copoule the following day. She wanted to tell me her life story. She had gone through hell when she was young, travelling around looking like a girl, but having to show her passport with a boy's name on it. She also told me about how she met

the mirror, I could see a horse with a rider ever so clearly. The rider held a sword in his hand. I was taken aback. How did he draw that? It was magic!

Earlier, someone had given us two little pills. They were 'Sunshine', a new kind of acid that had just arrived in Paris from the USA. I'm guessing that someone was probably Marie France. Ulla had them in her bag while we were having tea with Dali, just in case. At one point Ulla showed them to Dali and in her wonderful Swedish accent said, 'Oh Signor Dali, Yennie and I are going to take a little trip around Paris tonight.' Dali replied, 'Oh pleeze Ulla, do not take them now. I have to be at the opera in one hour!' With that we left the hotel and floated around Paris, giggling some more.

We had heard something big was happening in Paris. There was to be an exhibition of Monet's

From the letters of Marie France.

MUSEUM BOUTIQUE
MONTREUX
SUMMER – 1968

Ari Onassis at Open One. He once told her he would pay for her to have the operation for her to become a girl, but he never did. 'He just bought me a dress instead.' she said. She also explained the reason she always left Open One around the time they served breakfast. That was when the first little hairs on her chin would start popping out, which meant she had to go home.

That hadn't been the first time I heard about someone having a sex change operation. I had read about a British woman named April Ashley who had publicly come out as having changed from a man to a woman. There was also a waiter who worked at a restaurant called The Casserole, which was at 328 King's Road back in London. Vern and I used to go there frequently and there was a young man who often waited on us. One day we went in and he proudly told us his name had changed. 'It's Lorraine now. I've just had it off!' I had heard that people would travel to Casablanca for the surgery since it was one of the only places you could have it done back then.

From Paris, I went back to Switzerland. I stayed in Zermatt through the summer, but eventually decided I had to leave. The Matterhorn seemed to be getting closer and closer. It seemed to be coming into my bedroom window. Karl had a nightclub in Montreux called The Museum Club, so I went there to help him open a boutique with the stock we had left over from the winter season in Zermatt. Montreux was rather different than Zermatt. Instead of having the Alps and snow, Montreux had Lake Geneva and one of the most famous annual jazz festivals in Europe. In Montreux I was able to to see many jazz musicians perform at the Casino music hall, including Nina Simone and Chicago. That was the same music hall that caught fire in **1971** during a Frank Zappa concert and burnt down. Deep Purple wrote the song 'Smoke on the Water' about that fire.

At the end of the skiing season in **1969**, Michael the DJ told me me was leaving and moving to the south of Italy to a small village called Positano. He had visited Positano a few times before and had relatives who owned a villa there. He was very excited about going back again. He suggested I should go too. He thought I'd love Positano. Apparently many of the so called 'drop outs' from London and other big cities were heading to Positano. So I had been right in my assumption that Swinging London wasn't so swinging anymore. He told me many of the artistic people from London were now looking for quiet retreats where they could paint, write music and create. Positano was one of the hot spots on top of the list. As Michael spoke, I suddenly remembered I had been to Positano some years before on my trip to Capri. Positano was that pretty little town I remembered being all pink. I told Michael I would go check it out.

On my way to Positano, I stopped in Rome to see Audrey, before heading further south to the Amalfi Coast. While I was with her she told me about Jean Du Dan, a medium she had met, who ran the modern dance school she was attending. I already had a card reader in Rome, who was so accurate with his readings that it was spooky. My medium was Yarian Yacinto and he worked out of a tiny studio in his mother's house just off Piazza Barbarini. I often seemed to get my appointments with him late at night. I usually had to wait until about midnight before he came home. One evening I was waiting for him and his mother came in. I asked her how her son had this power. She said she had the power as well. She discovered her son's gift when he was quite small. One day she told him to go down to the courtyard and play with his little friend, Francesco. He replied he couldn't, because Francesco just had an accident. When the mother went to investigate, the little friend was being taken off in an ambulance!

One night while I was waiting for Yarian, I happened to see his appointment book on his table and flicked through the pages and saw an entry which read: 'Fellini, Patti Pravo, etc. etc. *séance venerdì sera*.' I suddenly became very nervous. If he was powerful enough to have clients such as that stopping by Friday evening, then he would certainly know I was reading his private appointment book too!

Pastel-Coloured Houses Clinging to the Hillside

When I arrived in Positano, I felt as though I had been thrown back to swinging London. The little town was filled with colourfully clad hippies. In London we had wandered down grand streets and parks, while here in Positano the hippies were running down narrow alleyways and long stone staircases on their way to the beach. In the late 60s, the psychedelic era was coming to an end. Flower Power was becoming exhausting rather than exhilarating and hoards of people with their long hair, Indian shirts, beads and bells began their exodus. Many of them found Positano to be a hidden jewel. They settled here to paint, write and make music while being surrounded by beauty and nature.

Soon after I arrived, I had a call from Vern. He told me that Brian Jones had phoned him and asked if he could come out to his country house for the weekend. Brian said he was feeling depressed and would like to see Vern. Vern was very busy and couldn't make it that weekend, but promised him that he would come out to see him as soon as possible. A few days later, we were all shocked to hear that Brian had died. He died on my birthday, **3 July 1969**. He was only 27 years old.

A few weeks later, on **20 July 1969** Neil Armstrong and Buzz Aldrin landed on the moon.

In my diary, I jotted down a few notes of my early impressions of Positano.

Diary—Positano, Italy

Standing on the terrace overlooking the pastel-coloured houses, which seem to be clinging to the hillsides and dripping down to the Mediterranean sea. I can see the sun reflecting on the roof of a villa on the Galli Islands.

The Galli Islands are a group of three small islands off the coast of Positano. When I first moved to the Amalfi Coast, they were owned by Léonide Massine, the famous French ballet choreographer, who many remember for his small role in the film *The Red Shoes*. After Massine died, Rudolf Nureyev bought the islands. Long, long before either of them, it was said the islands had been where the Sirens had tried to enchant Ulysses with their songs in the Odyssey.

Positano has retained its lovely old charm. Over the years, the tiny town has been host to many well-known personalities from all over the world including John Steinbeck, Tennessee Williams, Anthony Quinn, David Keith, Moschino, Jean Paul Gaultier, Mick Jagger, Marianne Faithful, Liza Minelli, Barbra Streisand, Ann Bancroft, Mel Brooks, Dustin Hoffman, Elizabeth Taylor and Andy Warhol, just to name a few. The locals are used to famous faces passing through, so these stars know they will be left alone to relax in peace.

My friend Michael was living on the top of the town in a community living situation with a group of people from all over the world. He told me there was room for me to stay there too. It was a real hippie scene in that house—so far away from my chintz-covered bedroom at Vern's in London! Living like that wasn't really what I had bargained for when I decided to come to Positano, but I took any experience as a new education. I settled in and even helped them paint the walls of the apartment with fresh flower petals. How hippie can you get?

Patrick, a young boy from Paris, was living in the apartment over us. He was working as the DJ at the Quicksilver Club, a disco in town. We seldom saw him since he always came home in the wee hours of the morning and slept until late. Every now and then if he didn't show his face on his terrace later in the day, we would check on him. We knew he took pills to sleep and then others to wake up. Only once did we have to call the ambulance to bring a stomach pump. That reminded me of my nanny days in London…

There didn't seem to be any heavy drugs being passed around Positano, but everyone was smoking dope. I remember every few nights or so I would see some people going out of their apartments carrying white pillowcases. I couldn't understand why, until someone explained they had discovered a government zone nearby where cannabis was being grown. I think the government was growing it to make rope, but my friends had other uses in mind for the pot.

I spent my days on the beach either swimming or listening to someone strum a guitar. My nights were usually on the beach or dancing at the disco. It took me about two weeks to realise this was where I wanted to live. I loved the beauty and tranquillity of Positano. There were even some things about life there which reminded me of Mildura. The hot weather felt like home and there was flora I hadn't seen since I had left Australia. I made up my mind to move permanently and headed back to Switzerland to get my belongings and to say goodbye to Karl. When I left he told me to take care and said if I ever needed anything I could always give him a call. I never saw him again.

I returned to Positano and before I could even unpack, I was told that we were going to a beautiful, 18th century villa for a drink and then to a barbecue on the owner's private beach. So I got straight into my new social life with no time to settle in. The owners of the villa were the Count and Contessa Gaetani D'Arragone. Their two daughters, Raimonda and Fausta were hosting the party, while their parents were away. Raimonda and Fausta became close friends of mine. I would end up renting two of their houses in the years to come.

I found there were so many interesting people to meet and things to do in this little town. Nearly every night a group of us would eat at La Cambusa restaurant on the beach before we headed over to the Quicksilver disco or to Buca di Bacco down by the beach. It was at Buca di Bacco where I first met Vali Myers. For many years now I had been mixing with the most exotic and strange looking people in Europe, however none of that prepared

Positano 1969.

95

Vali Myers and Halgerd.

me for Vali. One night at Buca di Bacco, I was approached by a fascinating creature. Her white powdered face was surrounded by long wild red hair. Her green eyes were heavily lined with black kohl and her lips were bright red. She wore long colourful robes and had no shoes on her feet. What really set her apart were the finely tattooed whiskers that marked her fox-like face. She reached out and took my arm and asked me to dance. As she did, my eyes caught a glimpse of the intricate designs she had tattooed on her delicate hands. It looked as though she was wearing dark lace gloves. Vali and I became good friends. I'm not sure I can fully describe Vali. Vali was Vali, what can I say? She was originally from Sydney and in **1949** she had travelled to Paris where she worked as a dancer in the Taboo Club. She settled in Positano in a little house in a remote valley outside of town. She had a large group of dogs up there which she cared for, first with her husband, Rudi, and then with her partner, Gianni. They had collected a few stray dogs and they all had babies, so their doggie population grew and grew in the valley. I once asked her about an unusual necklace

she had on and she told me she had made it from the teeth of one of her dogs that had died. Vali had a pet fox which she named Foxy. She had another one later called Halgerd. No one tames foxes, but Vali did. Foxy wouldn't go near anyone else, but it loved her. There are some lovely photos of her and her foxes. In Positano we never saw Vali during the day, she avoided the sun so her skin would stay pure white, but every night she would come down to the bars in town to dance. She loved dancing more than anything. One time Vali and I were at a cocktail party and I was asking her about the tattoos on her face. She told me that she loved her whiskers and that she had them done when she thought she had earned them. Years later she moved back to Australia. There she had a dingo she named Gypsy. Dingo's are seldom tamed either, but again somehow Vali found a way. I had heard she had to get rid of Gypsy, because it wasn't happy living in the city.

One of the first people I met in town was Shawn Phillips, an American songwriter with an amazing voice. He played guitar and sitar. He actually gave George Harrison his first sitar lesson. Shawn had written songs for Donovan including *Season of the Witch* and he sang back up for the Beatles on *Lovely Rita*. Shawn lived quite near to us on the top of town, so we saw him often. During that time in Positano, it was common to see people such as Viva, the Andy Warhol actress, or the actress Tina Aumont and her partner who was a French painter named Federique. The French actor Pierre Clémenti and his talented friends were renting a villa on the Galli Islands around then too.

Positano was magical in many ways. I remember one night that first August I was on the beach with all my new Positano friends. As we looked up at the sky, we began to see falling stars. Not just a few, but masses of them filling the sky. I'm sure we all had something to drink or smoke that night. There were so many falling stars that we thought maybe we had had a little too much… The following morning when I went to the grocer I was amazed to hear all the people in the shop talking about the falling stars too. I left wondering, what had they all been on the night before? I found out that that night is called *La Notte di San Lorenzo* and the skies are filled with falling stars every year on 10 August.

Now that I was living in Positano for good I wanted to find an apartment of my own. I had a little money put aside so could afford something decent even before I found a job. Michael knew the perfect place for me. He told me Tano Festa, a well-known Italian painter, was currently renting the apartment, but Michael told me I should go look at it anyway. When Signor Festa opened the door and I asked him if I could see his apartment, he looked quite shocked. He had guests over playing cards and he didn't have time to show me his little house. He was kind enough to let me look around on my own though. I wandered around and thought it was charming. It was like a two-storey doll's house. The downstairs rooms were quite small and the main bedroom was on the top floor. What caught my eye was the fireplace in the living room. I imagined it glowing on cold winter nights with me snuggled up on a divan reading or listening to music. Perhaps, there would even be someone snuggled up with me. Then as soon as I walked onto the large terrace covered by wisteria, I knew that was the place for me.

I told the artist I wanted the house. He kindly explained he had just taken it for the entire summer and had already paid three months rent in advance. I said I would give him the money he had paid for the house. I gave him my name and told him where he could find me. I left him knowing the apartment would be mine. A few days later Signor Festa contacted me. I gave him his money, he gave me the keys and departed so I could move in.

I knew nothing about the actual owners of the property, except that they were from Naples. No one had informed them that a new tenant was living in their house. Then one afternoon as I was painting over the classic white walls with pale lilac paint, a well dressed Signora appeared at my door. She asked me who I was and why I was painting her house. I kept on painting as I explained that the painter from Rome had left, after I had paid him his money and I lived there now. Surprisingly she accepted my reply. She was very kind and we ended up becoming friends.

Now I had the perfect house and a little money left over to put it together the way I wanted. What I needed next was a dog. I had my mind set on a big reddish-blonde setter type of dog. I had planned to visit a kennel to find one in need of a home, but before I had a chance, one found me instead. Late one night as I was coming home from the club, I saw a small black and white dog sitting under the tree in front of my house. It was raining and this poor doggie was soaking wet and I had the feeling she may have been ill. I couldn't leave her in the rain, so I took her in. She was almost the exact opposite of the type of dog I had dreamed of, but she needed a home so I kept her and I called her Emma.

In **1970**, I had gone out to the *festa* for Ferragosto, a big celebration which happens every year on the **15th of August** with fireworks, brass bands and fairy floss. When I arrived home I called for Emma, but she didn't welcome me—not even with a bark, which was unusual. I searched the house and found her in the spare bedroom downstairs. She was lying on an antique velvet dress, which I had left out that afternoon. She looked at me with eyes which seemed to say, 'I have a present for you.' I noticed something

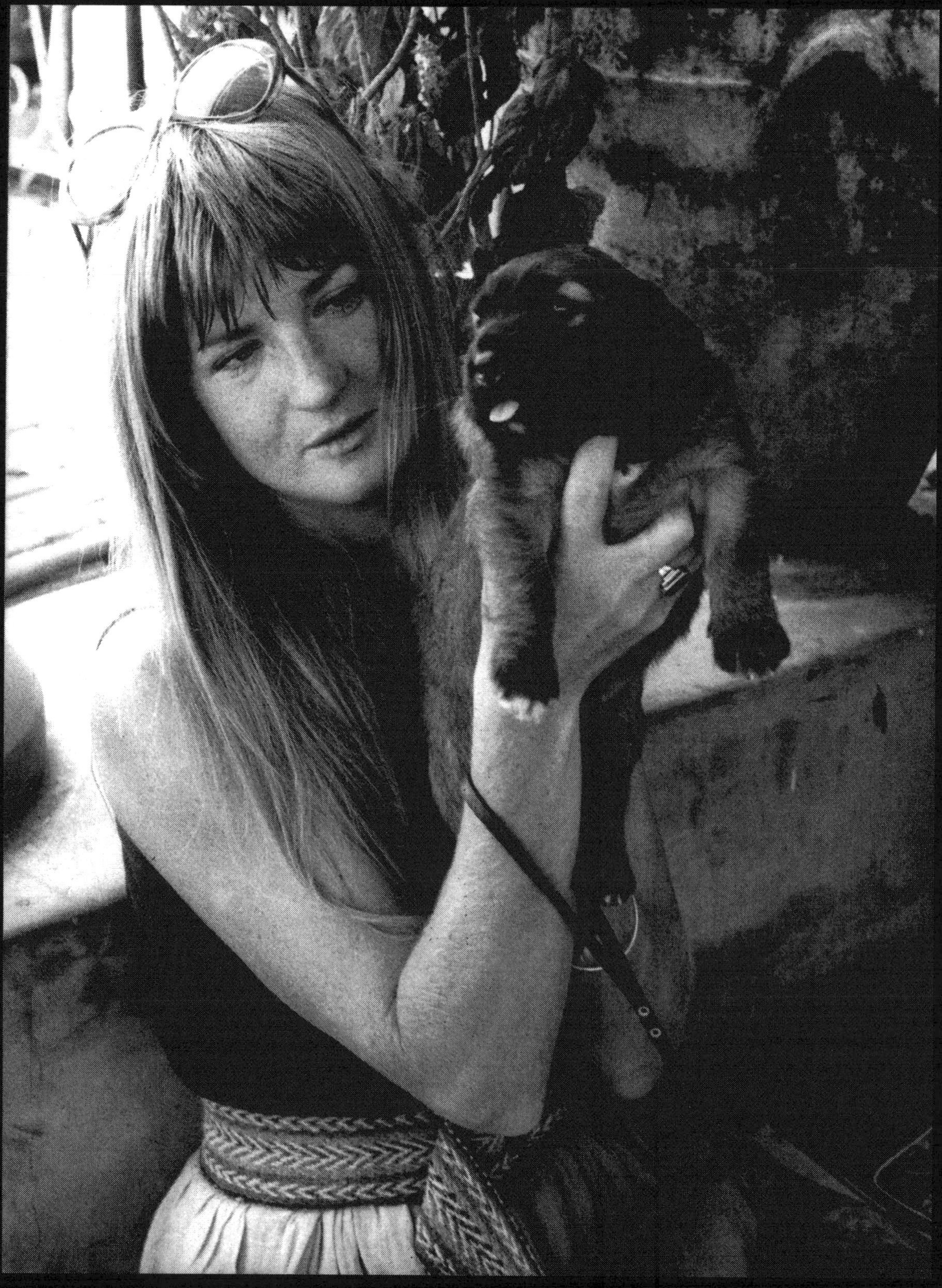

Jennie and Favola.

next to her. It was a big, greyish coloured blob, which began to move. I couldn't believe it. It was a puppy! I didn't even know she was pregnant. I searched everywhere for the rest of the litter, but there were no others to be seen. It was as though a messenger had laid this one puppy on the bed next to Emma to fulfil my dreams. The next morning a few of my young Italian friends passed by to visit. When they saw the puppy and heard the story, one of them exclaimed *'Che favola!'*, which means, 'What a fairytale!' I decided that was what I'd call her—Favola. Her arrival was just like a fairytale and after a few months she grew into exactly the big reddish-blonde dog I had dreamt about.

My life was settling in nicely—apartment, dogs, friends… Now I needed a job. I couldn't just keep running around with the crowd all the time. There was a well-known art school in Positano run by an American woman named Edna Lewis. Edna was a small, dynamic woman, who came to Positano and created an art school she called the Positano Art Workshop. It was an artistic institution for Americans who wanted to learn to draw, paint, sculpt and make ceramics in this magical town. Her sister Irma Jones ran a travel agency in New York and together they directed clients towards Positano and helped put the town on the map back in the **1950s**. The Art Workshop became a very serious venture. Soon people were coming in droves from all over the world.

The teachers at the workshop were all notable artists including: Sigmund Polizer and Reg Dixon, of England, Nellie Guiterraz, a Bolivian ceramic teacher, a Dutch painter Hans Harloff, Vali Myers from Australia, Peter Thomson from New Zealand, Vasilis Voglis a Greek-American, Giuseppe di Lieto, of Italy, Ibrahim Kodra from Albania and the English sculptor Margot Scott Williams. Edna supervised everything and everyone. She never missed a trick.

Edna was a small woman in her 70s, but she had a very grand personality. One evening I found myself at Bar di Martino with a group of people including Edna and the painter Vasilis. Edna was wearing a long black cape as she held court. Vasilis was in a joyous mood after a couple of glasses of wine. As the night drew on, Edna got up and said, 'Okay boys, how about a little boogie woogie in the Bucca disco?' Up until then, I had only seen Edna at art shows or in the school. I didn't know this social side of her! I learnt that she loved men, especially young beautiful ones. Whenever I introduced her to any of my male friends she would be soon flirting with the beauty of the bunch. She once proudly showed me photos of one of her lovers, a young African-American named Rocky. Around town, Edna was known for her miserly ways. She would often eat at Chez Black, where she would order a plate of grilled prawns. She would eat them all except for one or two and then call the waiter to complain they were not good, so they wouldn't make her pay for them.

Someone suggested I ask at the Art Workshop for a job as a model. The idea suited me. I knew it would be interesting to meet people coming from around the world to study at the workshop. The job was perfect for me. I usually spent my nights at the Quicksilver dancing until the early hours of the morning and often only slept a few hours a night. I was often so tired when I went to model for a class that I would lie down in the pose they wanted and then immediately fall asleep. The students adored me. I was the perfect model, because I never moved at all until one of them would gently shake my shoulder and say, 'Jennie, could you please turn over and change your pose for us?' It was wonderful to get paid whilst catching up on my sleep!

The Quicksilver was booming and bursting at the seams. The owners, Luigi and Tom, put a huge mirror on one whole side of the big room with the dance floor. Everyone was shocked. None of us had never seen something like that before. For the first few nights, no one would go near it or even look in that direction; people felt self-conscious dancing in front of the mirror. It only took a short time before people were fighting to dance in front of it. They were pushing and shoving to look at their own faces and movements. On top of the disco was a vast covered terrace with a bar and a restaurant that stayed open until 3.00 am. On each side of the bar were two cave-like spaces. Luigi wanted to turn them into two small boutiques. He asked me to take one of the spaces and stock it with clothes from London. My friends Judy and

Maria with Emma and Favola.

One day at my shop, I met three young women from New York. Andrea Feldman was on a free promotional trip given by Andy Warhol in exchange for her role in his film *Trash*. Andrea was travelling with Geraldine Smith who had starred in Warhol's film *Flesh* a few years before. I had heard Warhol often paid his actresses with trips rather than cash. Geraldine's sister Maria, who was also an actress, was travelling with them. They came into my boutique and we all just clicked and quickly became close friends. Andrea was mad as a hatter, but I loved her. She was obsessive compulsive and was constantly washing her hands. She was a very talented performer. One day we were at La Cambusa and Andrea got up on one of the tables and started giving a little show. The owner was so upset. He turned to me and told me to get my friend 'off the God damn table!' La Cambusa was one of the nicest restaurants in town. People didn't do things like that there. Andrea didn't listen. She went on singing and dancing. Soon everyone from down on the beach started coming up to see what was going on. By the time she finished, there was such a crowd gathered around applauding that the owner started acting is if he had planned the whole thing himself. He was proudly telling people Andrea was one of their regular clients.

Drugs were in full force in Italy then and particularly in Positano. Everyone, the young and not so young, was smoking dope and growing it up in the mountains. When you went out at night you would often have to wait ages to use the toilet because the loo was always occupied with people rolling their joints. The owner of the Quicksilver had been told he should be careful with what

Ben were asked to take over the other space. Our two boutiques gave the club a touch of class.

There were a group of people from the American experimental theatre troupe, Living Theatre, who were renting a huge villa in Praiano, a small village near Positano. They had renamed it the 'House of Angels'. Billy Berger, the Austrian-American actor, became the Lord of the Manor in this villa on the coast. We never saw much of their group during the day. They would spend most of their time at the villa. Then at night, they would get dressed in all their finery, which was usually black and sparkly. Then they would drive to Positano and make their entrance at the Quicksilver. Their presence would immediately take over the whole club.

Geraldine Smith

Andrea Feldman

was going on in the disco. There were rumours that there could be a big drug bust on the way. Luigi passed the information onto us and warned everyone not to bring any of their goodies inside the club.

One night in **August of 1970**, I was at the Quicksilver with Andrea, Geraldine and Maria. Suddenly about 200 policemen, most of them in civilian clothes, poured into the club. At first we didn't realise they were all police, because of the way they were dressed. We had no idea what was going on until one of the policemen shouted at the DJ to turn off the music. The DJ turned it off, but at the same time he turned on the strobe lighting, which totally confused them. I was never sure if he thought that would give

people a bit of time to get rid of whatever they had or if he had just touched the wrong switch by accident.

The head of police told everyone in the club not to leave. They planned to do a personal search of each and every person on the premises. The police began searching for drugs. They used torches and lit matches as they groped around in the dark on their hands and knees looking under all the benches and chairs.

My friends Geraldine, Andrea and Maria started screaming, 'Take your hands off us. We're American citizens. Don't you touch us or we'll report you to our Embassy!' That got the attention of the police. They were the first ones to be searched. The head of police became suspicious of them and told some of his men to take them home and search their house as well. I was searched next and remember warning the policewoman not to ruin the Victorian blouse I was wearing. Everyone in the club had to line up and be searched, only then were they allowed to leave.

Several of the police went up to the terrace and began pulling apart everything in both of the boutiques. My exquisite artificial flowers, which decorated the large straw hats, were stripped of their petals. Antique dresses and gauze robes were thrown in the air as the police scrabbled around searching any box or bag they could find.

Nothing was found anywhere or on anyone, so the police decided it was time to move on. Most of the guests had left by then, but I was at the bar with Luigi. We overheard one of the police say, 'There's nothing here, so let's move on to Praiano.' We knew they were referring to the House of Angels. We learned someone had given the police a list of places, both public and private, that they should search. Of course, the House of Angels would be on that list.

The town was more or less closed off. It looked like a war zone. I decided to go home as quickly as possible, in case they went to my house. I knew I had no drugs for them to find, but I was worried about two male friends I had staying with me from London. They were already tucked up in bed for the night—together. I wasn't exactly sure what the law regarding homosexuality was in Italy at that time. It had not been so long ago that the law legalising homosexual relations had been passed in England. I was afraid it would scare my friends to see police coming into their room and wanted to warn them what was happening.

As I passed by Edna Lewis's house, I noticed her door was open and there seemed to be a few men standing around. I went in and found her in the hallway sitting in a chair in her nightgown. She seemed a bit confused. When she saw me she said, 'Jennie, these nice men are here and I tried to offer them a cup of tea.' The painter Peter Thomson was with her. In a rather drunken voice he slurred, 'Edna, these are cops and they're looking for drugs not tea.' At that, Edna snapped out of her haze and screamed, 'Get out of my house or I'll call the mayor! Stop fiddling with all the paintings on the walls and go!' It really was a joke for someone like Edna to be on the list of houses to be searched.

The next morning everyone gathered on the beach checking to see who was in prison and who wasn't. Edna strolled down amongst the younger group and chuckled, 'Its great to see you're all here. I was lucky as well.' Not everyone was so lucky. Many people didn't show up that day.

The police did go to the House of Angles. Luigi from the Quicksilver had warned them that a bust might be on its way, so Billy and his guests had everything well hidden. We heard that when the police arrived at the villa, all the people there were sitting in a large circle on the floor chanting *omm – omm – ommm*… Candles were burning in every crevice and there was complete silence, except for the soft hum of their chanting. The villa was large and would take a while to be searched. Billy and his guests were told not to move from the room where they were in. The treasure hunt was on. Soon, one proud policeman found something wrapped in silver foil. The police had been told drugs might be wrapped that way. He came up to Billy waving the little silver parcel saying, 'Aha Signor Berger, now we have found something!' Billy just smiled and told him to open it. Inside was a bar of chocolate. The search went on for hours until it was nearly dawn and still nothing had been found. Some of the police said it was time to leave, but another suggested they should wait until sunrise and check the domed roof of the villa. When they did, they found about half a gram of hash. This tiny amount of hash put so many people away.

Those who were arrested weren't sent to prison, apparently there was a lack of space for them, so instead they were held in mental asylums near Naples for several months. The men and women were separated and Billy was held apart from them all. The charges against him were greater, since the villa had been rented under his name.

That wasn't the end of it. The following day the police busted another villa in Praiano and found more drugs, sending more foreigners to the asylums. There was an English girl in this group who was the lover of an Arab prince or sheik. He came to the rescue with money to get quite a few of those people out fairly quickly.

Carol Lobravico, Billy's wife, was sent off with all the other women. She had been ill with hepatitis when she was arrested. She told them she needed to take her medicine, but the people running the asylum refused to let her have it. As a result, Carol died from complications. No one could believe all this was happening and just because of a tiny bit of hash! Billy was given permission to attend his wife's funeral, but only if he agreed to wear handcuffs. They would have been the heavy old-fashioned kind with a long chain dragging on the ground. Billy refused, so I ended up going to her funeral on his behalf. I had known Carol better than I knew Billy and I always liked her. She was a nice woman and it was so crazy that she had died this way. Carol was buried in the small cemetery in Praiano, which has a beautiful view over-looking the sea.

Some of the women who were locked up sent me lists of things they needed while they were being held. Most of them were used to travelling around the world in style, performing in theatres and attending chic parties. Now they were missing their mascara, face creams and eye liners. I would pack up parcels to give to their lawyers to deliver to them.

One of the people arrested was Teddy, a black American who cooked southern-fried chicken on the terrace of the Quicksilver. One of the newspapers had written an article about the drug bust and they stated Teddy's age. That made Teddy so upset. Apparently he was much older than he looked. He didn't seem to care about being busted for drugs or being imprisoned in an asylum, but having the world know his real age was something else!

One morning after all the arrests, the police raided the art school whilst I was there modelling for a lesson. Edna had organised a 'Box' exhibition and anyone interested could enter their boxes. You can't imagine the sorts of things the police found in those boxes. Peter Thompson had put a stool in his small cardboard box and not a stool you sit on! Raimonda's box was full of little glass phials with coloured liquid in each of them. The police sent those away to be analysed. The head of the police walked into the studio where the students were sketching and there I was in the nude, lying on a small platform. He was shocked and said it was

a disgrace. What if small children came into this room? I thought that was such a strange remark coming from a man whose country has long been known for its art.

After several months, everyone except Billy was released. There were no trials, so I presume they had come up with enough money. They were given 48 hours to leave the country. Being expelled wasn't as bad as it sounds. They could come back immediately once they crossed the border. However, I only saw a couple of them in Positano again. I think the whole event must have soured their view of Italy. The bust made head-lines all over the world. Even the Washington daily paper ran an article with photos of people protesting the treatment Billy and his friends were receiving. Protestors were marching up and down in front of various embassies holding banners and shouting about the injustice of the case.

Billy was still locked up in Salerno by himself. He was the only one who had to go on trial. I decided to go to the trial to see for myself what was going on. I went with my friend Alain who had been arrested during the raid at the second house in Praiano. He had been sent to the asylum with the rest of them. While they were being held, Alain became the group's guru. He kept their spirits up and kept them moving physically and mentally to stop depression from setting in on them all.

Billy's trial was quite something. American tele-vision crews were there filming everything. Billy arrived with his hands in those heavy medieval handcuffs with a long chain which noisily dragged behind him as he was led down the aisle. I've never been good at public speaking and I nearly fainted when some American reporters asked to inter-view me and Alain. I don't remember what I said to them, but I was glad someone had lent me an artificial white fur coat that day. At least I looked good for the cameras. Billy was finally released. It had been nearly eight months since his arrest.

Billy went back to the House of Angels to write a book about life at the villa and all that had happened to them. I had never been that close to Billy. He was extremely good looking and he was quite a presence. To be honest, he had always rather intimidated me. I was quite surprised when

Jennie and Judy in Positano, 1970.

he called and asked me to come to the villa to help him with his book. I had never stayed at the villa before and had always wanted to, so I accepted. I thought since so many of those people had left the country, the villa would be quiet. I packed a small case and took off to Praiano. I was looking forward to having some time to get to know Billy a little more and was hoping I could learn to be less shy in front of him.

When I arrived at the villa, I found Billy's daughter, Debbie, was also staying there, along with a beautiful black American model named Patti. The villa was large and had several floors. As I wandered around, I bumped into a few young English men who were there as well. When it was time for dinner, one of Billy's friends told us there was only homemade apple pie to eat. Freshly baked apple pie was fine by me, but I suppose in retrospect, I should have suspected something.

We ate early and I retired to one of the cave-like rooms to listen to music. The villa was wired with speakers and headphones scattered about in every room. No matter where you were, you just had to put on a set of headphones to have access to continual music. It was amazing. Even the domed roof had a supply of these magical gadgets. I put on some headphones and heard Pink Floyd thrashing

out *A Psychedelic Trip*. As I listened, I started to feel rather weird. The music seemed to get louder and louder and I had to keep taking the headphones off. I was laying on big cushions staring up at the high domed ceiling. I saw incredible drawings up there and wondered how someone could have climbed up on a tall ladder to draw on that high ceiling. The more I looked, the more I saw. New designs began bursting out all over.

I began to feel as though Carol's ghost had returned to the house. I threw off the headphones and decided to go for a stroll around the villa. When I walked out of the room, I couldn't believe my eyes. The corridors were ablaze with hundreds of candles. The whole villa was glistening like a Christmas tree. It was stunning. I bumped into Billy in the corridor and saw he was amazed too. He took me by the hand and led me into his bedroom. He told me to sit on a throne-like chair which was positioned in front of some windows that stretched from ceiling to floor. He told me to look outside, but I don't think I saw whatever it was he wanted me to see. In my imagination, I saw hundreds of policemen, walking up the driveway and into the villa, as they had actually done a few months before. I left his room and found many more people around long tables covered with

Michael, Jenny Kee and Jennie, 1970.

platters of food visible in the glow of candles. I wanted to leave, but knew I couldn't at this time of night, so I relaxed and tried to make the most of the experience and enjoy the beauty of it all. The next morning I got up, packed my case and told Billy I was going home. I also told him I wouldn't be eating apple pie again for a very long time! He laughed and told me he hadn't known anything about the pie either and was just as surprised about all that had happened the night before as I was.

The Quicksilver was still full every night, however the atmosphere had changed. People seemed nervous after the bust. You could tell it had left a mark on everyone. I was still going almost every night, escorted by my two dogs. Many people brought their dogs with them to the disco. The dogs would sit on a bench near the dance floor and watch their owners jumping around to the music. They kept a close eye on their owners to make sure they wouldn't be forgotten when the evening was over.

I began to think it may be time for a change. I began mixing with a new interesting group of painters from Paris. They had taken a big villa overlooking the sea for the summer to paint and have fun. One of these friends, Eduardo Arroyo

later went on to become a big name in the art world in Paris. These artists were far removed from the drug world. They were more into liquid highs. I felt safer hanging around with them and enjoyed their company.

A beautiful young painter named Katinka Neidestrasse arrived from Hamburg and became part of our group. She and I used to go to Resina, the big outdoor market in Herculaneum not far from Pompeii to buy up lots of old clothes. It reminded me of my days at the Chelsea Antique Market. Katinka and I would bring the clothes back to my house. I would get out my sewing machine and we would fix up the garments to get them ready to sell in my boutique. Katinka married Luciano Nuvolari, a man she had met in town. They had two children, Davide and Amelia and for many years they lived in a beautiful villa near the beach.

In addition to the Quicksilver there were three other nightclubs in Positano back then. Privilege was up in Fornillo. They had a little stage which served as their dance floor and a big cinema screen where they played music videos. There were stairs inside where everyone's dogs would sit waiting for their owners to go home. The back of the bar at Privilege was completely covered in peacock

feathers. That freaked me out. In Australia, having peacock feathers indoors was considered a sign of very bad luck. Privilege stayed open all night and they served pasta for breakfast in the early hours of the morning. Bucca di Bacco opened a year after I arrived in town. It was a charming club and was very smart. It was the club that rich visitors felt comfortable sending their kids off to alone. Music on the Rocks was owned by the same people who ran the restaurant Chez Black down on the beach. Music on the Rocks was at the far end of the beach. Katinka and I used to go there with a group of our friends. We would dance all night and then leave the club and walk right into the sea to cool off with a swim with all our clothes on. We must have been quite a sight walking into the waves with our long chiffon dresses blowing in the night air. Katinka would have on one of her beautiful flowing dresses and her signature long gloves. I guess it was a good thing we often dressed in chiffon then, the material would dry quickly after our night time swims.

That year there were two more deaths from my past in London. Jimi Hendrix left us all on

18 September 1970 and Janis Joplin on 4 October 1970. Both of them were 27 years old, the same age as Brian Jones.

Around this time, Judy, who ran the other boutique at the Quicksilver, introduced me to her Italian boyfriend, Antonello, whom she had met at the club. He was very amusing and charming and after we chatted for a while, he told me I should meet his best friend, Eduardo. He said I would fall in love with him. A week or so later, Antonello raced into my shop saying, 'He's here, Jennie. Eduardo is here!' I wasn't looking for an Italian lover, however after hearing so much about this man, Eduardo Sorrenti, I was curious. I wasn't sure what to expect. When I met Eduardo, I thought he seemed like a man from Mars compared to all the hippies and rock stars I had known. Eduardo wore rather conservative clothes and wasn't into any of the craziness of the ex-London scene in Positano. He seemed very young to me, although I learnt he was just a couple of years younger than me. What I did notice was that he had a pleasant face and was absolutely charming. He seemed quite smart as well.

Eduardo began to spend nearly every night in my boutique. After a while, he asked me if I would like to go to his stepfather's villa in Massalubrense, near Sorrento. I accepted, at least I did after he agreed I could bring along ten of my friends and my dogs. I think Eduardo thought seeing his family's villa might help win my heart, but actually by that point I was already quite keen on him.

A few days later we all drove out to the villa. Eduardo quickly went around setting up lights in the pool and the gardens. A few minutes later, water was on the stove for pasta and sauce was being made. Along with my friends, Eduardo's brother, Ricardo, and his girlfriend, Francesca, were there too. We spent the evening having fun and playing music. We stayed up until the wee hours of the morning and then cleaned up some of our mess and headed off to get some sleep. Eduardo had been in bed for some time—waiting for me. I'd been having such fun with my friends I had nearly forgotten with whom I had come to the villa and why. Just as I was beginning to undress, the telephone rang. It was Eduardo's mother. She told him their neighbours at the villa above had called her in Naples and told them their villa had been taken over by a bunch of crazy people who were having a big rave party in the garden below. She said her husband had just left Naples with his coat over his pyjamas and was furiously driving to Massalubrense to stop the crazy party. As soon as Eduardo hung up the phone, everyone in the house was quickly woken from their beds. Within minutes, they were all up and in action: beds were made, ashtrays emptied, garbage taken out and before you knew it we were all in cars heading back to Positano. By the time Eduardo's stepfather arrived, he found his villa empty and in perfect condition. He was furious with the neighbours for making him drive all that way for nothing in the middle of the night! Eduardo and I went back to the villa again a few nights later, but that time the two of us went alone.

I began to notice Eduardo was changing. His classic shirts were disposed of and he was now

Eduardo and his mother, Carmen Sorrenti.

sporting Indian print shirts or funky T-shirts and small beaded necklaces. I realised he was trying to look and act more like my friends. He was trying to turn into what he thought I would like. That wasn't important to me. I was happy being with him and happy with our new life together. We had lazy days in the sun and quiet dinners together. I didn't miss the madness of my previous group of friends at all. It felt as if I were returning to the Jennie I had been in Australia.

Soon Eduardo insisted on taking me to see his family's house in a newly built up area on the outskirts of Naples. His stepfather, who he called Zio Angelo, was a construction engineer and he had built the entire block of apartments where they lived. Zio Angelo had sold them all off except for the penthouse, which he kept for his family. We pulled into the garage and Eduardo told me to stay in the car whilst he checked with the porter to see if his mother was home. He came back and said she was, which meant he couldn't take me in. That couldn't happen until we knew each other better. He told me to wait there for a few minutes as he went in alone. He closed the garage door and left me sitting in the car in the dark. I sat and waited and waited and waited… Finally after about two hours, he returned holding a salami sandwich for me. When I asked what took so long, he simply said he had to spend some time with his mother. Later, I found out those two hours had been spent taking a shower, eating a three-course meal, reading a comic on the loo and having a short nap—all whilst I waited in the dark!

When I first met Eduardo he had been attending an acting school in Rome. He gave that up after we met and returned to Naples, so he could be closer to me. Eduardo was now working with his stepfather in his construction company. I was glad he was closer to me, but I never thought construction was the type of work Eduardo should be doing. A short time after that episode in the dark garage, Eduardo brought his stepfather to Positano to meet me. Eduardo had taken me to some of the construction sites he was working on, so he thought it best if he introduced me to Zio Angelo before he found out about me from someone else. Zio Angelo Frascino from Calabria was a self-made man, a successful construction engineer, club owner and wine exporter. Eduardo was sure Zio Angelo would approve of me, and he did. We got along very well.

Now I had met one of his brothers and his stepfather, but had yet to meet his other brothers, Michele and Franco, or his mother, Carmen. Carmen was Sicilian and had worked as a school-teacher. Her first husband, who was the father of her four boys had been a Neapolitan lawyer. He died when he was only 39 years old. Eduardo was just 11 at that time.

Eduardo and I became very close to Ricardo and Francesca and the four of us spent a lot of time together either in Positano, in Naples or at their family's villa in Massalubrense. One day Eduardo and I were staying at the villa with Ricardo and Francesca, when Mamma telephoned to say she and Angelo were on their way to spend the night at the villa. When I heard they were coming, I wanted to leave immediately, but Eduardo had another plan. He said he would introduce me as Francesca's friend from New York. When Mamma arrived I was upstairs in the bedroom trying to get up enough courage to come down and meet her. I was led to believe she would cut off her right hand for any of her sons, and especially for Eduardo, who was the eldest. Woe be to the woman who would take him away from her! I finally worked up my courage and went down to the living room. I saw a small, beautiful older woman. She looked at me and asked Eduardo, *'Chi e' lei?'* Francesca quickly said I was her girlfriend from New York. At that moment Zio Angelo walked in, saw me and casually said, *'Ciao Jennie. Come va?'* Carmen quickly turned to me and asked, 'How do you know my husband!?' Her husband always had his eyes on younger women and it made her suspicious of everyone. I was praying Eduardo would have the decency to get me out of this mess. He did—eventually, but not until the next time we all met. Mamma Carmen and Zio Angelo stayed that night at the villa and as they were leaving, Zio Angelo whispered in my ear, 'We're leaving now, so you can go back to Eduardo's bedroom.' I shouldn't have been so nervous about meeting Eduardo's mother. From the moment she really knew who I was, I never had a problem with her. In fact she adored me.

In the typical Italian fashion I suppose you could say by that point I became Eduardo's property. I learnt this meant that whatever he did had nothing to do with me—that even included the other woman he had during our relationship. However, whatever I did was *most definitely* his business. I had to watch what I did and who I was with or I would get punished for my crimes.

One evening I was sitting with Eduardo and his friends in a restaurant, when someone mentioned they had seen me leaving the house of a certain Positanese in the wee hours of the morning. Just for the record, that event had happened quite some time before I had even met Eduardo and it was just the house of a close friend of mine named Giulio. When Eduardo heard the comment, he immediately got a strange look on his face. He beckoned his two friends and the three of them marched out of the restaurant. With them gone, I decided to leave myself. I had to buy dog food before the shop closed. I stopped at the shop and when I returned home, the devil walked in. He had a strange sweet look on his face as he asked me where I had been. I told him the truth—I had bought the dogs some food. Thank goodness it only took one swipe across my face for the blood to gush out of my nose. That stopped him immediately. I found out later that he and his gang had gone and broken all the windows in Giulio's house. They rammed his car into the mountain and made a real mess for him. A while later, Giulio asked me, 'Jennie, why did Eduardo break up my house and my car? I was going to have him beaten up and thrown out of town, but I didn't because I knew he was your boyfriend.' I told him that someone had seen me leaving his house early one morning and Eduardo was jealous. Giulio was Italian too, so my answer made complete sense to him and all was forgotten.

Life went on as usual. Eduardo and I were a couple. We were always together and we had our ups and downs. Then, one day I heard Eduardo was courting a rich older French woman who had a villa in Positano with her husband. Naturally, I didn't like it, but I suppose by then I had accepted Eduardo's rules about our relationship and just decided to wait for it to pass. I didn't complain. I even ironed Eduardo's tennis shorts when he went to play tennis with the woman. I did even worse than that. Alain and I would play doubles with them. They would always win, which really made me upset. Eduardo wined and dined this woman whenever her husband wasn't in town. Then when the husband came back, Eduardo would return to me. Once Eduardo even had the nerve to ask me to sew something special for this woman to wear. I refused to do that. I couldn't stoop that low.

The woman's husband was more angry at Eduardo than I was. He ended up leaving her and selling the villa. She was left with nothing, so Eduardo had to keep her. Even Eduardo's mother told me they couldn't ask her to leave, because she had nowhere to go. I felt rather sorry for her at one point. She was at least twenty years older than Eduardo, and she had had everything before she met my boyfriend, the Latin Lover. Now she had nothing. I don't think Eduardo had been with her

for the money, more likely it was sort of a challenge which backfired. Personally I wasn't that upset. I was still in love with him and he with me. My friends told me I was crazy to accept all he put me through, but somehow I always knew he would come back to me. His mother thought so too. She used to tell me, 'He will change one day Jennie. Please be patient.'

There were times when Eduardo would get very frustrated with me. One time we went to a ski resort in Roccaraso near Naples. I was still nervous on skis, and it made me even more nervous knowing Eduardo was a very good skier and I wouldn't be able to keep up with him. We were riding the ski lift up the mountain and as we were approaching the top I somehow fell off the chair lift. He jumped off after me. I felt so happy that he had come to save me from sliding down the mountain and told him so, however I was in

Eduardo, Jennie, Antonello and Judy in Venice.

Grand Canal. Venice was beautiful and exciting and so was the fog which enveloped the city. The fog was so thick we couldn't see more than a meter in front of us. None of the ferries were running, so we had to walk everywhere holding onto one another so we wouldn't get lost or fall into a canal. We went to a casino and Eduardo gave me a few chips to play with. I put them on number 31 and won a little money on the roulette! After that, 31 became my lucky number for a long time. We had a wonderful time in Venice and I'm certain our child was conceived there on **31 December 1971**.

When I got back to Positano, I waited a week or so before having a pregnancy test. It was positive. Eduardo was very happy when I called him with the news. Eduardo still had problems with his older woman, but that would be settled soon. I think he was already thinking of me as the Madonna with child. I was so happy and I felt nothing negative could come near me. I had left the doll's house and was now living on the same street, but much higher up. Actually, it was a terrible location, right in the middle of a long steep staircase. I still had a wonderful terrace, but the house was much newer. It didn't have domed ceilings or any of the old Italian feeling to it like the doll's house did.

I always corresponded frequently with my family in Australia and I kept promising them that I would return home soon. Now that I was pregnant, I wondered what I would tell them. I couldn't tell my mother, but I did tell my sister. I asked her to keep it a secret, just in case something happened. No use having my mother worry when she was so far away. I was always sending them photos, so now as my tummy started to get bigger, I sent them photos of me dressed in large flowing robes. I told them I was into my spiritual period!

for a surprise. He started prodding me with his ski pole screaming, 'Save you? You stupid twit! No one falls off a chair lift just a few meters from the top!' It was so embarrassing to have all the other skiers slowly passing over us as he yelled at me. It may sound strange to say, but it was actually on that trip that I first really knew I was in love with him.

Coming back to Naples from the mountains, Eduardo asked me if I wanted to get married or have a child first. Without even thinking, I told him it would be better to have a baby first and then see what happens. I was in love with him and I knew I would have a baby with him one day, but I couldn't really see the point in tying everything up at the same time. He suggested we could plan a romantic ski trip to Austria. I didn't think a dreary town in Austria was where I wanted to conceive my baby. I finally convinced him to go to Venice instead. What could be more romantic than Venice?

We drove to Venice in a Fiat 500 with Judy and Antonello. Travelling with four people from Naples to Venice in the winter in such a small car really takes some courage. At the first Autogrill stop on the highway, the cases we had strapped on top of the car were stolen. We arrived in Venice and booked into the Hotel Monaco on the

I actually was in a spiritual period. When I was two months pregnant, a group of friends and I went to Rome to attend a transcendental meditation class. We had our initiation ceremony and were each given a secret mantra. Before we returned home, I decided to see a card reader I knew named Pina Tadolini. I was only two months pregnant and was very thin, only about 56 kilos, so she couldn't have guessed my condition. As she was shuffling the cards, one fell out. She bent down to pick it up and exclaimed, 'Oh you are pregnant!' Well, that spoilt my secret! After spreading my cards on the table she told me some very bad news, 'The baby is going to die.' She saw the expression on my face and must have quickly realised she shouldn't have said that. She examined my cards more carefully and then said, 'No. I see the baby being born, but you are going to have a big problem in the very near future.' When I asked her what I should do, she assured me everything would be fine and I must remember to stay calm. *Stay calm?!* I lived alone in a small apartment in the middle of a long staircase and I didn't even have a telephone! It would be hard to stay calm after hearing what she had said!

I returned home and in the days that followed I tried not to think too much about what she had told me. Then a week later, I woke up at 5.30 am with the feeling that I had wet the bed. I turned on the light and I found I was swimming in a blood bath. I ran out of the house, down the long winding staircase to the main road and then up more stairs to the home of my friends Franca and Alain. I started banging on their door screaming, 'Franca, let me in. I am going to lose my baby!'

Now I know that when someone is haemorrhaging they should lie down and not move. Certainly not run up and down endless stairs, but I had no other choice, unless I wanted to lay there forever and ever, Amen! Franca called the doctor, who was more interested in who the father was rather than my bloody problem. He told me I was having a miscarriage and there was little he could do. He gave me a shot and left, saying he would return the next day. My friends were instructed not to let me go home for three days. Personally, I wasn't terribly upset by what the doctor said. I had more faith in my card reader than I did in that doctor. Later when I was alone, I called Pina in Rome and told her what had happened. She wasn't at all surprised. She asked me for the father's name and said she would do some white magic for me.

Three days later, Alain and another friend literally carried me all the way home and put me to bed. They called another doctor from out

of town to come see me. He assured me my baby was still alive. Each day a local woman from a family I knew well came to the house to give me a painful shot of something, but the bleeding still continued. I began to think I might end up losing the baby after all. Even the doctor gave up after a few days. He said he felt bad taking my money for daily visits when he couldn't resolve the problem.

I had a book called *Pregnancy and Problems*. It became my bible. I read it over and over again, hoping I could find a solution. Throughout all this I had not seen or heard from Eduardo, but that was the last of my worries. I was advised to bring in the local midwife, Angela, who had delivered many babies in Positano and the surrounding villages. She came from a family of doctors and had even been awarded a gold medal from the government for her work. Angela saved the day and she became my guardian angel. She said she had seen similar cases to mine and told me not to worry or get stressed out. Everything would be fine. I had faith in her and felt safe under her care.

A month had gone by and Favola, who was also pregnant, gave birth to eight puppies right near my bed. She would never leave my side even when she gave birth. She was so exhausted after the first four puppies popped out that I had to get out of

bed and get a pair of scissors to cut all the sacs to let the little ones free. Afterwards my friends came by to play cards, keep me company or help with the puppies.

A few months later, the bleeding finally stopped and my crying stopped too. Angela told me I could get out of bed. In my bible I read that if you have a problem in the first two months, you must be very careful in the seventh month. When that time came around, I put myself back into bed for the next month or so. In my eighth month I had to go to a clinic in Vico Equense. That was where many local pregnant women went in those days. The doctor there had studied in New York, which sounded good to me. During one of my check ups they told me I was having twins and I needed an X-ray to find out what position they were in. I wasn't that surprised. My brother had twins and my father had twins with his second wife, so why shouldn't I have twins too? However, I was rather nervous about raising two children on my own. I knew their daddy wouldn't be much help. It was a relief when the X-ray showed only one baby with a very big head. However, the baby hadn't turned at all. It was sitting straight up like a little Buddha for the whole eight months and didn't intend on turning now. After consulting my book, I insisted

on having a caesarean birth. The book said having a baby with a large head coming feet first would be difficult, especially since it was my first pregnancy. My doctor was very happy with my decision.

Around this time I saw Edna Lewis for the last time. She died on **15 August 1972**. I passed by her house to pay my last respects. My friend Suzanne Charlton had dressed Edna in a red satin evening gown with red polish on her nails and powder on her cheeks. I sat my huge pregnant body down near the bed where Edna lay and thought to myself: *Here is a person who lived a very full life right up until the last moment. Now she is gone and a month from now there will be another being brought into this world—my child.*

I hadn't been able to work at all during my pregnancy, so as the months went by money was getting tight. My landlady, Maria, came by to collect the money for my rent, which I didn't have. I remembered what Angela and the cards had said: No stress and no problems. So I looked Maria straight in the eye and told her, 'I'm having a baby. Please do not discuss money with me now.' She looked down at her shoes, as though she realised she had done something bad and shuffled off. I now weighed 84 kilos. It was all in my tummy, which made it great for reading. I could prop the book upon my enormous stomach. I read *Lord of the Rings* through my pregnancy, which years later became one of my child's favourite films. She must have been reading along with me when she was in my womb.

The morning of **14 September 1972** was warm with a slight breeze blowing. The day was calm. Most of the tourists had left and given the town back to the locals. I felt extremely peaceful that day, but I found all I wanted to do was to sleep and to pee. I began to feel very strange and had someone call the midwife. Angela arrived and checked me out. She told me she was going home right away to get her car. She said I was going into labour and we had to leave for the clinic immediately!

I dressed, packed my little case and pulled my enormous tummy up all the stairs to the road. I was feeling uncomfortable as I waited for Angela to arrive and was hopping up and down. By then, it was late in the afternoon. I was standing on the main road leading into Positano in my white mini dress, which was now shorter than ever since it was being pulled out of shape by my big belly. I had an overnight bag in my hand and was desperately trying to keep both feet on the ground. I was trying to keep my balance, but found it difficult, especially knowing that we had a forty-five minute drive to the hospital in Vico Equense. I was wishing this little creature inside of me hadn't decided to come ten days early! My two close friends Marmory and Suzanne drove by and asked me what I was doing dancing up and down in the street. When I told them I was about to give birth and was on my way to the hospital, they said that they would follow in their car and stay the night with me.

Finally, Angela arrived in her old Volkswagen and we began our drive to the clinic. It was bad enough being in labour in an old VW with a long drive ahead of us. It got worse when Angela told me that if my water broke before we got there, not only might the baby die, but I could also have a big problem as well! Oh dear, if only the baby had turned and was in the right position. Then it could have popped out in the car, but we both knew I had to have a caesarean.

I had been crossing my legs, hoping that might slow things down. When we finally reached Vico Equense, I had to untangle my legs, which seemed to have gotten into some weird yoga position. I followed Angela as she barged into the clinic with authority and screaming, '*Emergenza! Emergenza!*' We were told the doctor was still in the hospital in Castellammare and wouldn't be

Jennie and Carmen.

back for an hour or so. Just my luck! I guess I needed to cross my legs again. My two girlfriends arrived, making my small room quite crowded. When the doctor came, they wheeled me into the operating theatre. I was scared. I almost wished I was a good Christian or believed in some god, so I could ask for help, but I wasn't. Just before I was poked with a needle to send me off to Never Never Land, I asked the doctor to please look at the clock the second the cord was cut. I needed that information for the baby's horoscope chart.

At **10.20 pm on 14 September 1972** my daughter was born. She was Virgo, with Gemini ascendant. I hadn't known the sex of my baby, but everything from the Tarot cards to the pendulum, which had been held over my tummy, had predicted it was a boy. I hadn't even thought about a name for a girl. I decided to call her Rebecca Edwina Hanlon. All the nurses hated the name Rebecca and they weren't shy about letting me

know it. I have no idea where I got it from, but being an unmarried mother, I felt I had a certain right to what my child was to be called. However when her father arrived the next day, he changed her name on all the documents to Carmen Sorrenti. Of course, he chose Carmen after his mother. When he told me what he had done, I was lying there with metal stitches in my stomach and not feeling great and I just thought, *What's in a name, anyway?* As I looked at my little daughter, a white-skinned beauty with blue-green eyes and the first wisps of blonde hair beginning to show on her head, I wondered if the name Carmen was right for her. I didn't get any support from the hospital staff, which had all gathered around to listen to our dispute over her name. They all preferred the name Carmen and patted daddy on the back cheering *Bravo!* as he walked out.

After the caesarean section, I was fed by a drip for four days and was getting very hungry. The

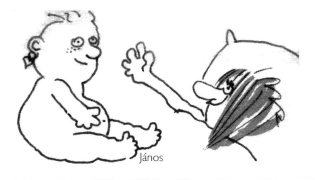
János

doctor told me I couldn't get out of bed or have any solid food until I had passed wind. I don't think that happens anymore these days. I asked him how I would know when I passed wind and he replied, 'Oh, you will know and so will everyone as far away as Positano.' He was so right!

During my pregnancy, I had been told I should increase the amount of milk and fresh fruit juices I had so I would be able to breast feed without any problem. I may have slightly over exaggerated my intake. I produced so much milk I could have nursed every baby in the entire hospital. That continued for three years. I felt like a cow. While I was in the clinic, I didn't know what to do with all the excess milk I was producing. So after Carmen had all she wanted, I would get rid of the rest in the pot of a plant someone had sent to me. I decided that when it was time for me to leave the clinic, I would give the plant to a certain nurse who had never been nice to me. She had already figured out I wasn't one of the big tippers. Imagine being presented with a plant which had been well-nourished for a couple of weeks with mother's milk! The plant blossomed, but the perfume was a little off putting!

The clinic was private. I had my own room and bathroom. I had chosen it because I knew several women from Positano who had had their babies there. There were some public hospitals in the south, which were either very inexpensive or free, however I heard there was a risk of coming out with hepatitis or something worse. I knew I had made the right choice, but I didn't really have the means to pay for it. My own money was running low since I had stopped working during my pregnancy, plus Carmen had arrived ten days early, so I didn't have the time to get some money together. I always had faith that things would work out if you think positively. I also hoped Carmen's father would help—after all he had just signed all of her documents. In those days they only kept you in the hospital a few days after a caesarean birth. Ten days had passed and I was still there. Each morning when the nurse came in and said, '*Buongiorno, Signora.* You can go home today.' I would just lay there playing Miss Rich Bitch and cooly reply, 'I think I will stay on a little more to relax and get my strength back.' As soon as I was alone, I would be on the telephone to Eduardo pleading for help. The staff was fine with me staying longer. They didn't have to take care of us much, so it was as if I was paying for an expensive hotel.

Eduardo came by to see us and sometimes he would stay over night in the spare bed in our room. The staff would bring him breakfast early in the morning, but he would keep sleeping. Then when he woke up, he would send it back complaining it was cold. One of the times he visited, he pulled up to the front of the clinic in a gold sport's car which belonged to his French mistress. I told him never to do that again. The staff would think we had money. I told him to park it a long way off and then take a bus up to the clinic. Eduardo didn't offer to pay the clinic himself, but he did give me a cheque from his brother once, although it wasn't for that much money. It probably only paid for a couple of days. After that Eduardo suggested I should simply inform the office that I didn't have any more money and then walk out with the baby. Finally Jimmy James, an Australian painter and a wonderful friend of mine, paid the bill for us. He said everyone in Positano wanted to see me and meet baby Carmen and the only way to get us there was to pay the clinic. Jimmy was so kind to me and he became like a grandfather to Carmen.

When we arrived home, I found Elenora Appuzzo, a local woman, waiting for us. She had put our house in order and stocked the cupboards and refrigerator with food. I will never forget that gesture she made. We were not close friends and it was so kind of her. The day after I brought Carmen home, I was passing the grocer shop and Anna, the owner, ran out to greet us saying, '*Signora* Jennie, let me look at the baby!' How quickly things changed… I had gone into hospital as *Signorina* and came out as a *Signora!* I was rather

taken back when Anna said, 'Che bella. She's so beautiful. Have you given her to Jesus yet?' I told her I had just gotten her myself and didn't intend to give her to anyone, yet!

I had a close friend named Guy, who I had met when he was working as a waiter at the Quicksilver. He was just returning to Positano after living in France, where he was from. He was looking for a place to live and I had a spare bedroom, so he moved in with us. Eduardo knew him well, so there were no bad feelings. It was the perfect situation. Whenever I could pick up an odd job, Guy would babysit for Carmen. Autumn was coming on and there were many trips to Naples to Eduardo's family. Carmen was the first female grandchild in the family and Nonna Carmen was very proud.

I thought it was wonderful having a baby, especially a little girl. It was like playing with my favourite doll when I was a child. Changing her clothes and putting bows in her hair. However, my dog Favola was quite upset about the intrusion of this new thing in our household. When I first brought Carmen home, Favola stopped eating for a few days. I began to worry that she wasn't getting any nourishment. *Nourishment*, I thought. *That's what she needs.* I had an idea to keep our little family united. I was still having problems with my never-ending supply of milk, so I decided that Favola would find mother's milk in her doggie bowl each day instead of the usual meat and rice. It wasn't long before she accepted the new arrival and soon she wouldn't leave my side when I was with her new 'baby sister'. She actually became a great babysitter. Whenever I had to run to the grocer shop across the street, I would leave Carmen in her cradle with Favola sitting guard. When I returned, Favola would be in the exact same position as when I left. How I loved that dog.

I tried to be the perfect mum for Carmen when she was little, however I really don't believe there is a perfect mum or dad in the end. When she was about three weeks old, I thought it would be good for her to take a little of the gentle autumn sun before winter set in, so each morning I would put her on the terrace in her pram. One morning I was ironing and probably dreaming about her wonderful future. I was so involved in my fantasy that I didn't notice it was raining and, by the look of the terrace, had been for some time. I raced out and more or less had to fish little Carmen out of the pram. She was sort of swimming in her own little pool. I often wonder if that is why she loved swimming at a young age.

I would like to write one more note about my midwife, Angela. When Angela was older, she developed a bad problem with her legs and began using a cane to help her walk. After a while the pain must have gotten too much for her. One day her husband came home and found her in the bathroom—dead. She had hung herself. The authorities said she couldn't have a priest at her funeral, because she had committed suicide. It seemed so unfair after all the good she had done in the village. Someone contacted the Vatican. In light of all she had contributed to the people of Positano for so many years, she was pardoned by the Pope and allowed to have a priest at her funeral after all. Whenever I go to the cemetery in Positano I visit her tomb and thank her for being my guardian angel when I was pregnant.

Around this time, a young couple moved to Positano. Carlo Rizzi was the brother of Gigi Rizzi, one of the lovers of Bridget Bardot. His wife was Simona, the daughter of an Ambassador to Persia. We became good friends and we were frequently invited to their house for dinner, which was a help to me while I was living on a tight budget. The Shah of Persia was planning a large event over the course of several days to celebrate the 2,500 anniversary of the founding of the Persian Empire and Simona's family would be attending the celebration. I was asked to make a dress for Simona. If I remember correctly, I made it out of curtain material, much like Snooks and I used to do with our fancy dress gowns back in Mildura. Simona loved it and so did everyone else. I was quite proud, considering I was a no one in the world of fashion at that time.

There were always so many interesting people in Positano, either living here or just passing through. One day, I was at the Cambusa restaurant on the beach and I met a young French woman named Dany Coudert. She told me she was a writer and wrote under the pseudonym Jeanne Cordelier. After a few minutes, she admitted she had been a well-known prostitute in Paris. I was rather surprised. I couldn't imagine this small, intelligent young woman being a whore! She and her husband at the time had rented a house on the top of Positano in Chiesa Nuova and we all became friends. I met her shortly before Carmen's first birthday and Dany wanted the four of us to celebrate it at her house, which we did. We started seeing them often and our friendship became much closer. Dany confided in me that her husband had been involved with a big court case, which revolved around the Waldorf Astoria Hotel in New York. The film *The French Connection* was made about that case. She told me she and her husband were living under the protection of the U.S. government and had been told if they saw or heard anything that worried them, they should immediately call a direct number they had to the FBI in Washington. I was rather worried about knowing people who were involved with the U.S. government, the FBI and international drug smugglers, but fortunately nothing bad ever happened.

Ghosts at Casa San Matteo

In **1974** Guy and I had met a young American man by the name of Scott Kemper. Scott had graduated from Harvard University and then worked as a waiter in Provincetown on the tip of Cape Cod in Massachusetts. There he had met friends who told him so much about Positano that he decided to come check it out for himself. The three of us got on well together and we all decided to look for a bigger house where we could share expenses and live as a family.

We found a wonderful house, which had once been a monastery. There was a little church outside the front gate called the church of San Matteo, although it never seemed to be open. The house, which was about 450 years old, was called Casa San Matteo. I had heard it had been built for Caroline Bonaparte and her husband General Murat as a holiday home. I'm not sure that's true; it may be just another Positano Whisper. It might be true though, because when standing on the long terrace of Casa San Matteo, you do look down onto the Hotel Palazzo Murat and Palazzo Murat means Murat's palace.

The house was lovely. There were spacious rooms on the top and even larger rooms on the bottom floor. The long staircase inside the house had a noble look to it. It made a woman feel as though she should be dressed in crinoline rather than in jeans and T-shirts. Actually, some of my male friends felt the same way! On the roof was a garden with a pomegranate tree and at the entrance of the house on top of the staircase coming in from the street there were two enormous datura trees. When they bloomed, their huge white bell-shaped flowers gave off an exotic perfume so heavy that you could hardly breathe.

I loved my bathroom in San Matteo. It was not very big, but it was wonderful. It was the only room in the grand old villa which could be heated enough to warm us during the colder months. The room was long and narrow with a small bathtub at one end with blue and white tiles along the outside of the tub. At the opposite end of the room, I squeezed in a small divan with colourful cushions. An electric heater was all we needed to heat the space. Someone had given us a black and white television set and I put it in the bathroom on a small table. We had never had a television before, but now bath time for little Carmen felt like going to a premier. Carmen's older sister, Favola, would join us and curl up on the thick bath mat and dream away.

Favola gave birth to 13 puppies in that bathtub. When she was ready to give birth, she jumped in and the fun began. The first puppy was born around three o'clock in the afternoon and it wasn't until the wee hours of the morning when the last one came out. After each birth, she would jump out of the tub and take her little one by the scruff of the neck outside to clean it off. It was as though she didn't want to mess up the bathroom.

Casa San Matteo was such a magical old villa. Soon after we moved in, we decided to give a costume party in the enormous rooms down below, which were still empty. The theme was 'The Night of Celebrity Couples'. Scott and I dressed as Adam and Eve. As our guests arrived and came down the garden staircase, Scott and I were perched high in one of the datura trees. We were scantily robed in white chiffon and had our bodies coated in white powder. Most of the guests were very arty people and they put so much thought and creativity into their costumes, each trying to outdo the others. It was a fabulous night.

There was something else which made Casa San Matteo special. There was a ghost. It was one of three well-known ghosts around Positano. My ghost was so well-known that most of the locals couldn't believe I would live there with a small child. One day a man stopped me in town and asked how I was doing in THAT house. I could tell by his voice that he meant how was I doing with the ghost. I said I was fine. He told me he had done some construction on our house years ago. He had

brought his dog along with him to the job and the dog refused to enter the house and all its fur began to stand straight up on end. Someone else had told me my ghost was a he and he had been a monk from the San Matteo monastery. I was actually completely fine with the ghost. I accepted him and always felt very peaceful and serene in that house. I never felt the need to lock the big ancient doors. I felt the ghost was watching over us. I began to think of him as another member of our family. Carmen did too. She used to ask her little friends to come over and play with the ghost. Whenever she said that, the other children would go berserk! Years later after we had moved out of the house, a woman named Raffaella moved in. I heard that one night when she was alone in bed in the dark there was suddenly a torch in her face. I actually heard that same thing had happened more than once to other people as well. I'm not sure why the ghost was kind to us, but I always felt nothing bad would happen to us there.

Although I was at peace with the ghost, I wanted to know more about it. I called Jean Du Dan, the psychic I had met years ago in Rome with Audrey Rose. I told him about our ghost and asked him to come to Positano for the weekend to give me some advice. I told him I would find other clients for him here to make his trip worthwhile. I knew with all the wacko friends I had I could find him lots of work. He agreed, but said he would need to bring his boyfriend, Franco, with him. Apparently Franco had powers of his own and could sniff out ghosts. Although I was quite sure I knew just where in the house our ghost lived, the idea of having my thoughts confirmed by a professional was very interesting to me.

Jean Du Dan was quite powerful. When he was 13 years old he had met Carl Jung who told him he had very special powers, which he would come to realise in the near future. Jean was a dancer and when he grew up he ran a dance school in Rome. He only did readings on the side. He didn't want to use his power for financial gain. However whenever times weren't as good and he wasn't making enough money from teaching, he would give readings to people seeking advice as a way to help make ends meet. When he gave a reading, Jean Du Dan would ask the person to write a question

on a piece of paper and fold it. Then Jean would hold it to his forehead without reading it and fall into deep concentration. He would begin to see fascinating symbols—some beautiful, some not so beautiful, which he would describe out loud. By the time he had finished describing what he saw and felt, the person's question would be answered. The process of translating the symbols would take about an hour and a half and it felt like a Magical Mystery Tour. At least that's how it worked for me. I only went to see him three times in Rome. He used to call me 'The Ghost of Positano', because of the way I would appear every now and then at his house.

When Jean and Franco arrived at Casa San Matteo, I explained to them all I knew about the ghost. Franco offered to sniff the ghost out and the hunt began almost immediately. Jean, Carmen, Scott, Guy, Favola and myself all followed in a line behind Franco. Franco continued heavily sniffing his way through the rooms of the villa. We all found ourselves sniffing as we went along as well, even Favola!

I was quite certain our ghost monk lived in a room on the lower floor of the villa. The room had once been a kitchen and it had a huge wood stove made of beautiful old blue and white tiles. It resembled an altar. Franco sniffed around the room and agreed this was the place we were looking for.

Their weekend with us turned into a month and their stay was full of surprises. There was never a dull moment. Jean was very busy. People were actually lining up for appointments with him. He could only see about three people a day, because his work was so emotionally draining. Two friends of mine Arianna and Cornelia had recently been robbed and they came to ask Jean for help. He didn't like to get involved with that sort of thing. He had worked on two big cases for the police in the past and didn't like it. He was far too mystical and sensitive for crime cases. However, since these were friends of mine, he agreed to help them. The day after they met with him, they saw a man from Salerno who matched a description Jean had given them. The man was travelling with a woman who was wearing one of the necklaces which had been stolen from them. The case was solved!

Our evenings together were fascinating. I adored our after dinner games and conversations. Jean told magical stories of his years in Paris, Cuba and Brazil. They were stories filled with voodoo, black and white magic and tripping with the Indians of South America.

I had wanted to see Jean make a table move, as I had seen in films, but he insisted it was a bit like a game for children and didn't want to do it. I kept asking him, until one night he finally agreed. Carmen was in bed asleep and Scott and Guy were out for the evening, which I thought was just as well. They didn't believe in any of that stuff. I invited Suzanne Charlton, who lived next door to join us. Suzanne and I were both dressed in black. I lit candles all around my enormous bedroom and positioned a three-legged table in front of the large arched windows that looked out over the datura trees in the garden. Jean told us to put our hands flat on the table with our fingers slightly touching each other. I was very excited and ready to be taken into the past or wherever we would be heading. Jean began sort of mumbling and chanting. He was probably telling the table to hurry up and get moving so he could go to bed. He told us that when the table was ready, it would lift off the floor and come towards the person it wanted to speak to.

All of a sudden the table started doing little jerks, like a woman in labour. It began lifting slightly off the floor. The jerking got more violent. Jean asked it who it wanted to talk to. Suddenly I felt the table pushing against my stomach and heard Jean say, 'So, you would like to speak to Jennie?' At that moment, Scott walked into the room. Instantly the table fell back into place. The spell was broken. I stared at Scott. He stared back, looking rather pale and angry. I could just imagine what he would say to his friends the next day when he told them this story!

Jean Du Dan

Jean and Franco's visit with us was not all exciting and fun. There were some rough patches too. Their relationship was not going smoothly. Franco was rather aggressive and Jean was the complete opposite. Jean didn't drink much alcohol, but Franco often drank much too much and then he would become angry. There were several nights when Jean woke me up asking for help with Franco when he was in one of his violent moods. They both had powers and sometimes when they fought and the situation between them got heavy, the electricity would go off. I found this sort of amusing, but it was also rather annoying. Scott didn't like it at all. Once I actually saw a light bulb shoot out of a bedside lamp in Jean's room and smash against the wall during one of their fights.

Guy

A month had gone by and it was time for Jean and Franco to return to Rome. Scott, who was a great cook, had offered to make them a farewell dinner. However he had one condition. There could be no fighting between them, because he needed the electricity to stay on so he could prepare the meal. We all hoped we could get through the evening without any fighting. The dinner went well, but then I noticed Franco was drinking more and more. Towards the end of the evening, Franco disappeared downstairs. When we finished the meal, Jean went to sleep and Guy went up to the garden on the domed roof to get some fresh air. I prepared to go to bed and Scott put on his long white night robe before going downstairs to make sure all of the doors and windows were closed tightly in case it rained.

Guy came into my room to have a chat and all of a sudden we heard an incredible scraping noise coming from one of the rooms below. It sounded as though chains were being dragged across the ancient tiles. Guy went down to check what it was. I remembered that Franco had been down on the lower floor for quite some time. I had no idea if he was still there. I waited on top of the staircase. Then I saw a very serious looking Jean trying to

half-carry, half-drag Franco up the stairs. Franco's eyes seemed to be popping out of his head and there was a little froth dripping out of his mouth. When I asked Jean what was going on, he just told me not to worry. He said he would handle everything.

Guy and I went back to my room wondering what on earth could have happened down there. Then, Scott appeared at my door. He was furious and said, 'Damn it. Can't I even move around my own house without having some freaky guest fainting and muttering, "Scott… Death Scott. Beware of death!"'

Apparently, what happened was Franco had too much to drink during our dinner and he went down stairs to cool off before he made trouble for Jean on their last night. He fell asleep down there. Then Scott came downstairs in his long white nightgown to close the windows and doors. In the dark, Franco saw this white figure flitting silently by in the half darkness and thought it was the real ghost. There was a big old chain hanging from the wall close to where Franco was lying. He grabbed it for support, but the chain detached itself from the wall and Franco dragged it along the floor. Just as Franco began to faint, he looked at the ghost and saw Scott's face, which is why he called out, 'Scott… Death Scott. Beware of death!' before he passed out.

Jean and Franco left the next morning before I had time to tell them what had really happened, so Franco left thinking he had really seen the ghost. About six months later, I met them again. I began to bring up the ghost story, but Jean kicked me under the table. Franco still wasn't over the experience yet. When I told them the truth, we all rolled around the floor in fits of laughter.

Not long after that exciting month, I received a postcard which felt as though it had been sent by another ghost—a ghost from my past. It was from my father. Although I had corresponded with my father over the years, this postcard was different. It was posted from Tahiti and on it he had written that he was on his way to see me. I hadn't seen my father since I was one and a half years old, the same age Carmen was now!

Over the past 34 years I had hoped I would see my father again, but now that he was actually

Jennie's father.

few weeks where he would be receiving a prize from The Lions Club.

It was nice having my father with me. He loved to talk about his past. He told me all about his time in the military where he had been a great organiser for the troops. I'm not so bad at organising myself, so I suppose I should thank my dad for passing on that ability to me. After dad had left our family in Australia, he ended up marrying the other woman, Ann. Together they had a son named Lex and then twin boys, Peter and Tony.

The morning after his arrival, Dad met Scott and Guy. There were no problems between them as I had feared. Dad told me they both seemed to be good people and Dad actually became quite fond of Scott, even after seeing him come to breakfast in his long floral satin housecoat. After breakfast Scott would often sit doing his nails whilst chatting away with Dad. Dad was fine with the whole scene and he enjoyed Scott's company. Each day I would take my father out to meet my friends around Positano. As we walked around town, I noticed he frequently had to keep stopping to rest. I asked if he was okay, but he said he just wanted to look at the beautiful view.

The time had come to make our trip to Rome, so Dad could receive his prize from The Lions Club. It was to be a grand event held in the Excelsior Hotel on the Via Veneto. I asked what I should wear. Although I didn't have much money to spend on clothes, I knew I could sew something nice for myself. Shoes were always my problem, so I was happy when Dad offered to buy a pair for me in Rome. I arranged for my friend Mimi Barba, the number one driver in Positano, to take us to Rome for a couple of days and then on to Naples. I asked Mimi not only to drive us around, but also to babysit for Carmen when Dad and I went to the big event at the hotel. Carmen was happy. She knew Mimi well and I was certain he would take very good care of her.

I knew nothing about The Lions Club. Apparently, the members are given badges and the bigger the badge, the more important you are. Dad's badge was quite big. We entered the hall and Dad had us wait by the door for someone to come over to take us to our table. I told him I could call someone over in Italian, but he insisted there

on his way, I was having second thoughts about meeting him. Maybe he wouldn't be as he seemed in his letters. Perhaps, I should just remember him as he was on paper. He didn't give a date for his arrival, so I just had to wait. I wondered what he would say about me living in a villa with a gay man and a French playboy.

Quite late one night the big old cowbell that hung outside the main entrance to the villa began to clang. I raced down the long staircase and opened the door to find a man standing there with a suitcase in hand. He looked at me and said, 'Jennifer?' I was amazed. I recognised his eyes immediately and said, 'You have the same eyes as my daughter!' He smiled and replied, 'Well, I am her grandfather…' Both Scott and Guy were out that evening and Carmen was asleep, so I had a little time on my own to start to get to know my father by myself.

One of the first things my father said to me was, 'Jennifer, where can I find the lions?' I had no idea why he wanted to see lions, but told him we could go to the zoo in Naples if he wanted. He explained that he was talking about The Lions Club. He said he would need to go to Rome in a would be no need, once they saw his big badge. No one came for us and I grew tired of waiting, so I waved someone down behind Dad's back. When they came over, I told them my father had come all the way from Australia. We were seated at a large table with a group of Italians, none of whom spoke any English. The man next to me spent the whole evening asking where I lived and what my telephone number was hoping to pick me up in the typical Italian fashion. My father heard our conversation and wanted me to translate what the man was saying to me. I didn't want to tell my dad that the man was hitting on me, so I had to keep making up stories the entire evening. The new shoes I had chosen were obviously too small for me and they were beginning to hurt my feet. While I was sitting there I had taken them off under the table. Then when they called my father's name to go up to the stage to receive his prize, Dad insisted I go up with him. I quickly had to squeeze my feet back into the little shoes. It wasn't easy, but I managed to do it in time to go up with him without too much embarrassment.

When the evening was over, we found Mimi in his Mercedes waiting for us. Carmen was jumping up and down with joy to see her mamma. Mimi told me he had taken her to a pizzeria and after they had eaten, Carmen had jumped up on the table and danced to the Neapolitan music!

From Rome we went to Naples to visit the Sorrenti family. We stayed in a charming hotel on a hill in Posillipo with a wonderful view of the bay. It was a nice trip and I was rather proud to introduce my father to my Italian family. They have been very important to me and Carmen. From the time Carmen was a few months old until she was about three, my life had been divided between Positano and Naples. Carmen and I would often stay over with Ricardo and Francesca and their two little children, Mario, who had been born a year before Carmen, and Vanina, who was born about a year later. I think Carmen and I spent more time with Ricardo and Francesca than we did with Eduardo. I always enjoyed our visits to Naples. Occasionally, we would all go to Zio Angelo's villa in Massalubrense together. I loved staying there. It was on the sea with a view of Capri and they had their own private swimming pool.

Jennie's father in Positano.

Christmas was coming and Scott and a friend prepared a grand Christmas dinner at our house. There were 16 guests sitting around our table, all dressed in elegant clothing, including my father who had brought his smoking jacket. Later that day, my Italian family came by to join in our Christmas celebration. Eduardo came along with Ricardo, Francesca, Mario and Vanina.

We celebrated New Year's Eve at Da Vincenzo's restaurant with some of my friends, including Gene and Suzanne Charlton and Oliver Campbell. Afterwards, we all decided to go to the Buca di Bacco nightclub to ring in the New Year. What a group we were. I had little Carmen on one side and my father on the other. The Charltons weren't getting on well. Suzanne was having an affair and Gene was upset. At the end of the evening, I was getting ready to take my little family and walk home, but Suzanne kindly offered to drive us instead. I heard that when Gene couldn't find his wife, he thought she had run off to her new lover. Gene headed towards the beach in a drunken haze. He filled the pockets of his trousers with big rocks and began walking into the waves with his heavy load, intending to end it all. He went so far into the water that a group of Neapolitan tourists had to drag him out. What a scene it must have been! Gene always dressed so elegantly. He must have been quite a sight walking into the waves in his white lacy frilled shirt, tails, a black velvet cape and beautiful boots. We never ever seemed to have normal outings in Positano. Nothing really amazed anyone after a while. We all became used to odd dramas unfolding around us.

My father ended up staying with me for three months and it gradually became obvious that he was ill. I later found out he hadn't been well back in Australia, but he didn't want to tell me. I called the doctor and then had to get him a nurse to give him his treatments. To tell the truth, I wasn't sure what he had. I didn't suspect it was anything drastic; he was only 69 years old. So I was shocked when the doctor insisted we needed to get him better as quickly as possible so he could go back to Australia. The doctor told me my father's condition was very serious and he didn't want my father to die in my house, since I had only just met him again recently. I was stunned, but I agreed with the doctor. My dad stayed in bed for quite a long time to build up some strength for his return trip.

My brother in Australia called me and said our dad had withdrawn a large amount of money from his bank. His other family had contacted Alan. They were concerned that our father was staying in Italy so long. They were worried that perhaps he planned to stay with me. I explained to Alan that the reason Dad was not going home was because he was so ill. The only money he had spent here was for doctors and medical treatment and quite a few expensive presents for his second lot of children as well.

When he was well enough, I arranged my father's flight back to Australia. Dad asked me to reserve a wheelchair at the airport in Rome, which was waiting for us on our arrival. As we were on our way to the departure gate, Dad said he wanted to take out travel insurance before he left, in case anything happened on the plane. I wheeled him over to the office and as he was filling out the form he turned to me and said, 'Now, to whom should I leave this 125,000 dollars?' I shrugged. '... to my boys in Queensland, of course', he replied to his own question. I just shrugged again. I had never expected to receive anything from my father anyway, so it really didn't matter to me.

Just about three weeks after he left Italy, I received a telegram informing me that my father had died on **20 April 1974**. I cried for him, although he was someone I never really knew. I was grateful though to have had that little time with him before he died.

Carmen and Our Strange Family of Friends

I was extremely happy being a mum and totally enamoured with my little daughter. We never had much money, but we lived in an enormous old villa. Money just didn't seem to worry me. Somehow Carmen and I managed to eat well and pay the bills. I knew I had to begin thinking about getting a job, but I needed to find one that wouldn't separate me from Carmen, the greatest treasure I ever had in my life. I began picking up odd jobs whenever I could and I started making some clothes to sell in a few boutiques in town.

I was still seeing Eduardo from time to time, but I had so much going on that it didn't bother me that he wasn't around more of the time. It never occurred to me to look for another man to share my life. That was fine with Carmen; she was incredibly jealous of anyone who ever came near me. I began to worry about the fact that Carmen didn't have a passport or at least some official identification document. I had tried to get one for her earlier, but Eduardo had refused to sign the papers for a passport. He was afraid I might try to take her out of the country and away from him. Carmen had Eduardo's surname, but my name was on her birth certificate. In those days, only the father had the legal power to make those types of decisions for a child. The father was the boss, even if he didn't pay for anything, which was the case with Eduardo. I never tried to get anything from him. He really wasn't that involved with Carmen's life. Carmen didn't even want to be with her father, unless I was there with her. I began to get very nervous. What if I wanted to take her to Paris, or London or anywhere for a holiday outside of Italy? I decided that Carmen and I would take a train to Rome for the day so I could talk to the authorities at the Australian Embassy.

I spoke to the consulate and told him I wanted to go to Australia with my daughter. I showed him her birth certificate, which had my name and Eduardo's on it. He asked me which of our surnames I wanted on her passport. I quickly said mine, Hanlon. I knew immediately I had done the wrong thing. Then, I made it even worse... The consulate asked me if the father was in agreement. I replied, 'Father? Who knows what happened to her father. You know when you're young and come to Italy. You happen to meet a good looking Latin Lover and it's possible you may get pregnant... I don't know what happened to him. Maybe he's dead.' The consulate listened sympathetically and then told his secretary to prepare the passport for us right then. I felt bad to have made up such a lie, but I was desperate to get Carmen a passport.

Eduardo never found out about Carmen's Australian passport. Then not so long after, he decided on his own that we should both go to the Italian consulate and get her an Italian passport, which we did. Now Carmen had two passports—with two different names! For years I had problems straightening that mess out. It finally was corrected years later when I wrote to the Australian embassy and told them I had found her father. Everything worked out and Sorrenti became her name on both of her passports.

Carmen in kindergarten.

Carmen and Eduardo.

In **1975** when Carmen was three years old, it was time for her to begin kindergarten. It was so difficult for me to let her go. Up until then we had done nearly everything together. On her first day of school, Carmen was wearing the standard uniform, a white cotton smock with a yellow bow under her chin. Clutched in her little chubby hand was her lunch basket. The school gave the children a plate of pasta for lunch, but the extras were brought from home. The other toddlers thought the food in Carmen's lunch basket was strange: boiled eggs, yogurt or vegemite sandwiches. Not exactly the traditional Italian diet.

I'm afraid my crying and worrying as we walked to school did not give Carmen the confidence she needed for her first day. Sister Vincenza met us at the door. She was about the same size around as she was high and was very cheerful. She took Carmen in her arms to welcome her into the fold, but Carmen responded with a couple of kicks to her shins and a handful of fists against the poor nun's tummy. Carmen screamed that she wasn't staying and wanted to go home with her mamma. But she did stay and she loved every minute of it for the next three years.

Everyone at the school was Catholic except for Carmen and a little French boy named Alexis. I told Sister Vincenza it was Carmen's decision if she wanted to become a Catholic. Perhaps that was a big decision to give to a three year old, however I felt she had to make up her own mind, after all it was her life. About a year later Carmen did make up her mind; she decided to become a Buddhist. She had a little American friend in town named Ila. She was about three years older than Carmen and she was a vegetarian and a Buddhist. Ila had convinced Carmen she should become a Buddhist too. One day the Mother Superior telephoned me regarding this news. I asked Carmen what was happening, but all she would say was, 'It's a secret. I can't tell you I'm a Buddhist.'

None of that mattered to the nuns. They loved Carmen and spoilt her with attention and gifts. She was always coming home with presents from the nuns. I would ask if all the children had gotten presents and she would always say, 'No, only me.' Occasionally, she was even invited to have lunch with the nuns in the convent. I often wished I could have been a fly on the wall when she ate with them. I would have loved to have seen my

Carmen and Ila.

little girl sitting at the head of a long wooden table surrounded by nuns eating bread and cheese. I imagine Carmen saying between bites of her sandwich, 'No, I'm sorry. I cannot become a Catholic, because I am a Buddhist.'

What Carmen had learnt in school must have rubbed off on her in some way. When she was about four years old, Carmen announced that she wanted to be an actress and not long after that her religious crisis began. She loved the pageants and drama of the Catholic church and I could see the dramatic side of her come out whenever she was around anything religious.

To get to our favourite restaurant, the Grottino Azzurro, we had to walk up a staircase and under an archway. In the archway, there is a small statue of the Madonna, which always has a little light burning and a small vase of fresh flowers. It is one of many little shrines around Positano. Carmen

had a ritual every time she passed the Madonna and since we often walked to the restaurant with a group of friends, it didn't take long for everyone to learn the routine. Carmen would stop at the Madonna and begin her prayers. We all lined up behind her in silence. She always ended by crossing herself, kissing both of her hands and sending the kisses off to the Madonna. Only then could our little procession continue up the staircase to the restaurant.

For many years when she was young, Carmen had a morning routine. At about 5.00 am every morning she would get out of bed, cross our spacious house, come into my room and get into my bed. I often thought she did this in her sleep, as she never said a word. One of the first presents Carmen received from the nuns was a set of rosary beads, but they weren't normal rosary beads. They were iridescent and shone in the dark. Of course, Carmen had to wear her rosary beads to bed that night (and would continue to do so for a long time after). The next morning she came into my room, as usual. It was winter, so my room was pitch black. I must have been half asleep when I opened my eyes and saw a green shining cross moving across my room towards me. I nearly fainted. For a minute I thought the ghost of San Matteo was up to his old tricks.

I was always involved in whatever was happening in the kindergarten and the church during this time. There were many processions for various celebrations and I would be in the middle of the crowds walking behind the priest, the mayor and everyone who marched along the winding streets in town. During one of the Easter services, I took Carmen and her friend Ila to church. It was so full that people were standing in the aisles. When it was time for Communion, I glanced up the pew, but Carmen and Ila were nowhere to be seen. There was a long line of people slowly making their way up to the altar to take Communion. Then I saw the children. They were lined up with the rest of the crowd, hands folded on their chests with very solemn expressions on their faces as they moved towards the priest. Oh dear, I thought to myself, Carmen hasn't even been baptised, let alone had her First Communion. I started to

Carmen (on right) in one of her early acting roles.

dressed as Vali Myers.

Carmen in a school procession

hiss at them, '*Psst, psst*, get back here.' I'm certain they heard me, but they ignored me. When they had finally eaten the bread and sipped the wine, they came back to their seats. After the mass, when I asked them why they had done that, they said they had just wanted to practice.

When Carmen was a child, people often used to stop us and comment on how strikingly beautiful she was. I wasn't sure she was as beautiful as everyone said. I often thought she seemed special to the Italians because of her pale colouring. I was sure however that her beauty did not help her character when she was little. By the time she was four, she had been touched, pinched, pulled, photographed, cornered in shops and smothered by people. Carmen didn't like

Carmen, 1976.

all the attention and as a result she became quite antisocial and rather anti-people.

I remember one day when we were surrounded by about six Italian women in the hardware shop. One of the women was trying to touch Carmen. She started screaming, 'Just let me touch her hair, so I will have good luck!' It was traumatic for Carmen and her response was to become rude and cheeky. I would attempt to keep the interaction polite and say, 'Carmen, smile and say hello to the signora please.' Instead Carmen would stick out her tongue, stamp her foot or worse—say something I hoped they wouldn't hear or understand.

A perfect example of her rudeness happened one day at the Buca di Bacco bar. She was about four years old and was wearing her white lace dress and frilly Victorian cap. Sitting beside us was a group of elegant Italian women in designer clothes having their late afternoon cocktails. They began to talk about Carmen saying things like, 'My God, look at that exquisite child. She's a real

jewel. We must take some photos of her. She must be a foreigner with those eyes and that hair. She seems to be made of wax.' They went on and on. Meanwhile, my little jewel was misbehaving and picking at the flowers in the vases decorating the wall of the bar. One of the waiters, who knew us, called across the bar and told her to stop ruining the flowers. Carmen stood up, put her hands on her hips and screamed in her low raucous voice in perfect Neapolitan "*Va fa in culo!*", which is not very nice—at all. Certainly not what you would expect a four year old to say! I was wishing I didn't know her and I couldn't imagine where she had learnt that phrase. However, I have to admit I also wished I had a camera to capture the expressions on the faces of the women at the next table. As Carmen grew older, she received fewer pats and pinches and gradually became sweeter and much more tolerant.

There was another time I had wished I had a camera to capture an exchange between Carmen

and one of her admirers. I was always in the need of odd jobs to make a little money and I was doing some modelling for Vasilis Voglis at the Positano Art Workshop. Vasilis told me his good friend Tennessee Williams was in town and asked me if I would 'lend' Carmen to him. He wanted to show off my beautiful daughter and introduce her to Tennessee. I said, yes, of course. I loved Williams' work and asked if I could meet him too. The answer was NO. I had to stay behind. I will never forget sitting in the bar at the Buca di Bacco watching Carmen dressed in a long Victorian lace dress with a matching bonnet holding on to Vasilis' hand as they walked together along the empty beach towards Tennessee Williams. He was dressed in a white linen suit and a white Panama hat and was holding a cane. If only I had had a camera in those days! The light of the sun was shining on the famous writer and my little blonde girl as Tennessee shook her hand in the middle of a totally empty beach. It was really too much.

Our little family already included two dogs, but in a moment of madness, I decided to add a little cat to our crew. The kitten's mother, Issey, was from Queens, New York and had been brought to Naples by Carmen's Aunt Francesca. Issey devoted her life to having kittens and I decided to bring one of her latest babies back to Carmen as a surprise. Carmen wanted to call him Giu Giu Giuliano, but I said that was too long, so she cut it down to Giu Giu. In Italian *giu* means 'down'. So Giu Giu means 'down down'. I think right from the start, his

name totally screwed up the poor creature. We always spoke to the cat in Italian, so when he was up somewhere eating something he shouldn't have been we would say *giu giu!*, telling him to get down. Of course he thought we were just calling his name, so he would meow and keep on doing what he shouldn't have been doing. The poor thing just didn't understand. He was rather an odd cat in general, but his name certainly didn't help matters.

One day I noticed my washing machine was quite full of dirty clothes, so I pressed the button to let the soap powder go to work. As the machine was washing, I passed by and saw something which made me do a double take. I couldn't believe my eyes… I thought I saw a little face and two paws pressed against the inside of the door of the machine. They disappeared and then as the clothes spun around, I saw them again. It was Giu Giu! I stopped the machine to let him out. He was surprisingly alright—and very clean too. It's difficult to keep a story quiet in a small town like Positano. More than once when I was introduced to tourists at my friend's villas, they would say, 'Oh you must be the woman who washes her cat in the washing machine.'

On **16 August 1977**, Elvis Presley died.

My social life was very limited at this time. I was a devoted mum and my life was centred on my daughter and my close friends. Around this time, Scott and I went to a party and met Ed Wittstein and Bob Miller, a couple from New York. Ed had come to Positano back in **1955** to meet Edna Lewis at the Positano Art Workshop. Ed and Bob fell in love with the town and they

began returning for a few months each year. Bob worked for a big time advertising agency in New York City and Ed worked on films, plays, operas and television. He was the original Set Designer, Costumer, Prop Master and Lighting Designer on the off-Broadway play *The Fantasticks,* the world's longest-running musical. He worked as the Production Director for the film *Endless Love* starring Brooke Shields and directed by Franco Zeffirelli and he was the Art Director on *Fame.* He worked for Woody Allen as the Production Designer on the films *Bananas* and *Play it Again Sam.* Ed purchased a house in Positano in **1971** with the money he made on *Play it Again Sam.* They named the house Casa Sam, after the movie. Their dog was named Sam too. Bob and Ed's house was close to ours, so we would often see each other on the street and we all became friendly. Soon they became part of our group.

Casa San Matteo overlooked the Hotel Poseidon and I came to know the owners, Liliana Aonzo and her two grown children, Marco and Monica, well. I actually had met Marco because his Dalmatian, Luca, had raped Favola. Luca was the father of her 13 puppies. I saw Marco on the beach one day when I was walking some of Favola's little ones. I introduced myself and asked him for alimony—at least a few tins of dog food. Marco denied the puppies belonged to Luca. I told him their mother was a large reddish-blonde dog and all of her litter were white with black spots, yet he still denied paternity. What a pity DNA testing wasn't available at that time to solve the crime.

There is another very important friend of mine I need to mention. One day Carmen and I were sitting at a local bar with my friend Jessica when she introduced me to a man who was walking by with his dogs. His name was János and he was someone I had often seen around town along with his friend Justus Pfaue. You couldn't help but notice János and Justus. They made such an impression. They were both quite attractive and were always seen with their two large Hungarian dogs as they made their way to the beach or to restaurants. Their white dog was named Curva and she was the mother of Busi who was black. The dogs had long Bob Marley dread locks that

János

dragged along the pavement picking up all the garbage along the way. You could hardly tell which way the dogs were headed, forward or back, because their fur was so long.

János told Jessica he was feeling rather lonely. He seemed to be such a sweet and simple young man that I felt sorry for him. The following morning was Easter and I was at the bar again with Carmen and her friend Gennaro. We were on our way to the beach to have a picnic. János walked by and I asked him if he would like to join us. He was so happy to be asked and said yes, so we all trotted down the stairs to the beach.

It was a great picnic, at least it was until we came to the hard-boiled eggs I had prepared. János took the first one. He broke it open and it was raw! All of them were raw. I watched in dismay as the yellow yokes dripped into the sand, but János just started to laugh. He laughed and laughed and rolled around in the sand. I think that was when he fell in love with me. He must of thought, how could anyone be so sweet and kind and yet so stupid at the same time.

I saw János a few more times over the next weeks, but we still didn't really know each other very well. In many ways, I knew nothing about him. Then, one morning at three o'clock I was woken up by the telephone. I thought it was an odd time for someone to call unless it was urgent, so I got out of bed to answer it. It was János. He told me he was sitting on the floor looking at his little penis and it reminded him of a small pink hamburger. I was standing there in my kitchen in my pyjamas trying to take in what he was saying. What was going on? Since I had met Eduardo, my life had become very straight and normal. Now all of a sudden, this male beauty who I barely knew

Bob Topol, Carmen, János, Jennie, Ricky and Marmory.

was calling me in the early hours of the morning and telling me that his cock was very small and he didn't like the way it looked! What should say to him? I let him talk on and on until he was exhausted. I was even more exhausted and I knew I had to get up early to take Carmen to school. It was such an odd telephone call, but somehow after that night I started thinking of János in another way. Don't get me wrong, it had nothing to do with the subject of his call. I just felt closer to him. I found myself drawn to János. I wanted to see him more and more and I wasn't exactly sure why.

We began seeing a great deal of each other. The first time he invited me to see his little house in Positano, he loaded me up with piles of cushions,

linens and other special things for my house. Such generous gifts, I thought. It wasn't until later when I got to know him better that I realised none of those things he had given me had belonged to him. He had taken them from other people.

János loved to talk about his past and I loved hearing about it. He told me his full name was János Zigmond Von Lemheny and he had been born in Hungary on **11 June 1949**. He said his father had died many years before and was buried in a cemetery in Transylvania. I told János I wanted to visit his father's grave someday. I thought maybe he was a vampire!

In the late **1960s**, a German film company had been shooting in Budapest and Justus Pfauer was there from Munich to work on the film. Justus was a writer and many of his books had been made into films. Justus and János met and there was a strong attraction between them. When the crew left, János decided to move to Munich to be with Justus. János had no passport, so he had to escape from Hungary. He told me he more or less walked over the border and into Germany. In fact, when I met János in Positano, he still only had exile status instead of a passport. Munich became home for János and Justus and later they divided their time between Munich and Positano.

János and Justus were together when I first met them. Over time they decided they shouldn't be a couple, but they still continued to share apartments together in Positano and in Munich. Even though Justus started dating other people, he was always very possessive of János. He even became jealous of my relationship with János as our friendship became closer. That was a problem for me, since János and I spent so much time together. We sort of became a weird and wonderful couple. There were times János and I would even go out together with Justus and his new young lover. Although I spent time with Justus, I was never really comfortable around him.

In **1978** Carmen was six years old and it was time for her to go to the elementary school. Now she wore a blue bow on her smock instead of a yellow one. Mamma shed a few tears once again. Carmen found this school a bit boring. It offered no painting or music lessons and very little sport, but she was bright and her grades were good and she made many friends there.

In a small town in southern Italy a 'different' child could potentially run into problems. Compared to most of the children in Positano, Carmen's childhood was definitely different. She had a non-Catholic mother who was not married. Our friends consisted of artists, writers, homosexuals, pot smokers and dropouts. You name them—we knew them. I was worried when she was little that she may have problems with her school friends. Fortunately, she didn't. Carmen took everything in her own stride. She understood at an early age that being 'different' wasn't at all negative and she became more tolerant towards others as a result. She had no problems making friends and many of her friends liked to come to our house to eat, play or to sleep over.

Carmen and János.

Not only did Carmen take our weird mix of friends in her stride, she embraced our strange family of friends. One day, Carmen's teacher asked all the children in her class to draw themselves along with their mother and father for Mother's Day. Carmen drew herself and me with János in the centre. You couldn't mistake János, because she drew his moustache. She casually explained to her teacher that the man was her mother's best friend and her father lived in Naples with his other girlfriend and that was that. None of it troubled Carmen. She always spoke only the truth.

There was so much going on in Positano at that time. There was a cinema at 25 Via Cristoforo Colombo where we could see the latest films. We also had a Cine Club, which used the same space about once a week. They showed old classic black and white films. Each time we went to the Cine Club, they passed out a list of possible films for the

Costume parties with János (left) and Bob Miller (above).

next showing. Whichever film got the most votes would be chosen. It was often like a party when we went there. It was the place you would meet all your neighbours. The building was always cold, so we would bring blankets to keep us warm. We also brought in pizza and bottles of wine to have while we watched the films. Monica Aonzo and her boyfriend Raffaelle were among those who ran the club. There were also book readings and discussion groups around town. There were art shows popping up in various locations and concerts on the beach. Of course, there were endless dinners and amazing costume parties hosted at the homes of all our friends.

Even after living in Italy for nearly ten years, there were times when something would happen to make me realise I still didn't really think like an Italian. I remember that happened to me on **16 October 1978**. That day the whole world was waiting for the announcement of the new pope in Rome. When the white smoke started fuming out of the Vatican chimney, I was excited to hear Karol Wojtyła had been elected as Pope John Paul II. I had read about his life and had hoped he would be chosen. He had been involved in the theatre and arts and he wrote poetry. I thought the life he had lived made him a more interesting choice than many of the earlier popes. The morning he was announced, I went to the grocery shop across the street to do some shopping. The shop was crowded with women and they all seemed rather nervous. When the owner saw me come in, she gasped and said, 'Jennie, the new pope has just been elected and he isn't Italian... He's Polish. This is terrible!' I told her I had heard the news, but couldn't understand why they all were so upset. I said I couldn't see why the pope couldn't be Polish. After all, didn't the Romans crucify Jesus? The looks I got from the other women in the store made me decide I probably had enough food at home and I quickly turned around and left.

János

The Woman Who Made Gauze Look Like Chiffon

My boutique at the Quicksilver had only lasted that one season before the drug bust. Now, I needed to find some way to earn a living which was flexible enough for me to spend all the time I wanted with Carmen. Looking around, I saw people coming to Positano from all over the world for their holidays and I knew while they were here many of them bought clothes. The town was full of little boutiques. I had been in the fashion business in London and Switzerland, so I decided I would do the same here, only this time I would design my own clothing. I began to tell everyone in town I was a designer from London and they believed me. People seemed to like the clothes I made and the news of my work began to spread by word of mouth through my friends.

I knew gauze was big in London at that time. They had gauze in Italy too, but it was dense and heavy. It seemed to me something one would wrap cheese in. The gauze in London was much finer and I knew that when it was treated correctly it could became soft and flowing. It was also incredibly cheap—cheap as dirt. It was perfect for the type of clothing I wanted to make, so I decided to bring English gauze to Italy. I had bolts of unbleached, light cotton gauze sent to me from London. Then I dyed it to the pastel colours I had in mind. I knew pastels would be a sharp contrast to the bright colours which were currently favoured by many Italian women.

My friend Jessica helped me dye my fabric. To me that was the most difficult part of producing my clothing. I was very exact. The colours had to be perfect. I would often mix the dyes myself and then Jessica and I would dye the cloth down in the two enormous rooms in my basement at Casa San Matteo. We strung up clothes lines around the rooms to hang the dyed cloth to dry. Jessica worked with me for a while, then when she had to leave, I met Susan, a young English woman who had recently moved to town. Susan was looking for work, so I took her on as my new dyer. When I first started out, I sewed most of the clothes myself. Then as I began to produce larger quantities, I found I needed help. I hired Rosetta, who lived next door to me, as my dressmaker.

I did all of the designing myself—with the help of Chloe. I spent so much time with Chloe. She was one of my closest friends, a member of our family and my main partner in designing my clothing. I seldom used a pattern, instead I just draped the cloth over Chloe. She was wonderful. I would raise her to my own height, measuring by the shoulder. To raise her, I would have to unscrew a screw at the bottom of her torso until the iron tube was free to slide down to the required height, then I would tighten the screw and she and I would be shoulder to shoulder—like identical twins. Chloe would then be ready to be draped with the fabric, which I fastened down with pins which I pulled from Chloe's neck. That was a handy place to keep them, since Chloe had no head. It may sound like a horror film, but Chloe was my dressmaking dummy, although personally, I prefer to think of her as my model.

I would often have long conversations with Chloe when we were alone. I would say to her, 'You know Chloe, after Favola you're my best friend. There aren't many friends I can stick pins into, scream and curse at and knock over and yet you never get angry at me. Seriously, I don't know what I would do without you. The more I touch

Carmen and Charlotte modeling at the Sirenuse Hotel.

you and the more I fiddle with you, the more successful I become. I can tell if a design works on you that it will be a smash hit with others. I get so nervous when I have to prepare a new collection. I often can't sleep at night. I get up and try to sketch something I think might work, but by the time I put pencil to paper the idea has gone. Then I see you and I know you'll help me. Only you can get me through those wretched times. You are the creator, Chloe, not me. Please don't ever let me down.' It may seem strange for someone to talk so seriously to a dummy, but then again I guess it's really no different than talking to a ghost.

When I first started draping fabric on Chloe, I found the gauze was so light that I could use it in layers. If I made a mistake, I would just cover it up with another piece of fabric or some lace. My 'mistakes' were sometimes my most successful designs. They had a more artisan feel to them, which was very popular.

I started to sell my clothing to a couple of well-known boutiques in town. Then, I was asked to take part in a fashion show at the Sirenuse Hotel along with Princess Sibylla Ercolani. Sibylla's family owned the big old stone watchtower on the water in Positano. She prepared a winter line and I was to present a summer collection. That was

the first time I had to prepare a collection specifically for a show. It was a challenge, but I enjoyed it. I even included some children's clothing, which were modelled by Carmen and Susan's daughter, Charlotte.

Word continued to spread about my designs. I was close friends with Paula Chandon of the Moët champagne family. They had a villa not far from Positano. Paula used to invite me over to stay with her and I became very friendly with her whole family. When I stayed there, I would be given the same suite Coco Chanel was given whenever she stayed at the villa. While at their villa, I was always amazed that whenever we went out to the beach for the day, we would return to find the clothes we had worn earlier had all been washed, ironed and hung up in our closets again. I sold a number of dresses to Paula's mother, Francesca, the Countess of Chandon. I was rather proud of that. After all, the Chandon family owns the House of Dior and now the Countess was buying dresses from me. I was told that Princess Margaret had once stopped by their house for a visit and saw Francesca wearing one of my dresses. Apparently the princess complimented her on it and asked where she had bought it. When I heard the princess had admired my dress, I was so pleased.

Francesca Chandon

I thought perhaps I would have a chance to sell to her as well, but my hopes faded when Francesca told me she had refused to tell the princess I had made her dress. Francesca said she didn't want the princess wearing the same clothes she had!

In **1976** I met an American couple who were very close friends of Bob and Ed. Marvin Segal was a big time lawyer from New York. He had just arrived in Positano from Sicily, where he had been defending Tommaso Buscetta, one of the top mafia bosses at the time. Marvin's wife, Josephine, who everyone called Jo, was the fashion editor for *Sports Illustrated* and later for *Look* magazine.

Jo loved my clothing and asked if she could become my manager. I had never thought about having a manager, but I was thrilled and agreed. Through Jo's connections, I was able to get publicity for my designs. I had a full page article in *The Australian Women's Weekly* on **30 March 1977**, with the heading, 'A Typist Whose Clothes Have Become the Spirit of Positano.'

The article described my clothing as, 'A free flowing line, of subtle pastel colours with a floating dreamy kind of look.' They said I 'instinctively developed the layered look before it took the fashion world by storm' and they called me '...the woman who made gauze look like chiffon.' Not bad for a woman who invented being a designer by herself.

There was another article in *The New York Times* by Bernadine Morris, which described how Jo had partnered with 'an Australian, who had worked in a boutique in Swinging London and then moved to Positano.' The journalist wrote that my designs were, '...rather special dresses of cotton gauze dyed in soft shades of mauve, blue or yellow and always made in double layers. Some were tunics of varying lengths meant to be worn over harem pants, flared pants or double skirts... What customers liked about them... were the shear quality of the cotton and the shadings from pale to deeper tones. The top layer is usually a paler colour than the one underneath... The skirts and pants are made on drawstrings and two sizes are enough to fit most figures. They all have ripply hemlines and the tops vary from camisole to long-sleeved. There are children's versions, which were originally made for Miss Hanlon's 4-year-old daughter, Carmen, which will be at Saks Fifth Avenue next month, when the store will also have the grown-up styles.'

With Jo's help, I was able to sell my designs to Bonwit Teller and Jeane Eddy's shop in Manhattan, as well as to the upscale women's specialty store Henri Bendel. I used to ship boxes of my clothing to Bob Miller in New York. He would iron them, put them on hangers and then carry them by hand for me down to the Henri Bendel shop on Fifth Avenue.

Having Jo as my manager seemed to be working out well, however I didn't realise that Jo and Marvin were having marital problems. When everything came to a head between them, Jo stopped being my manager, which was a pity since Jo and I had a good working relationship.

Around that time, my friend Dany Coudert contacted me. She said she would like to come to Positano and stay with me for a while, so she could work on a new book she had just begun writing.

Her first book, *La Dèrobade,* had been a big success and was translated into over 17 languages. The English version of that book is titled *The Life of a Hooker.* Her new book was to be called *La Passagère.* Dany spent a few months at my house. We were both working hard. Dany would write all day and I was preparing a new collection, which I hoped to take to Paris. The only time we would take off to have a little fun would be on Saturdays. We would get all dressed up, Carmen included, and go down to the Cambusa restaurant for dinner. We usually invited people back to the villa to have a drink and the party would go on until the wee hours of the morning. One day Dany had great news from Paris. A producer and assistant were coming to Positano to meet with her and discuss making her first book into a film. She took me with her to meet them in a restaurant on the beach. After they left, we giggled and celebrated with a glass of champagne!

Dany was content with the writing she had done and I had finished my collection, so the three of us took off to Paris where Carmen and I stayed with Dany and her husband. I handed over my new collection to a woman, who I hoped would buy them, but instead she took off with all my samples and I never saw her again! Oh well, I didn't let it bother me too much, after all we were having so much fun in Paris.

When I returned to Positano, I met another woman who made an offer to be my manager. Ann Sterling was from California and she told me she knew many people who shopped on Rodeo Drive in Los Angeles, including a number of well-known actresses such as Lauren Bacall and Candice Bergen. I knew nothing about that world. It all sounded so exciting to me and Ann was fun and enthusiastic, so I said yes.

I liked the idea of working with the stars, however Ann told me that before I started to work with them, I should do mass production for some of the big stores. Mass production didn't excite me at all. I wanted to be on a more personal level with a smaller selection of clients, but Ann convinced me I should follow her advice. Once a year, the

Ed Wittstein, Elli and Marvin Segal.

Plaza Hotel in New York dedicated one floor of the hotel to fashion designers to show their newest collections. Ann arranged a three week show for me at the Plaza, where I would be grouped with the Californian designers.

Now I had a big job in front of me. I had to design a collection I would be proud to show to the American buyers. That would take a lot of work on my part. I got to work on my collection, but not long after I started, I began to feel rather ill. I couldn't figure out what was wrong. I was certain it had nothing to do with the excitement of the show. I just felt as though everything was off. I lost weight. I couldn't sleep, yet I was full of energy. My eyes seemed large and had kind of changed shape, as if they were popping out of my head. I also hadn't had my period for about three months. I went to a local doctor in Positano who told me I was pregnant and had conjunctivitis. I knew for sure I wasn't pregnant and my eyes didn't weep, so I didn't think I had conjunctivitis either. One night I was at a restaurant with a friend of mine who was a doctor. He took one look at my neck and told me to go the hospital early the next morning. He said there was something very wrong with my thyroid.

Jennie and Carmen with Guy and Scott.

Jennie working on a collection.

That was the last thing I needed whilst working on my grand collection. The specialist told me I should go to hospital for one week. I couldn't do that! I didn't have time to lay around. I told him I had a little girl at home and I needed to be there to look after her. I promised that if he would let me go home, I would stay in bed and follow the treatment he ordered. I told him my friends would stop by often to check on me and make sure I was resting.

I went home, but knew I couldn't stay in bed—not now. I had to finish my collection. The dates were already set and our tickets were booked. I had to keep working. My bedroom had enormous bay windows, through which I could see anyone who was coming down the steps to my house. I set to work, but kept my eye on the staircase to watch if anyone was coming by to check on me. If I saw someone, I would quickly jump into bed and pretend to be a good patient.

By **November 1978,** I had finished the collection and was ready to fly off to New York. I packed all my special medicines, but by then I actually felt great, not sick at all. Carmen and I were meeting my American friend Lisa at the airport in Rome and we were all to fly to New York together. On a train to Rome, Lisa had been robbed of everything, including her passport, money and jewellery. She managed to get a replacement passport in time, but she had no money. I had no money on me either. I hadn't brought any, because I knew Henri Bendel was going to pay me for my last shipment to them when I arrived in New York. Before we left Positano, Bob and Ed had given Carmen some 'mad money', a hundred dollars in one-dollar bills, for her to spend in New York as she chose. Lisa and I ended up having to ask Carmen to pay for our Bloody Marys on the plane. The hostess must have thought it strange to see a little blonde angel in her black velvet dress counting out her money for our drinks.

Diary — 11-1978 — plane to New York
Oh God, what on earth am I doing on this jumbo jet heading for New York? I have the feeling I've bitten off more than I can chew this

time and I will end up choking on it. All I did was pretend I was a fashion designer. Now, I'm on my way to the Big Apple to show my collection with the Californian designers, on the 8th floor of the Plaza Hotel. I'm nervous just being on this plane. I can't stand flying. Damn you Carmen, for making me sit in a non-smoking section, just because you can't bear the smell of smoke. Double damn you TWA, for showing the film 'The Buddy Holly Story' for our evening entertainment. Everyone knows he dies in a plane crash in the end!

My show started on **8 November 1978**. Carmen and I stayed at Bob and Ed's brownstone on East 87th Street. This was our first trip to the Big Apple and we preferred staying at a house with our friends rather than at the Plaza. Besides we knew we would be spending most of the next three weeks at the hotel. Carmen had fun at the Plaza. She was always up to something. Each day as we came down the stairs, she would stop in front of the large portrait of *Eloise at the Plaza* inspired by the books written by Kay Thompson. Carmen would stand there trying to make the same face as the little girl in the painting. Carmen often wore her best dress, a little black velvet number with a white lace collar by Jean-Paul Gaultier. People would stop and watch her trying to match her expression to Eloise's. One couple came up to us and asked where this child came from. I wanted to say she was from Mars… While I was showing

my clothes, Carmen spent most of her time in the rooms of some of the Californian designers. Their makeup girls loved trying new makeup looks on such a cute six-year-old and Carmen loved all the attention. Carmen was happy and I was happy too. This was all a new world for us.

When I had first arrived in New York, the buyer from Henri Bendel asked me to show her my collection before my show. When she saw what I had brought, she told me I didn't have enough pieces. They liked my models, but they knew I needed more to have a successful show. They offered to lend me the last shipment I had sent them to use, as long as I gave it back to them when the show was over. I was quite chuffed that such a famous store would do a favour like that for someone like me.

149

Bob and Ed's TV House on Fire Isalnd.

In the show room at the Plaza, Bob had set up an Italian coffee machine and we had Italian music playing. The space felt like a little Italy. The show went on for three weeks and my room was always busy. Many buyers came and looked through my collection. Most would view the collection without commenting and then just leave. At first I thought they weren't interested in my clothes, but I just didn't know how the fashion business worked in New York. I soon learnt that the next day they would be back.

By the end of my show at the Plaza, I had many orders from several stores in New York including Henri Bendel, Bloomingdales and Saks Fifth Avenue, as well as Betty Dorso in Los Angeles and a children's shop in Miami called General Store. I was thrilled all these well-known shops liked my clothes and I was eager to get back to San Matteo and begin working on all the clothes I would need to fulfil their orders. I was also hoping this show might lead to other possibilities in the future.

Now that the show was over and Thanksgiving was coming up, a small group of us made plans to spend the weekend on Fire Island. We stayed

at Bob and Ed's TV house in The Pines. It was called the TV house, because it was actually shaped like a TV. I had heard they had designed the house themselves and had it built with the money Ed had made working on the musical *The Fantasticks*. The day we arrived the island was quiet, hardly anyone was there. The next day it was packed with people who were all coming in for Thanksgiving. Bob and Ed showed us around. We walked across the Judy Garland Memorial Path over to Cherry Grove where all the gays lived. I loved seeing the signs on the houses with two men's names listed together. It was wonderful to see how open they could be about their homosexuality. We went out to The Sandpiper, the only disco on the island, and had a great time. Then after a few days on Fire Island, we headed back to their place in Manhattan.

Since Carmen was missing a few months of school, we tried to do as many things as possible in New York that would be educational for her. Bob and Ed sent us to many museums and Broadway shows to expand her experience. Ed had worked on many films and on Broadway and he used his connections to get us in to see several shows. We went to see the musical *Annie* on Broadway. Carmen loved the show so much I could barely get her to leave the theatre. Ed also got us tickets to see *The Fantasticks*, the show he had worked on back when he was in his twenties.

Christmas was approaching and it was exciting to see the city decorated for the holiday. Carmen had always believed in Father Christmas. Back in San Matteo, I would have someone drop a black rubber boot down the chimney when she was about to leave her note for Father Christmas on Christmas Eve. I did all sorts of tricks so she couldn't help but believe in him. I even cooked spaghetti for Santa, which Favola would happily eat after Carmen went to bed. Now in New York I had a bit of a problem. One day we were in Woolworths and I saw a big fat Santa walking towards us. Carmen had her back towards him. When he touched her on the shoulder, she turned around and saw who it was. Within seconds, her fair skin seemed to turn even whiter. She started to tremble so much that I was afraid she might have a fit. He asked her what she wanted for Christmas, but she just stared at him without speaking. I hurried her out of the store only to be met with more Santas on every street: black ones, white ones, tall ones, short ones. There seemed to be Santas everywhere. I tried to explain to Carmen that Santa had many helpers, but soon we would go to see the real one at Macy's.

Going to Macy's was was a trip and a half. We lined up with all the other excited children to wait our turn to see Santa, while his elves chatted to me about Fire Island and other fun places they had been. We had to wait quite a while, but it was worth it. Carmen was completely convinced she had finally met the real Father Christmas. Later when we returned to Positano, she excitedly told her school friends who she had seen in New York. They all told her Santa didn't really exist. Even their parents said the same thing, but Carmen would have none of that. She was certain Father Christmas was real.

It was now time to leave New York. We had been there for a few months. The whole trip had been a great experience for us. It was certainly an amazing opportunity for my business. Nevertheless, I was happy to get back to Casa San Matteo with Favola, Giu Giu, Chloe and our ghost. I knew I would be very busy over the next few months and I couldn't wait to get my hands on Chloe and start creating again. Carmen and I both had many exciting memories to bring back with us and our future seemed to be looking very positive.

Carmen and Santa at Macy's.

I spent a few months making the clothes for all the orders from the New York show. After that, I continued to work in the fashion business for a while longer, but I was mainly working on my own. I knew that in order to go higher in the business, I would have to be totally committed. I wasn't sure I wanted to do that. I still occasionally made clothes for my friends, but I never really charged as much for them as I probably should have. Gradually, I began to realise that I really didn't want to be in the fashion business anymore. I did have another small fashion venture with Jànos a little while later. We bought up lots of plain white T-shirts and Jànos, who was a talented designer and painter, painted them. People seemed to like our shirts and the money we made kept us going for quite a while. Eventually that business went away too. Over the years I've had a few of my Tarot Card readers tell me I was frightened of success. Looking back, I think they had been right.

Favola, Carmen, Jennie, Scott, Guy and Maria.

The End of Casa San Matteo

I loved my life at Casa San Matteo. I didn't think anything could ever get me to leave that house. In fact, a friend of mine once said that I loved that villa so much, only an earthquake could get me to leave it. The house was beautiful and we had good neighbours who all helped each other out. Gene Charlton had taken over the Positano Art Workshop after Edna Lewis died and he was now running it out of his house next door to us. His wife, Suzanne, had gone back to America with their two children, so Gene was alone. I became closer to Gene after Suzanne left. He would often come over to have a drink with us or we would all go out to restaurants or bars together.

One afternoon in **July 1979,** I was at home when I heard a woman's voice screaming over my back wall, 'Jennie, come immediately! I think Gene is dead!' The voice was Dorothy, an American art student I knew well. I dropped everything and ran up the stairs to Gene's house. I saw Gene lying in a foetal position on the floor of his small study and Dorothy began screaming at me to give him mouth to mouth. I could tell right away that I couldn't help him. Gene's face had turned kind of black. I knew he was dead. I called my neighbours Rosetta and Giulio to help us and then I called the police. When the police arrived, they asked Rosetta and me to help carry Gene to his bedroom and put him on his bed. As we tried to straighten his legs to get a hold of him, the air inside of him escaped and it made the most horrible groaning noise. It scared both of us so much that we dropped Gene on the floor! The police yelled for us to hold on tighter and not let him fall again. On the second try we managed to get him onto his bed.

Gene always loved to dress up for special occasions, so I knew he would want to be dressed properly now and that I was the one who would have to do it. I decided to dress him in his favourite outfit, black trousers and a white laced-trimmed shirt with his white boots and maybe a jacket, if I could manage it. I left the single diamond earring

in his ear. Gene never took that off, so I thought it was only fair to let him take it with him to wherever he would be going. Jimmy James went to the Town Hall to take care of all the legal matters. Bob Miller helped me get the house ready. When someone dies in Positano, all their friends and acquaintances come to the house and sit with the body to cry, chat, drink wine and reminisce about the past. Bob arranged the living room with plenty of bottles of wine and glasses for the guests who would soon arrive.

I was alone when I was preparing Gene for his last visit with his friends. As I was making sure he looked good, one of his eyes kept opening. I kept closing it gently whilst begging him to please keep it closed for me. Thankfully he did so in the end. Some of the coffin bearers couldn't arrive in town until the day after, so the burial had to be delayed by a day. Gene's maid, Maria didn't have the courage to sleep in the house with the body, so she told me I had to stay with Gene. I did, but I was very glad Carmen happened to be in Munich that night with János. The next day when the hearse arrived to take Gene to the cemetery, I decided at the last minute to put Gene's special cane into the coffin with him. We held his funeral, said our goodbyes and buried him.

Gene never had much time for small children and he wasn't Catholic, so I was quite stunned when I went over to put his house together after his funeral and found a piece of paper still in his typewriter. On it he had written that he now liked small children and had started to believe in God and wanted to give himself to Him. I'm sure Gene didn't know he was going to die that day, so I wondered why he had written that then? His wife, Suzanne, hadn't been able to fly in from the U.S. in time for the funeral. When she

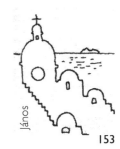
János

153

arrived a few days later, I talked to her about what had happened and I gave her the writing I had found in Gene's typewriter. As Suzanne looked around his house, she asked me if I knew where his cane was. Apparently it was very valuable and had once belonged to someone famous. Oh well, there was no getting it back now! I hope Gene is happy with it.

Over the next year or so, I helped Suzanne take care of some things that needed to be done locally after Gene died, including selling some of Gene's paintings for her. On the evening of **23 November 1980**, I had some friends in from Naples who had come to look at Gene's paintings. When my friends left at about 6.30, I bolted the huge wooden door in the kitchen, which led to the winding staircase in the main entrance of our house. Carmen was at the kitchen table dressed in a white gauze summer dress and drawing whilst I prepared supper.

The weather had been rather strange for several days. It was very warm—a little too warm for that time of year. It was also very still; not a leaf was moving on the trees. I remember the light from the moon was incredibly strong for about four nights. It was as though the moon had been full for several nights in a row.

At about 7.30, I heard a scraping noise from the kitchen door. That was odd, because I knew the door was securely locked. I opened it, thinking perhaps Favola had been locked out, but then I realised she was in her usual position by the stove waiting for her supper. The scraping noise grew louder. Then the heavy old door started to slightly open and then close, as if some tremendous force was pushing it from the outside. The solid iron bolt on the door had no possibility of resisting against whatever external force was moving it. I stood there trying to understand what I was seeing and began to get nervous. I was so worked up that I didn't hear people shouting in the streets or the dogs outside who were all barking (although Favola remained silent as usual).

My mind turned to the Red Brigade terrorists who I knew were still up to their tricks in Italy at that time. *'Che è?'*, I whispered. 'Who's there?' Nobody answered. I began to feel very scared. I imagined a group of masked men on the other side of the door armed with machine guns. Then

I heard Carmen cry out, 'Mamma, there's no one outside. It's an earthquake. Look at the tiles dancing up and down!' *Merda!*, I thought. *What do we do?* I remember hearing you should get under an archway in an earthquake. We had plenty of those in our house, but I began to worry. Our house was 450 years old. Just how much shaking could the old house take?

Carmen wanted to run. I only had a couple of seconds to decide what to take with us. Money, possessions, documents…? I quickly decided to take nothing but myself, Carmen and Favola. I was sorry to leave Giu Giu behind, but I knew he was a survivor and would take care of himself.

Time was running out. I grabbed a piece of cord to tie around Favola's neck. We had a long hike ahead of us down the winding staircase, up the garden stairs to the street, then another long set of stairs to the road. I thought maybe the ghost might try to follow us, but I knew he would be safe in his room. By the time we got to the top of the stairs and reached the main road, all I saw was confusion. Everyone was out in the road. No one knew what to do. It happened so quickly—from the time I first heard the door scraping to when the earthquake was finally over was only about five minutes. Now the town was in total chaos.

Many people were frantic. I saw the Salvati family near the top of our staircase. Little Silvia was crying hysterically in her mother's arms. I tried to be very calm and cool in my Anglo-Saxon sort of way, hoping I could put them at ease, but I guess I wasn't as calm as I thought. Carla Salvati looked at me and said, 'Jennie, you're so white! It looks as though you haven't got a drop of blood in your body.' So much for my coolness…

Evening was setting in and it had become quite cold. I saw Carmen standing there shivering in her little summer dress. She was still holding her paintbrush in her hand. I knew I would have to return to our house to get her a jacket. I also had to turn off the gas. I hadn't had time to do that in our hurried escape. I was nervous to go back in the house, but I had no choice. I went back in, grabbed a poncho for Carmen, turned off the gas and blew a kiss to the cat. He was fine and was probably just upset that the door to the fridge hadn't been forced open by the quake.

Masses of people were hurrying down the road. They were carrying whatever they could: blankets, cases and pots and pans. There were so many people and they were all moving very fast towards the beach. I didn't think that was a good idea. What if there was a tidal wave? I decided to head up to the top of the town instead to Jimmy James' house. Jimmy and his wife, Rosie, were always so calm and collected about everything. I felt sure they would know what to do.

As we went, Carmen and I passed the convent of Chiesa Nuova, where Carmen had gone to kindergarten. I noticed the nuns were all gathered on the street. 'Signora, Signora!' they called out to me. They told me there was a white light in the mountains. They thought a bomb had exploded, so they had gone into the church to pray. I told them it wasn't a bomb and they should not go back inside the church. It might not be safe. I told them that if they wanted to pray, to please do it in the street instead. We still had quite a way to go to get to Jimmy's house. Favola was the only one who was happy. It was unusual for us to go for such a long walk at this time of the evening. When we reached Jimmy's door, I started babbling to him about the earthquake. Jimmy just calmly said, yes he knew about it. They had hardly felt a thing in their house. There had been a strange noise in the electrical line and a Japanese lantern in the centre of their living room began swaying back and forth, but that was it. I was very glad when Jimmy offered to let us stay with them for the night.

Rosie wanted to go up to the Bar Internazionale to see what was happening in town, so Carmen and I went with her. When we got there, it seemed as though the entire town was in the street. The bar was empty. Everyone was afraid to be indoors. Poor Angelo the barman had to stay inside in case anyone wanted to order something. We decided to sit down and have a drink to keep him company. To this day, I can still remember drinking that glass of port so clearly. There was a radio on in the bar. Each time the news came on, people would swarm inside trying to hear the latest news of the quake. Then the minute the news was over, they would all rush out again to the safety of the street.

The early news reports said, 'This evening at 7.30 there was an earthquake in the south of Italy. The central point was near Avellino. Naples and many other towns nearby felt the tremors. The death toll is about three people.' After about half an hour the number of deaths climbed into the hundreds and then later into the thousands. Andrea Milano, the mayor of the town, was in the bar. He was handing out packets of cigarettes to those who needed them to calm their nerves. We left the bar and walked up the stairs to the square in front of Chiesa Nuova, where I had seen the nuns earlier. The locals had dragged their belongings out of their houses: beds, television sets and cooking utensils and set them up around the square. It almost felt like an outdoor party rather than the aftermath of an earthquake.

The next morning, when I awoke I felt my whole life in Positano had exploded. I hated the idea of returning to Casa San Matteo. I had eight years in that magical house and in only a few minutes it was all wiped away.

Before the quake, I had been crating up Gene's paintings in one of my basement rooms and I wanted to go back and get them out to send to Suzanne. Jimmy offered to accompany me. He knew I dreaded the idea of going back there alone. We were there about four o'clock that afternoon and as I was closing one of the crates, I suddenly felt dizzy. My head began to spin. I told Jimmy I felt like I was going to faint. We found out later that there had been another tremor in the central zone at the exact time. It didn't reach Positano, but it did reach me!

Carmen and I were now homeless. I wasn't sure what to do. Eventually when the telephone lines were repaired, I got a call from Bob and Ed in New York. They had been trying over and over to call us to see if we were safe, but it was impossible to get through. They told me Carmen and I could move into their house and asked us to keep in touch to let them know we were alright after the quake.

I went over to collect some more of our things from San Matteo. I found there had been a tremendous windstorm, which had forced open the double windows and ripped off one door. It created an enormous opening in one of the walls and looked as if a bomb had exploded in the house. I looked around and thought, *This is it. This part of our life is over.*

Jimmy James and Jennie.

Friends helped me carry our few things over to our new home at Casa Sam. We set up Carmen's bedroom in the front of the house with all her toys and dolls, which we had rescued from the quake, however she rarely slept there. She preferred to sleep on the extra bed in my room. I suppose she felt safer being close to me.

Thankfully there were no deaths in Positano and after everything settled down over the next few days we found there was really relatively little damage in the town. The Positanese all believed we were saved by the mountain range surrounding us. The quake had registered 6.9 on the Richter scale and there were many deaths and much damage in towns not far from us. Throughout the area the death toll was reported to be between three to four thousand people, and more than eight thousand had been injured.

Back in about **1976**, my brother and his wife had experienced another major earthquake in Italy when they came for a visit. I was thrilled when I heard they planned to come see us. My brother and his wife meant so much to me and I was excited for them to be able to finally meet Carmen. Before coming to Positano, they stopped for a night in the northern city of Udine, which is northeast of Venice. They booked into an inexpensive hotel there and that night when they were tucked in bed, suddenly the bed started jumping up and down. Alan told his wife they should have paid a bit more and booked a better hotel. Obviously this one was built over a railway track. 'No!', cried Barbara. 'It's not a train. It's an earthquake! We have to run!" They had a problem just trying to get down the staircase, because the stairs were moving up and down from the quake. That was an enormous earthquake. It hit a vast area killing hundreds of people and leaving thousands homeless.

By **November 1980** we were finally settled into Bob and Ed's house. Casa Sam was a very old building and Bob and Ed had left nearly all of the construction and fittings in their original state, which made the house wonderful. The location was great too. Carmen didn't have to use the school bus anymore, instead she took about 280 steps from our house to her elementary school. It was good exercise for a little girl. There was a small grocery shop across the road from us and a large hotel next door. Janòs and Justus were now renting a house close by too. I loved living at Casa Sam. Almost every weekend during the winter I would invite a group of my friends over for dinner. Marco from the Poseidon Hotel supplied our cocktails and wine and there was always plenty of food. Through Marco I had met Francesco Maione, who owned the Hotel Royale. He and his girlfriend, Bettina, would come and sleep over. All my other Italian friends would join us. We would have a roaring fire in the fireplace in the kitchen to keep us warm as we ate, drank and played cards until early in the morning. I felt safe at Casa Sam, even though we didn't have our ghost to watch over us anymore. We lived there for about two years, except during the summers when Bob and Ed came to Positano. Then Carmen and I would move out so they could have their place to themselves. While they were in town, I would find a room or house to rent for those few months. It made us feel a bit like gypsies.

One morning while we were staying at Casa Sam, I was stopped by several people on the street asking if I had seen the flying object in the sky the night before. They all said more or less the same thing: the UFO had appeared near the Galli Islands off the coast of Positano. It soared through the sky towards Positano and then made a sharp turn south towards Praiano. The next night many people saw the same thing. There was talk that they were alien ships. People in town were beginning to get scared.

A couple I knew from Milan were staying at Janòs' house. I went over to ask if they had seen the flying object too. To my amazement they had and they were rather shaken about it. I decided I would get to the bottom of the mystery and call the authorities myself. I think the first call I made was to NATO and then to the Italian Air Force. They listened to me, but probably thought I was a tourist who had too much wine. The last person I spoke to told me to call the local police and then he abruptly hung up the phone. The next morning, a friend told me he had just come back from Sorrento. As he was nearing Positano, he saw several large computer type machines on the side of the road hidden amongst the trees. I went out on my terrace and and saw a huge naval ship going around and around the island. *Oh my God!*, I thought to myself. *What have I done?*

My friend Vittorio suggested I call a woman who had a small hotel in Fornillo. He said she may know something. I called her and asked about the flying objects. She knew all about it. She told me not to worry. Apparently a German guest at her hotel had been taking a boat out to Li Galli each night. He would go behind the islands and send up some large illuminated balloons. They would be visible for miles as they floated up the coast. She said the German had left that morning and assured me it wouldn't happen again. I thanked her and went out onto the terrace again. Thankfully the ship was gone. I was glad I hadn't given the authorities my name or telephone number. I didn't want to get in trouble with NATO over some strange balloons!

I was still taking odd jobs when I could find them. Jimmy James asked me to help him transcribe some of the old hand-written diaries he had kept when he was young, back when he had left

Rosie and one of her sons.

England on his way to Australia. I loved Jimmy. He was a very intelligent man, an avid reader and a great painter and now he was writing his autobiography. I read through his diaries. They were much like a travel guide filled with so many amusing stories about his travels and his life. His wife, Rosie, had already published a book about her own life in Prague. It covers the post-war years, through the Stalinist purges, up to the Prague Spring of **1968** and its aftermath. She had been married to Pavel Kavan and they had two boys, whom I got to know well. Her book had originally been called *Freedom at a Price* but in the second edition the title was changed to *Love and Freedom*.

8 December 1980 was a day I will never forget. That was the day John Lennon flew away and left us all.

In those days, many people in Positano were growing pot. I once had a bush so large people told me I should have won a prize for it. One night in **1982**, I was at the Hotel Royale with Francesco Maione in his office. Some police officers walked in and Francesco went white as a sheet. He thought they were there to see him, but they said, 'No, we want her.' They told me they wanted to take me back to my house to search it for drugs. As they walked me home, I knew I had nothing of my own to worry about in the house. The problem

was that just a few days before I had been at János' and had seen he had big glass *demigianni* jars filled with grass all over his house. He liked to smoke pot when he made his art and he had been growing quite a bit, so he would have a supply on hand. I thought he had far too many jars there, so I told him I could store some for him over at Bob's. I took one of the big *demigianno* of grass to my house and left it on my kitchen table downstairs. Now the police were going to search my house… When we got there, I told the police my little girl was sleeping in her room and I wanted to check on her. Carmen asked me what was going on. I told her there were some police in the house and I needed her to call out that she needed a drink of water. Carmen was always up for a performance, so she did what I said. I asked the police if I could get some water for her and they said ok. They didn't know the house had another floor below, so I was able to go down and take the jar and bring it out to the terrace, where I hung it on the clothesline by one of its handles, so it was swinging over the garden below.

The police finished searching the house. They found nothing and left. Once they were gone, I took the jar inside and spent the next few hours trying to flush all the pot down the toilet. There was so much, I ended up clogging the toilet. I called Marco and told him what had happened and the word spread. People were busy clogging up toilets all over town that night. I was glad I had gotten rid of the pot, because the police were back early the next morning. I asked them what they wanted *this* time. They said they wanted to search the garden in the daylight. I had just finished planting some flowers a day or so before and when the police saw all the new little plants and they said, 'Ah, now we have something!' I told them they were just flowers and pointed to all the signs I had put up identifying the plants as pansies and geraniums. They realised their mistake and once again, they left.

A number of people were arrested around town that night. Most were kept in the jail in Amalfi for one night and then released. Later that morning, I had a call from the local police who told me János had been arrested for possession of pot. They were holding him at the station before he was to be driven to the prison in Salerno. They said I should come by if I wanted to say goodbye to him. He had been arrested by a vice squad from out of town, not our local police officers, whom we all knew. Someone must have denounced János to the police for them to single him out. We thought they kept János the longest because he was a foreigner and they thought they could get more on him. We found out later that the vice squad had put a tele-camera on János gate and for several weeks they had been watching everyone who was going in and out of his house. I went to see János at the police station and then went to his house, where I found a note he had left for me.

> *Dear Jennie, The police tuk me. I go to prison but come back soon. Pleaze give food to dogs, Busi and Curva. Luv János.*

I called Justus in Munich to tell him the news and he came immediately. Justus and I took his Vespa motor scooter and went to go see János at the prison in Salerno. The lawyer had told me I shouldn't go inside to see János. He thought it would upset me, because I was so close to him. On our first trip to the prison, I had to bring János some clothes. Like an idiot, I took his cashmere sweaters and his best trousers. János called me later and said, 'Are you crazy? You brought me my best clothes. Now I have to sleep with all

my clothes under my pillow or else my cellmates will steal them!' I had never dealt with anyone in prison before (only mental homes), but I would learn… János actually ended up getting on very well with his cellmates. They had facilities to cook in their large cell, which was for about twelve people. János was a good cook, so everyone liked him. János was constantly drawing wherever he was. He managed to continue drawing in prison, where he made portraits of his cellmates, which kept them entertained.

We went to visit him a number of times. I think that was when Justus and I finally became friends. All the time we spent going back and forth and trying to help János together created more of a bond between us. I remember waiting for Justus while he was in with János, I would look around at all the people waiting to see their friends and family in the prison. Nearly all of them were carrying large crates or bags of food for their loved ones. I heard one small child ask his mamma when daddy was coming out. The mother replied 'Oh you know Daddy, he always takes a long time to say goodbye to all of his friends, so we have to have patience.'

Justus found a good lawyer for János' trial, which was a few months later. A group of us from Postiano all travelled to the court house in Salerno. Even Marco's mother joined us. We were quite a chic looking crowd of witnesses. I had the chance to have a few words in private with János before the trial began. I told him he should keep his mouth shut and just nod his head in reply to the judge's questions. I was afraid he would hurt his case by telling his whole life story in his limited Italian. Unfortunately, my advice didn't last long.

Judge: 'Mr Zigmond, why did you have so much grass stored in containers in your house and growing in your garden?'

János: 'Well Signor Judge, I am a painter and when I paint and draw I like to smoke the best stuff, which is called sensimilla.'

The Judge turns quickly to his secretary and tells her to write 'sensimilla'.

János: 'Now to make sensimilla you have to have male plants and female plants. So

János

you have to keep on growing lots of plants until you have enough of both sexes…'

The Judge turns quickly to his secretary once again and repeats what János said.

János was eventually released. Marco and I went to pick him up and we celebrated with a bottle of Champagne, which Marco had brought in the car for the occasion. When we arrived in Positano, many people were on the road cheering for János as if he were a hero returning home from war.

Drugs were quite common amongst my friends then. Jimmy James once told me he and the musician Shawn Phillips were planning an LSD trip up in the mountains. I was surprised. It would be Jimmy's first trip and he was 68. I wondered if taking your first acid trip at that age might be dangerous. Maybe—maybe not. Who knows? I guess all went well, because when Jimmy returned from the mountains, I asked how it had been. He just said, 'Jennie, why didn't I try this before? It was amazing!'

Jimmy's wife, Rosie, died in **November of 1981** and after that Jimmy decided to move back to Australia. He didn't think he would be returning to Positano again. He told me he wanted to take care of me and Carmen and wanted us to move into his house when he left. The owner of Jimmy's house had made a deal with him. The house had been in ruins when Jimmy moved in. The owner had said that if Jimmy fixed it up, then he could have use of it until he died, rent free. Jimmy fixed that house up beautifully. Now that he was leaving, he said we could live there until he died. It was such a generous offer. I thought someone must have been watching over us—perhaps it was Rosie. I was so sorry that Jimmy was leaving Positano. He meant a great deal to me and Carmen and had done so much to help us over the years, but living in his

house would be a reminder of Jimmy and his time with us.

On **14 September 1982,** Grace Kelly was killed in an automobile accident.

One day in **1983**, Carmen surprised me by telling me it was now time for her to give herself to Jesus. As I was taking in that information, she immediately began talking about the kind of long white dress she should wear, what type of veil she should have and whom she would like to invite to her party. She had the whole event already planned in her mind. She didn't realise there was one big problem with her plans. She hadn't been baptised yet, which was required by the church before she could make her First Communion. I went and discussed Carmen's plans with Don Raffaele, the local priest. He was very kind and told me

Marco, Monica, Jennie and Carmen at her baptism with Alexis.

Carmen's First Communion with Marcella.

Carmen was accepted in the town even without being baptised or making her First Communion. I thanked him, but said Carmen had made up her own mind and was certain this was what she wanted to do, so he agreed to work with us. He said she could be baptised one week before the the rest of the children her age made their First Communion. Carmen's French friend Alexis decided to join Carmen, so Don Raffaele said they could be baptised together. The priest gave them both instruction booklets and told them to learn the answers to the questions they would be asked on the day of their baptism.

I told the Mother Superior we wanted Bob and Ed as Carmen's Godparents. When she heard that Bob was an atheist and Ed was Jewish, she politely said 'No' and suggested we find two more suitable people. I asked Marco and Monica and they agreed to become her Godparents instead.

As the word spread about the baptisms, interest amongst all the people in town grew. Typically children are baptised when they are just a few months old. A baptism for two eleven-year-old children had never happened in Positano before. Everyone began to fantasise about what kind of service it might be.

On the day of their baptism, the church was full of curious onlookers. Carmen and I were at the altar with Marco and Monica, who were holding candles and promising to guide Carmen in her spiritual life. Alexis' mother, Martine, and her partner Ernesto were there with him. When it was time for the priest to ask the children their questions, the priest started with Carmen. Everyone in the church was straining to hear as he asked her the first question in his gentle voice. He spoke so quietly that Carmen couldn't hear what he said. She had a rather loud raspy voice in those days and in the silent church she said, 'Would you mind speaking up? I can't hear a thing.' That caught Don Raffaele off balance. He repeated the question and then, trying to be kind, he mumbled the answer as well. As soon as I heard him, I knew he shouldn't have done that. It made Carmen ask in an even louder voice, 'Who is supposed to answer this question, you or me?!' They made it through the rest of the ceremony successfully and finally the water was poured over their heads and they were baptised. I shed a few tears and the Mother Superior was weeping, probably with relief that Carmen and Alexis were finally saved from sin. As we came out of the church, there was a crowd of people outside throwing sugarcoated almonds in celebration.

Then one week later on **29 May 1983,** Carmen made her First Communion along with 63 other children. It was one of the most splendid ceremonies I have ever witnessed.

The festivities had begun a month before the special day. The statue of the Madonna had been carried from Maria Assunta, the main church located down by the beach, and then placed in all the other churches around town. It was left in each church for several days. Before the Madonna was to arrive at each church, the people living in that area were asked to decorate their houses with flowers, leaves or coloured lights, so it would be beautiful whilst the Madonna was with them.

On the day of their First Communion, the Madonna was carried through the streets winding down the mountainside back to the main church again. All 63 children followed in a procession behind her. The girls were dressed like little brides in long white robes. The boys were in dark blue suits. Each carried a candle and a large white lily. They were followed by their parents and a Rent-a-Band blasting out joyous music on brass instruments. A monk, who had come from another town, joined the procession. He walked with outstretched arms with a white dove quietly sitting in each of his hands. Incense was burning in large barrels along the roadside and fireworks spurted out from the crevices in the mountains.

Since there were so many children participating, only their parents were allowed in the church for the service. My friend Toni Reichenbacher was visiting me from Munich. Since Carmen's father couldn't be there that day, I asked the ushers to allow Toni to come in with me instead. She was very religious and I knew she would love seeing the ceremony. Toni was a wonderful person. She was one of the owners of Deutsch Eiche, a well-know gay restaurant in Munich. She was friends with many famous German painters and writers and had even worked with the German film director, Rainer Werner Fassbinder in one of his films.

Inside the church, the children and their parents sat together. When the children were called to the altar to receive communion, their parents were to go with them. As Carmen and I headed towards the altar, I whispered to her that I couldn't receive communion myself, because I wasn't Catholic. I didn't want to have to explain that to the priest in front of the whole church. Carmen whispered back, 'Well then, just keep your mouth shut.' So I did.

There were more celebrations that night. Fireworks exploded over the town and the scent of incense lingered in the air. That evening I gave a big party at Bob and Ed's. Two of my friends, Maurizio and Claudio, helped me prepare platters of food for our guests. An American friend gave Carmen a medallion, which had been blessed by the Pope. The celebration lasted until the wee hours of the morning. It was a day never to be forgotten.

A few weeks later Carmen finished her fifth year at the elementary school. Some of my close friends were concerned about her future. They thought she should go to an English speaking private school in Rome. At first I was horrified with the idea. However they convinced me that although Carmen spoke English well, she wasn't learning to read or write it properly in the local schools. I realised I couldn't deny my daughter the chance to go to a good school in Rome. I could see Carmen needed more opportunities to expand her education, even though it felt like I would be losing the most precious part of my life.

My friends and I formed the 'Carmen's Future Committee.' It consisted of Bob, Ed, Francesco and Justus. I couldn't afford to move to Rome right away, so Carmen would have to board at the school. It would also take time for me to find a job to pay the tuition. The members of the committee all agreed to come up with a share of the money for Carmen's first year at a school in Rome, which

Carmen's elementary school.

would give me time to sort things out. I have to admit that deep down I had another reason for not wanting to move to Rome. Carmen's elder sister, Favola, who was getting on in age, had never even been to a city. How could I do that to my dog? You may think I was a rotten mum for thinking that, but it all worked out in the end.

Carmen and I planned a trip to the Eternal City to check out the few English speaking schools available to find the one which would be the best fit for her. It turned out that we had very little choice. There was only one school which offered to board students, The International School of Rome. It was run by a Christian Scientist couple and was situated outside of the city in a beautiful old villa surrounded by large trees.

Carmen was to start at the International School in **September 1983**. Maurizio offered to drive us to Rome in his old VW. I insisted on staying over that first night. Most of the students were still on holiday, so there was enough room for me to stay at the school. There were very few students at the school when we arrived and the first ones I saw seemed to all be the children of diplomats from Africa who were working in Italy. It was already late in the day, so I paid the office the initial fees for the year and then Carmen and I went up to bed. That was a horrible night for me. I had a bad feeling about the school and I couldn't sleep. I was worried it wasn't the right place for Carmen and didn't want to leave her there. More than once I wanted to go downstairs and ask for my money back and run. Even now, I get butterflies in my stomach when I think about that night. It was only me who was nervous. Carmen was just fine. She was excited to start her new school. So I drove away the next day hoping I was making the right decision. I returned to Positano and although I missed Carmen very much, life had to go on. Thankfully there were many school holidays when Carmen came back home. Whenever she did return, she usually brought some of her new friends from school along with her.

I still had my worries about the school. I frequently telephoned there, but often I couldn't get through. I spoke to Mrs Harris, the Head Mistress, who told me that often when there was a storm or strong winds the lines would go down.

That didn't ease my worries. The school had many problems. There were never enough teachers. At times, Mrs Harris taught all the subjects and sports by herself. Occasionally she even taught the students tap dancing in the kitchen after supper. While Carmen was there, they had to get rid of their bus driver and then one day the cook disappeared, so the students had to help with kitchen duty. In Carmen's second year there were only four students boarding at the school and they were often left alone. That worried me too since the school was in the middle of nowhere.

One day, I had an urgent telephone call from Carmen. She said something awful had happened, but she couldn't talk now because someone was coming in. She hung up and called again two more times with similar cryptic messages. I was getting frantic! What could I do when I was 200 kilometres away? Eventually, she called again and was able to talk. She said when the four boarding students were left alone, the other three students would get into Mrs Harris' liquor cabinet and mix her rum with their Coca Cola. Carmen was so worried. They were her best friends. She had told them if they continued doing that they would be dead before they were 20. She asked me to please not tell anyone, especially Mrs Harris. She just wanted to know what she should do to help them. I promised not to mention it to anyone and told her there was little she could do, especially since she was the youngest of them. I just asked her to *please* not do it herself. In spite of Carmen's crazy upbringing, she has always been very straight and moral. She's not a Miss Perfect, but she has her own rules and sticks to them without judging the behaviour of other people.

I would go up to the school whenever the children put on shows. I loved to see Carmen perform especially since I knew she had wanted to be an actress since she was very small. At the end of the first school year, Mrs Harris had plans to put on the musical *Oliver Twist*. It was to be performed just before the graduation ceremony took place. When Carmen heard this, she immediately got a hold of the words and music and learnt every song in the score. She seemed to know she would get the role of Nancy, the only female role in the show (apart from a very brief entrance of a nurse).

The International School in Rome.

An Italian girl played Oliver and Sue, who was an assistant in the kitchen, played Bill Sykes. It was a female cast playing the male roles. I had my doubts about Carmen being able to reach the high notes in the song *Who Will Buy,* but somehow she got through.

The setting was quite wonderful. A stage had been set up outside the villa using part of the balcony and the steps above it as a part of the set. The backdrops had been painted by the students. Rows of chairs had been set up in front of the stage for parents and friends. A large hand-painted sign which read 'Love Thy Father' hung from the balcony by a rope pulley. The sign was drawn up as the play began. Most of the cast were African, which gave this very English play an interesting twist. Sue was the only one who's voice sounded anything close to a Cockney accent. The rest of the cast had accents which were Spanish, Italian, American, English or one of several various African languages.

The show opened with a group of the African students singing *Food Glorious Food.* From that moment on, I knew this was going to be the greatest musical ever! It didn't take long for the mums and dads to start giggling. Soon some of them were practically rolling around the garden in fits of laughter. Even the sad parts of the show were funny. Carmen made her entrance wearing a bright red satin dress and a look of total desperation on her face, in keeping with the role she was playing. She never lost that expression even when the audience was crippled with laughter. The rest of the cast began to go along with the audience's reaction and started laughing too, but not Carmen. She never winced and by the time she got to her solo, I put my hands over my eyes and pretended to be sad or else I never would have heard the end of it from her. When it came to theatre, Carmen was always very serious.

The nurse was played by a young African girl who was Carmen's good friend. She made quite

165

The International School.

the other child came to attack her, it looked as though she was being killed by a dwarf. She clutched her heart, staggered and fell to the floor—dead! Her fall was fine but she landed with her legs and arms spread out and since she was supposed to be dead, she didn't try to get herself into a slightly more graceful position. She played being dead so well that she didn't get up, even when the play was over. The other kids just stepped over her dead body as they moved back and forth across the stage. I wanted to call out and tell her that the play had finished, but she would never have heard me over all the laughter. So there she lay, until her little friends dressed as orphans finally dragged her off the stage so the graduation ceremony could begin. The new version of *Oliver Twist* had been an overwhelming success!

Mrs Harris came on the stage wearing her Head of Harvard expression. She took the microphone and began calling up the graduates. Meanwhile, two of the 'orphans' had crept up to the balcony above and loosened the ropes holding the 'Love Thy Father' sign. The sign unwound itself and fell—just missing Mrs Harris' head by a couple of inches. The diplomats from Africa were hysterical and the rest of the audience were practically falling off their seats.

I was excited when I heard Mrs Harris had decided to produce *The Wizard of Oz* the following year. It's one of my favourites and Carmen was cast as Dorothy. I hoped this show would be as entertaining as *Oliver Twist* had been and that Carmen would do well as Dorothy as she had as Nancy. On the way to that play, my driver got lost and we arrived about 45 minutes late. A fuming Mrs Harris met us and said they had to delay the play just for me, as 'The Star' would not perform until her mother arrived. To punish me for being late, Mrs Harris gave us the worst seats in the garden, right next to the speakers.

This year there was no stage. The show took place out in the open amongst the trees on what

an entrance. She was to enter from above, come down the staircase and walk onto the stage. She was wearing a white nurse's outfit and had a white cap perched on the back of her head. She had only taken about two steps down the stairs when she tripped and literally rolled down the rest of the stairs and landed in a heap on the floor. As she lifted her head, her cap slipped over one eye. By this time the audience was shrieking.

Now came the best part—the scene where Carmen is murdered. Although Carmen was younger than the other students, she was already quite a bit taller than most of them. So when was once a basketball court. You can imagine what the sound was like. The students' voices were whisked away by the wind. The only sound you could hear well was the piano, which was on a tape and blared out over the speakers, which were right in my ears. Dorothy was skipping around the basketball court. A mangy old lion would disappear behind a tree and then would reappear with the Tin Man. The Scarecrow was constantly running to catch up with them, because he had forgotten his cue. We could see their mouths open and close, but there was no sound, except for the piano. More than once during the show, Mrs Harris had to change the tape. Once she put on the wrong one. Another time the music was at the wrong speed. I could hear her cursing away behind the speaker. She was so nervous that day that I felt like telling her to give it all up. After all, by that time there were only about 13 students left at the school. There wasn't even a graduation that year, because there were no graduates.

I already knew Carmen was not going to return to the school the following year, but I had decided to keep it quiet and let her finish the year in peace. I knew this would probably be the last time Carmen would see most of her friends.

In place of a graduation, Mrs Harris had organised a game of tug-of-war between the parents and the students. That was the last thing I needed. I had been up since 5.00 am, I was exhausted and knew we had a long drive back tonight. Now I had to play tug of war... Of course I couldn't refuse, so I found myself squashed between two fathers from the Congo. They both had obviously come straight from their embassies wearing dark suits, white shirts and ties. I had on high heels for the occasion. None of us expected to be tugging on a rope in the middle of an old basketball court. I guess it's not surprising that the children won.

St.Carmen Sorrenti

After much exchanging of addresses and saying goodbye, I finally got Carmen into the car. I didn't tell Mrs Harris that Carmen wouldn't be coming back the following year. However when I mentioned that I was looking for a small place for us to live in Rome, I saw her face drop. Carmen was one of only four boarders she had left. That meant less money for the school in the next year.

Apart from the many defects of that school, I still feel those two years were an incredible experience for Carmen. She went through so much at The International School of Rome that being there was an education in itself.

The Dogs of Positano

When I first arrived in Positano in **1969**, there were stray dogs everywhere. They were not only welcome in the town, but they were considered members of the community. The only difference was that they couldn't vote, be baptised or make their First Communion. The dogs travelled around town in pairs or packs. They sought out food or a bit of love and affection wherever they could find it. The lucky ones found themselves a permanent residence. They were all very sweet and not at all aggressive. Some of them aimed high, in the direction of the tourists, knowing there was a slight chance they might be taken away on a plane or in a car in a newly purchased dog carrier.

Shortly after the earthquake, a friend of mine named Yvonne was in Positano on holiday. She wanted to find a stray dog to take back home with her to the east side of Manhattan. There were many strays around that winter to choose from. Yvonne fell in love with a short-haired, slanted-eyed charmer she named Lucy. Before Lucy left Italy, she had to have her medical certificates from a veterinarian to get out of the country. I travelled to Castellemmare with Yvonne and Lucy to visit the dog doctor. When we arrived at the address we had been given, we were surprised to find the building had been split in two by the earthquake. All that was left of the third floor was a washbasin still clinging to the wall. We had to go back the next day to find the new address where the vet's office had moved. Lucy did eventually make it to Manhattan and lived a good long life in the city. She became a favourite of all Yvonne's neighbours and even starred in a TV commercial.

In the late 60s and early 70s when groups  of musicians, writers, and painters flocked to Positano, they arrived with all of their old habits. There was a little psychedelic group of dogs who used to wander house to house and from party to party back then. I like to think those dogs got high on their nightly trips to visit all their friends. They were a small group of dogs, but they were extremely with it. The dogs belonged to everyone and they shared their time with so many people as they travelled all over town. There were so many dogs, each with their own personality. Heathcliff seemed to be the leader of the gang. He ended up with Fabrizio in Milano. Hustler was a rusty-coloured, yappy little dog. He ended up with a semi-permanent home with Judy, a close friend of mine from England. Hustler was probably the smartest of the group, especially when it came to getting around town. He would sneak on the local bus downtown and hide under the back seat. Then as soon as the bus stopped to let the passengers off at the top of town, he would scoot off to go wherever he was going. Edna Lewis once saw Hustler and asked me, 'Isn't that the little dog who catches the bus up to Chiesa Nuova at the top of town?' I suppose Edna thought all the strays took the local bus to get around town.

Some of the strays never left the beach area, which was where most of the restaurants were. Food was easier to come by there, although they did have to contend with the many stray cats there. Gianni, who had a small newspaper shop on the beach, loved the dogs. He would take a few of them home in the evening to sleep each night. The rest of the dogs would gather near his shop, knowing he would feed them. Some of the locals used to put a collar or a scarf around the necks of some of their favourite strays, so they looked as though they belonged to someone, hoping that might prevent them from being taken to the pound.

Personally, I was continually collecting dogs and finding them homes. When I found a new arrival in town, I would telephone Anna Sersale, one of the owners of the Sirenuse Hotel and together we would try to find them a place to

live. Carmen once got into trouble following my example. She found a stray dog on her way to school and took it with her into her classroom. The teacher wanted it to leave, but Carmen told the teacher the dog had to stay with her until the morning was over, so she could take it home to her mamma.

Once I found a short-haired stray who looked like a hunting dog. I called him Mario. Mario was ever so sweet, but a little stupid. When I found him, he was completely covered in fat ticks. I had heard the best way to get rid of ticks was with olive oil. It was such an Italian cure. The oil would smother the ticks, causing them to either fall off or make them easy to pick off without hurting the dog. I tried the oil cure on Mario. I covered him with about two litres of oil and rubbed it into his fur. It worked. The ticks all came off. I followed up with a bubble bath and gave him a fancy new collar. I heard one of the bank managers was looking for a hunting dog, so I told him I would bring Mario down to meet him. Mario had a wonderful karma, even if he was a bit stupid. Now after his oil treatment, he was clean and shiny and looked quite noble. The bank manager took one look at Mario and asked me how much I wanted for him. I just handed him the leash and that was that.

Another time I was walking home quite late one night and noticed I was being followed by a beautiful hunting dog. He had long silky white fur and was very friendly. He didn't seem like a stray. I took him home for the night to sleep in my bedroom thinking I would figure out what to do with him the next morning. In the middle of the night, he sort of went berserk. He began jumping from bed to bed, from one piece of furniture to another. I knew he wasn't dangerous, but he wasn't

a small dog so he caused quite a mess. He just seemed to be playing. The next morning I took him down to a boutique in the square. I knew the shop owner had other hunting dogs. He took one look at my new friend and said he would be happy to take him.

My friend Melino, the Baron from Naples, had a little silky terrier called Wa Wa. One day Melino drove his car to Pepito's clothing shop. Melino went inside and left Wa Wa in the car with the windows down. When Melino returned to the car, he drove off without bothering to check if Wa Wa was still there. When he arrived at Chiesa Nuova, he could feel something was stuck to the wheel of his car. Melino stopped to investigate what it was and discovered to his horror that it was Wa Wa. The poor dog must have jumped out of the window and caught his leash under the wheel. Melino called me that night to tell me what had happened. I went over to his house and found Wa Wa in his tiny bed lying on his back with his four little legs pointing straight up in the air in plaster and splints. Surprisingly, Wa Wa survived that crazy ride and lived to an old age.

My darling Favola lived for 15 years. She gave birth to 29 puppies in 3 different litters. I didn't want her to have all those puppies, but her boyfriends could smell her for miles away when she was on heat. I kept the little ones for a few months before giving them away, which meant our house was like a puppy playground at times.

I left Favola with Marco's sister, Monica, while I went to Paris in **1984**. When I got back I knew something was wrong. Favola was either sad or

sick. I called the vet who told me she had a virus and because of her age she might not pull through. When my friends heard the sad news they all came to see her. Every night my house was full of friends. Favola was one of the most loved dogs in town and everyone was upset about her illness. As she became weaker, she wouldn't pee, which the vet said was dangerous. I would carry her out to the garden, even though she was a big dog, hoping it would help. One evening a group of friends were at my house. One of them suggested we take her out into the garden and then each of us should pee in front of her. Maybe that might bring on the desired reaction in her. We all lined up and peed in turn, but to no avail.

As Favola grew weaker, Katinka's husband, Luciano Nuvolare, told me she wouldn't last much longer. He said I should be practical. It was time to have a coffin made. He told me his carpenter would make one for me, if I would take the measurements. I couldn't bring myself to do that, so Luciano did it instead. I asked him to have a plain white coffin made for her. We all cared for Favola for about ten more days. Every one of those nights she slept in my bed. Eventually the vet told me Favola would die soon and we should put her out of her pain and misery. It was such a difficult decision, but I finally agreed to have the vet put her down.

On her last day, **5 December, 1984**, our friends were there as usual. The vet asked me to leave the room when he gave her the needle. He knew I couldn't bear to see it. I left her in the hands of my good friend Maurizio Russo, who loved her very much. Afterwards, Favola was laid out on my bed on an antique white lace bed cover, so people could

pass by and pay their respects. She was surrounded by hibiscus flowers from the garden and we all wrote dedications on her white coffin.

Marco had agreed to let us use the top garden at the Hotel Poseidon as a cemetery. Luciano offered his Jaguar as the hearse. Favola's coffin was to have four bearers, including Marco. However Marco had been in Torino and was late coming from the airport, so we had to delay the funeral until he arrived. All of Favola's friends followed the procession from our house to the hotel. It was just like any other funeral in Positano; after all, she was a big part of my family.

As we were driving to the 'cemetery', Luciano asked if he could stop and pick up a friend of his who was visiting from Germany. It was a nephew of Albert Speer, the author of *Behind the Third Reich*. By the time we got to the hotel it was getting quite dark. To get to the burial ground we had go up on the domed roof of the hotel and then leap about one meter from dome to dome. There was complete silence, except for some sniffling and blowing of noses. Suddenly I heard Luciano's roaring voice. He was screaming at his friend, 'We're having a funeral and you nearly fell off the roof. You could have been killed yourself and you can't be buried with the dog, you idiot!' None of us knew the man suffered from epilepsy and was on medication that made him dizzy. I'm sure he hadn't anticipated going to a dog's funeral on a domed roof of a hotel that day.

It was an amazing funeral. So many friends were there to see Favola off. Most of them had been around when she was born and they saw her grow up by my side. Favola had always travelled with me to cocktail parties, restaurants, discos and art shows. She was a part of everything we did for 15 years. Her funeral was a way to mark our own passing years.

Luca, Marco's naughty Dalmatian, died two years later. He was buried next to Favola in the rose garden. Later, a cocker spaniel belonging to Patrizia from Naples found his way into the pet cemetery at the Poseidon too. There was only one cat who was privileged enough to be laid to rest in this exclusive space. It had belonged to Marco's wife, Laura.

Every year when Bob and Ed travelled from New York to Positano they would bring their cat and dog with them. Their dog, Sam, could sing. Whenever they said, 'Sing Sam, sing' the dog would put his face toward the sky and sing. Even when Sam was quite old, he was still flying across the ocean to Positano and still singing a few notes.

Bob had a very hard time when the vet told them Sam was not well and may not have time to sing many more songs. Bob loved Sam so much. He couldn't bear the thought of losing him. Bob planned a trip to Venice and asked if I would watch Sam while they were away. I think he knew Sam's time was coming up and he didn't want to be there when it happened. One evening while they were away I went to dinner with János. Before the meal was over I had a strange feeling in my tummy. I knew something had happened to Sam. I asked János to take me home. As soon as I entered the house, I began calling him. There was only silence. Frantically I searched the house and found Sam lying near a pot of geraniums on the terrace. He was dead. I felt so guilty about leaving him alone for those few hours and I was so sad he was gone.

Bob was going to be away for a while, so I knew we had to bury Sam. I started looking around for something to serve as a coffin. The only thing I found was a large cardboard box. I laid him inside it and asked János to carry him down to the lower garden, where I planned to bury him. I looked for a shovel, but couldn't find one. I began to get nervous. I didn't want the neighbours to find us burying something in the yard as the sun came up. They might think we had killed someone and were getting rid of the evidence. All I could find was a large soup ladle, so we began to dig the grave with that. It was slow going and the hours were

János

passing. I was getting frantic and crying and János was screaming at me. After what seemed like hours, the hole looked like it was large enough. I lifted the coffin over the hole to check the size and suddenly the bottom fell out of the box and Sam fell into the hole! The hole wasn't really deep enough. I screamed for János to pick up the dog so we could dig deeper. He screamed at me to just help him fill in the hole. By the time we had all the earth in place, there was a small mound of dirt with a little black paw sticking out. We tried to cover that with more dirt, but it didn't really work. The next morning, I called Bob in Venice and told him the sad news. Later that day Bob went to the cathedral and lit several candles for Sam.

As the years passed, the stray dogs continued to roam the streets, but our lives were changing. We didn't have as much contact with them and they weren't as much a part of the town life. It was now just a 'hi' here and a 'woof' there.

Unexpected Opportunities, The List and Falling Buildings

In **1985**, I was given an unexpected opportunity to enter a new profession and, for the first time in my life, to make some good money. Justus had recently written a new book for a German television production. It was called Oliver Maas and was about the life of a young violinist. Most of the series was to be shot in Germany, but since Justus had a house in Positano, he decided to use the Amalfi coast as one of the locations in the story. Justus knew I had many connections along the Amalfi Coast, so he thought I could be very helpful to the crew. He talked to the Production Manager about giving me a job and he agreed. It all sounded very exciting to me, even though I had never worked on a film before and had no idea what my job would involve.

The film was produced by TV60 and was directed by Gero Erhardt. I was introduced to the Production Manager, Dieter Graber, and the Assistant Manager,

Sylvia Monalti. Sylvia and I immediately became good friends and remained so for years. My job was basically to do whatever they needed me to do. I took Sylvia around the coast to meet locals who could be used as extras over the following months. We also visited locations they might use in shooting. It was a fun education for me to see how the preparation for a film was done.

Everything was going smoothly until Sylvia had an accident and hurt her back so badly that she had to stay in bed for a week or so. As her new close friend, she asked me to stand in for her. I didn't know much about film production, but I did know that being the Assistant Manager was a very important position. I told her not to worry, I would help her do whatever needed whilst she was recuperating. I suppose I took it as a challenge, as I did with most of the jobs in my past, doing all I could to learn quickly on the job.

Oliver Maas

172

Very early each morning, I would go to Sylvia's hotel room and we would run through the script for the day. She would write a list of the things that needed to be prepared for the shooting. I loved it. It felt as though a new and exciting life was beginning for me. The locals in Positano and in other towns along the coast thought it was wonderful to have Hollywood coming their way. I used many of them as extras in our scenes. I would hire a bus to pick up the locals *en route* and get them to wherever we were shooting that day. I had bought an old run-down car to get me around as I was organising everything. I usually had a dog or two in the car with me. The production had constructed a trattoria on the beach in Furore, a town near Praiano, so the set needed a few dogs, chickens and a donkey to make it look real. Later when the script called for the trattoria to be burnt down, a crew of well-known special effects experts were sent down from Germany to do the job. I was quickly learning what this work was all about, and I loved it.

The night after all the shooting was completed, Dieter asked me to arrange a party for the actors and crew. Of course the extras were invited to join us too. We set up the party on the beach in Praiano and even managed to recreate a set from one of the beach scenes from the film. It was a very special night.

I have often thought about Sylvia's accident. It was unfortunate for her, however for me it was a stroke of good luck. It gave me the opportunity to learn a great deal about the film business in a very short time. I had hoped this job would lead to more work on films in the future and it did. Just by word of mouth I was recommended for several more movies. Everyone knew if you were planning to shoot in Italy, you should call Jennie, the Australian.

It was time for Carmen to move on to a new school. Her years of growing up in Positano with all our wonderful crazy friends and her two strange years at the International School were the perfect preparation for the next step in her life. I had inquired around for the best international boarding schools in Rome. I needed a school where she could stay whenever I was travelling to work on films. I had heard about St Stephen's School, which was highly recommended. They had excellent teachers and the students came from all over the world. The children were from so many countries that there were 14 native languages spoken by the students. St Stephen's was very strong academically and more importantly for Carmen, it had a well-respected theatre department, as well as classes in dance and art.

When I took Carmen to have an interview with the Head Master, he said she was too young to begin the first year. She was 13 years old, which was a year younger than most of the other students in the first year class. I suppose the fact that he saw her carrying a stuffed Snoopy dog toy under her arm didn't help convince him. The Head Master asked me to leave her with him for a short time, so he could speak to her alone. When they were done, he told me, 'Carmen is young, but I will accept her. I can see she's very bright and talented.' What a wonderful surprise for both of us! Somehow I could just feel that St Stephen's would be the perfect school for Carmen.

Carmen was to start at St Stephen's in autumn of **1986**. I decided to move to Rome so Carmen could live with me rather than board full-time. My friends John Moss and Gianni Stargetti lived in a beautiful apartment on Via Vittoria. Attached to their apartment was another small flat that was vacant. I thought it would be just right for us. It was small, but had a wonderful big terrace overlooking a monastery. Both apartments were owned by Felicity Mason, an English woman who had lived in Rome for many years. She had been married to Richard Mason, the author of *The World of Suzy Wong*. Felicity was loads of fun and had many very interesting friends. Years before, she worked as a voice coach for Italian actors. She also had some small roles in Italian films herself. You can read more about her life in her memoir *The Love Habit: The Sexual Confessions of an Older Woman* which she wrote under the name 'Anne Cumming'. After her death, some Italian gossip magazines claimed Felicity was a distant relative of the English royal family. I do think her accent and the way she looked was quite similar to them, but her way of life was *quite* different… You really have to read her book to understand what I mean.

Friends in Rome.

Whenever I've lived in a city, I've preferred to live right in the centre and this new apartment was ideal for me. It was about two minutes to Via del Barbuino and about four minutes to Piazza del Popolo and the Spanish Steps. What more could I have wanted? It was good for Carmen too. She only had a short bus ride to get to her new school.

John and Gianni were wonderful people. Living next door to them was perfect. John was working for a well-known American architectural firm on Via Sistina. He was frequently flying off to Saudi Arabia to work on new buildings in the desert. Then not long after we arrived, he and Gianni opened a gay bar called Hangar at Via in Selci 69. Hangar was one of the first gay bars in Rome and it quickly became very well-known all over the world.

One night after Carmen and I had gone to sleep in our new apartment, I was woken by a thump from the terrace outside of my bedroom. Our apartment was on the fifth floor, so it shocked me to see the shadow of a man on the small balcony near the terrace. Within seconds, I woke Carmen and we ran to Gianni and John's apartment. We knocked and John opened the door immediately. He was already awake and told us to come inside quickly. They had also seen some men on the terrace and they had already telephoned the police. We all stood there barefoot and in our nightclothes waiting for the police to arrive. A few minutes later, several police were at the door.

As soon as we told them what we had seen, the chase was on. It all seemed so unreal. As they were searching the apartment, I noticed a couple of the police began looking at John and Gianni's video collection. Knowing they had many 'for men only' videos, I quickly tried to distract them by offering them coffee. The burglars had headed up to the dome on my roof. They didn't know there was nowhere they could jump to from there. They were trapped. The police caught four men up there. As the last one was taken off in handcuffs, I screamed at him, 'How dare you try to break in and frighten a small child and a family!' The four of us stayed up for a while after they had left. None of us could go to bed after all that. It was a little too much excitement for one night.

I knew quite a few friends in Rome from my past. Some of them were living near by, so I was never without company. I was also meeting many new friends. Most of my life, I've found myself in the company of gay men and have spent a lot of time in their world. I think I'm drawn to them because many of them seem to be more open and creative and fun. I believe it was one of my gay friends who introduced me to Piero Guanieri. Piero was a very successful architect and interior designer. He had a beautiful apartment in Via Condotti in the centre of Rome, close to where we were living. I became close to him and his interesting group of friends, many of whom were either in fashion or worked as window dressers. There were times when Piero would get rather jealous if I spent time with men outside of his group. That's another side of my story with the gay scene. Some of my gay friends would have jealous fits when I mixed with straight men. I never understood that. I was just happy being with any of my friends.

When I wasn't working on a film, Piero would occasionally ask me if I could work with him on one of his projects at some amazing villa. I agreed, thinking it would be fun and interesting and I could learn another trade in the process. One time I worked with his crew on a re-do of a majestic villa on the Grand Canal in Venice. That was wonderful. Venice is one of my favourite cities. The old city is so fascinating and beautiful, and of course I have fond memories of it since it was where Carmen had been conceived. Another time I worked with Piero redecorating the offices of Giulio Andreotti, a well-known writer, journalist and politician. His offices were located just off Via del Corso in the centre of Rome. I worked there for three weeks hanging paintings, cleaning his many framed photos and dusting his collection of hundreds of souvenirs. As we neared the end of the job, several well-known politicians stopped by. Piero gave the key to Andreotti just before Christmas. We had even decorated a large Christmas tree for him in the main room.

In **1986** I was given the opportunity to work on the crew of the film *Pax Questuoso*. It was a silent film, except for one line said by an old man. The director, Klaus Linderman, was shooting it in black and white, which made the job quite interesting. It was being filmed half in Brescia, which is near Verona and half in Caorli, near Venice. The lead actor was a young German man named Michael Tanneberger. He was to play Jesus.

In Brescia, the main set was the grand old church and the surrounding piazza and streets. I was told I had to find nearly two hundred extras who could work for a few days as part of a procession scene. The script called for all of the extras to be dressed completely in black. I explained they would only be used if *all* of their clothes, including their shoes and accessories, were black. The first morning of shooting this scene, I carefully checked each of the extras to see if they had listened to my direction. If I found any other colour on them anywhere, I sprayed it over with black dye. Very quickly they realised I had been quite serious about my instructions.

There were many bars surrounding the church. I noticed when there was a pause in the shooting many of the extras would go to the bars and have a quick drink. It was easy to tell who was doing this by the way they were acting. They were supposed to be serious and solemn, but the ones who had been drinking weren't. I had to go around to each of the bars and tell the owners they were not to serve alcohol to any people who were dressed as nuns or dressed all in black. That resolved that problem.

Pax Questuoso

175

Once the filming in Brescia was completed, we moved to the small beach town of Caorli. One day we were on the beach shooting a scene with four children. They were all dressed in black and told to lie down spread-eagled on the wet sand with their mouths open. Just as we had begun to shoot, a dark cloud and vicious sand storm hit, causing all of us to quickly run back to the hotel. No one had ever seen a storm like that, even the local fishermen were taken by surprise. They struggled as they tried to bring in their boats. At the hotel, we watched the news on TV. They said a black cloud from the nuclear explosion in Chernobyl in Russia was moving across northern Italy! Once the cloud passed over us, we resumed shooting and we were able to complete our filming over the next few days. When we were finished, I planned a trip to Milan to visit some friends before heading home. Michael, who had played Jesus in the film, went along with me. It was a very strange trip. None of the restaurants could serve any food. Any fresh food was considered contaminated from the cloud and had to be thrown out. Shops could only sell food if it had been sealed in packets and the only drinks for sale anywhere were those sold in closed containers. What an end to the film! In spite of the cloud, I have wonderful memories of working on *Pax Questuoso*.

Andy Warhol died on **22 February 1987**.

In **July 1987** I received a call from my sister Joan back in Australia. She told me that her husband, Les, had died. I really loved Les and felt guilty that I was unable to be with Joan at that time. Joan and Les didn't have children. I never asked her why. She would have been a wonderful mum. When my siblings and I were younger, none of us really talked about our personal feelings or problems. Everything and everyone was just accepted without judgement, but I suppose none of us really got to know each other that well either. It was only later in our lives, when I started going home again, that Joan and I began catching up and revealing little things from our past. It was the same with Peggy when I finally was able to see her again. Their attitude towards me took away so much guilt I had about being away from home for so long. I really loved them for that. I suppose I was always their baby sister.

Although I couldn't go back to see Joan myself, I told Carmen the news about her Uncle Les and asked if she would like to go to Australia to see the family and visit with Auntie Joan. She said she would, so I got her a ticket to leave a few days later. That was Carmen's first trip to Australia and her first time meeting Joan. She had a great time meeting my school friends, including my old boyfriend Barry. Joan took her all over, even to cities I had never visited. I was so happy Carmen was able to finally see my country.

Over the years Bob Miller and Ed Wittstein continued to travel back and forth between New York and Positano. Back in **1981**, I had an odd conversation with Bob soon after they had flown in from New York. He told me there was a weird new homosexual disease that had hit America and many gay men were dying from it. I thought he was kidding and said, 'Oh come off it, Bob. There can't be a disease only gay men get.' He just laughed a bit and said that was the word on the street in New York City. It seemed so crazy to me. Then a couple of months later, the front cover of the German magazine *Der Spiegel* had a drawing of the face of a young man who was so emaciated that he looked as though he had come from another planet. It was the face of AIDS. Unfortunately, within a few years, I became all too familiar with that look.

It took us all some time to understand what was happening. Young men were dying all over America. Bob had been right, it did seem to be mainly hitting homosexual men. No one seemed to be able to find an answer for what caused the disease. There were many rumours going around. Some said it had spread from monkeys. Others thought it could be transmitted simply by casual contact with someone infected with AIDS. We read that no one wanted to touch people who had it, for fear of contracting the disease. The men were being treated like lepers. Even nurses in hospitals were trying not to have contact with AIDS patients. Some would even leave their patient's meals by the door of their room rather than carry it in themselves. We began to hear more and more about how AIDS was spreading around the globe. For a while, we felt a bit distant from it all; we didn't hear much about it hitting Italy. I do remember one day when my close friend Ciccio, who was gay, asked me if I thought he should take the test for AIDS. I told him if he thought he should, then he should, but that was it. I never heard any more about it.

Ciccio came from a little town between Positano and Naples and he would often go back and forth between the two. At one point, we realised none of our friends had seen him for a little while. Then in **September of 1987** we heard Ciccio had AIDS and had been put in hospital in Naples. We were all upset and so worried for him. This was the first case of AIDS any of us knew of in Positano. When he was first admitted, I wrote to Ciccio asking if I could visit him. He sent me a very sweet letter asking me please not to come. He said he didn't want any visitors to see him.

After some time, Bob suggested we should go see him anyway. He suspected Ciccio must be nearing the end. We had to take a train and then a bus to the hospital. It seemed to be isolated from the city. Outside the hospital there were only a few stray dogs. Inside it felt just as isolated. We didn't see any nurses or doctors, so we had to find Ciccio's room by ourselves. I suppose those were still the days when AIDS patients were practically left alone. We were glad to see that at least Ciccio's mother was with him. She left when we arrived. I presumed she needed a break. It must have been unbearably difficult for her to see her son so ill. I was quite shocked when I saw him. In his bed, he looked so thin and long, even though he wasn't a tall man. The skin on his arms was wrinkled and shiny. His skin looked so strange that at first I thought he was wearing clear plastic gloves. He looked dreadful. Ciccio was silent, but when Bob went over to take his hand, he quietly whispered Bob's name.

Ciccio (Francesco) Borriello died just a few days later. His funeral was held on **12 September 1987** in the small town where he was from. A large group of his friends all boarded a train to go to the funeral. We knew Ciccio loved art, fashion and colourful people, so we dressed in a style we thought he would have liked. We wore long colourful skirts or dresses and Indian shirts. Some of us carried fresh flowers in wicker baskets. We looked almost as if we had stepped back into the 60s. When we arrived at the church, we were

confronted by other people who had come to his funeral soberly dressed in black. We all waited together outside the church for the ceremony to begin, but after a short time the priest came out and told us that Ciccio's coffin couldn't be brought there that day, because it was the weekend. He told us to come back the next day. We returned the following morning and it was the same scene: the other group dressed in black and our friends in our colourful clothes. However our long hippy skirts and Indian shirts were now quite rumpled and the flowers in our baskets were drooping rather sadly.

Ciccio was the first of my friends I had to say goodbye to because of AIDS. Over time there were more and more of them, both male and female. Many were not just acquaintances, but very close friends. I call that period The Black Years.

Over the next few years my time was split three ways between my life in Rome with Carmen, travelling to work on various film projects and going back to Positano to catch up with friends. Whenever I returned to Rome after being away for a while, John Moss would greet me with the same question, 'Jennie, do you want The List?' The List, was the names of our friends who had died from AIDS whilst I was away. There were new ones each time I returned to Rome. At first I said no, I didn't want to hear it. It was too much. Then John explained it would be worse for me if I didn't know. I might try to phone or visit someone only to find they weren't around anymore. It seemed there were just too many of them. It became overwhelming!

János and I were still in touch, but we had a falling out in our relationship when I took my apartment in Rome. Initially Justus had insisted on paying for it. He thought that way he and János could come use it whenever they were in Rome. I told him no. It was my apartment and I wanted to pay for it myself. I didn't want to feel that I owed Justus anything.

János came to visit me in Rome and I took him to dinner at Piero's house. I wanted my new and old friends to meet. They were both very charming to each other throughout the meal, but when we left János was very upset. I wasn't sure exactly why. I thought perhaps he had been put off by the luxury of Piero's apartment, but I wasn't sure. I had the feeling something had been upsetting János over the last few months. He seemed rather depressed and irritable.

This was still **1987** and I had not been feeling so great for a few months myself. I was afraid I was getting ill. There was one morning in particular when I wasn't feeling well. I didn't want to be alone, so after Carmen left for school I called my friend Susi. She was an American who lived in Positano with her husband, Sandy, but she was now staying on Via Sistina in Rome. We went out for a walk around the city and ended up in an area with crowds of people. Suddenly, I had no idea where I was. All I could see were hundreds of people around me. I couldn't remember what city or even which country I was in. Then, I looked up. It felt as though all the buildings seemed to be falling towards me. I couldn't see Susi anywhere and I panicked. I started calling her name until she finally found me. I told her I needed to go home—now.

It was all so strange. That feeling lasted several days. Each day, I would try to act normal when Carmen was home from school. I would cook her dinner and do my best to pretend everything was fine. Then as soon as she went to bed, I would go to my bedroom and drag heavy furniture in front of my balcony window. I was five stories up and it made me feel safer, just in case I began to think about trying to fly away.

I made an appointment with a doctor. When I went to see her, I was so scared that I packed a small bag in case I had to go right to hospital. Susi came over and walked with me up to the doctor's studio in Piazza Barberini. As we walked, once again I felt that the massive old buildings were all going to fall on me. The doctor examined me and asked questions about how I felt. She told me I was having a serious nervous breakdown. I couldn't believe it—a nervous breakdown?! Impossible.

She told me not to worry and wrote me a prescription. It was for Zanax, which I had never heard of before. She told me to fill the prescription immediately and take one of the pills as soon as I got it. I was to continue taking them daily until our next visit. Today Zanax is nearly as common as aspirin, but in those days no one knew about it,

not even my friends in New York and they knew a lot about little pills! Susi and I went to the pharmacy and bought the medicine. I took one pill immediately and, I swear on my daughter's head, within three minutes I was fine. I nearly started dancing in the street! I felt so well, I insisted Susi and I go shopping and have a little fun to celebrate. Susi was just so relieved I was feeling alright again and so was I.

The pills were like magic. I felt like my old self. I felt so good, I decided to paint all the rooms in our flat. I have always loved painting rooms and knew it would be a good project for me. I bought some supplies and began painting. Then one morning, I noticed I had finished the prescription and was out of pills. I didn't think that was a problem. I had been feeling just fine. The real problem I had was I had also run out of paint. So off I went to the paint shop. As I walked, I glanced up and saw all the buildings had started swaying again, as if they were falling towards me. I called the doctor immediately, but was told she wasn't in that day. I screamed at the person on the phone that I needed more pills and if I didn't get them soon, I would jump off the balcony. Within a few hours, the pills were delivered to me.

I stayed at home for several weeks and worked around the apartment trying to get my health together. It was my healing time for whatever had gone wrong in my head. I tried to figure out why this had happened. My life had been smooth sailing before this. I had enough work to pay for all we needed, great friends, a good social life and Carmen was happy at school. I couldn't understand what had brought on the nervous breakdown. It took me about a month or so before I really came back to normality.

After my world finally stopped spinning, I received a telephone call which felt worse than buildings falling on my head—much worse. János called to tell me he was HIV positive. I couldn't believe the words he was saying. It couldn't be possible—not János.

I suddenly remembered a few months before I had moved to Rome when János had asked me to look at two small lumps he had found on his neck. He had no idea what they were and I didn't either. That must have been the first sign of it. Now on the phone he said something to me like, 'Don't go telling everyone I gave you AIDS.' I wasn't sure what he meant. Sometimes when he was upset or angry it was hard to understand him.

I truly could not believe that this was happening. I began to wonder if perhaps it had been this horror which had been the cause of my depression. I've always been a bit weird with feelings and mental vibes. Could it be I had sensed this on some inner level? As I thought about the past few months, I began to realise why János had changed towards me. I knew he still loved me, but something was off between us. Now I understood. He had been acting different because he had been protecting me.

I began to wonder if I should take a test myself. To tell the truth, I didn't have the courage to go to the doctor. I was too petrified of what I might hear, so I just didn't go. I couldn't stop thinking about János' news and this horrible new reality, but life had to keep going on for me and Carmen. It even went on for János.

Later that year, I was contacted by Phoenix Productions of Berlin to work on a television film called *Die Versicherung* (*The Insurance*). Marco Serafini was the Director and Inge Meysel, a well-known German actress, was to star along with the Italian actor Guido Gagliardo. The film was to be shot near Positano in Amalfi and Massalubrense.

Some of the crew had warned me that Inge Meysel was not always easy to work with, but I didn't find her a problem. I won her over by learning the type of

food she liked and I made sure she had it. Others on the crew didn't have it so easy. More than once I saw a makeup girl in tears, as she was putting Inge's face together early in the mornings.

I knew so many people in the area, that it was easy for me to cast the extras and small Italian roles. I was even able to use Monica Aonzo from the Hotel Poseidon for a small role. A few of the locals I used have remained friends of mine, including the actor Enzo Salamone and Marianna Cafiero, who was just four years old at the time.

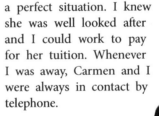

I loved my new profession. Whenever I had to be away from Rome on a set, Carmen would sleep at her school. It was a perfect situation. I knew she was well looked after and I could work to pay for her tuition. Whenever I was away, Carmen and I were always in contact by telephone.

Die Versicherung (The Insurance)

I had kept in contact with my family in Australia over the years. My brother and his wife and their children had visited me in Italy, but my mother and two sisters never came. Then I began hearing news from my siblings that our mother was not feeling well. Perhaps I should have gone home to see her, but I didn't think anything was seriously wrong, so I was shocked when I had a call from home on **3 March 1988** with the news that my mother had died. I asked my sister Joan why she hadn't told me that our mum was so ill. Joan told me my mother had totally lost her memory. When I would send photos of Carmen to her, Mum would think it was me in the photo. Joan explained that if I had have gone back to see her, she wouldn't have known who I was anyway. Joan thought it would be too upsetting for me. I suppose she was right.

I had always dreamt about returning to Magnolia Avenue to look at the little house where I grew up and to visit my high school to see if my name was still legible on the bike rack where I had scratched it back in **1954**. I could see myself arriving at the railway station in Mildura, taking a taxi to 6 Hunter Street, jumping over the small, white picket fence as I always did, banging on the front door and calling out, 'Open up, Mum. It's Jennifer. I'm home.' But now I had waited too long. Even if the house still stands, my mother was dead and I never had a chance to fulfil those dreams.

In the fall of **1988** I had a job on a film in Puglia. Around that time, Piero had decided to rent an apartment in Taormina, Sicily for a group of our friends to have for an August holiday. I realised it would be easy for me to travel from there to Monopoly in Puglia, where the film crew would be staying. At the apartment in Taormina we had a fun group of our friends, including Stefano, Guiliano, Ludovico and Maria Pia. It was a very gay holiday and lots of fun. We spent long days on the beach relaxing. At night, we went out to restaurants, followed by dancing at a well-known club, where most of the people were either men or men dressed as women. Those nights were so colourful and filled with great music and lots of laughs. When we occasionally ate at home, Stefano and Giuliano would put on fashion shows for us after going through my wardrobe and dressing up in all my evening wear.

I stayed with my friends for about a month before I had to take off for my new job working on a German TV series called *Peter Strohm*. An episode called *The Green Brigade* (*Grüne Brigade*) was being produced by Bayerischer Rundfunk Production Studios and was to be filmed in Puglia, Locorotondo and Bari. The director was Lutz Büscher and it featured the actor Klaus Löwitsch. That was my first time in Puglia. I enjoyed the location and I really enjoyed the shooting. We used a number of local police officers as extras to play the police force in the film. They seemed to have more fun being movie stars than anyone else.

In **1988** I worked on a video musical clip for the Italian singer, Francesco di Napoli. It was shot in Rocca di Papa, Frascati and Anzio. That was a short, but fun job. I was able to work with Rolando Belli, whom I had met back on the set of *Oliver Maas*. Rolando and I remained friends and we went on to work on several more films together.

The next production I worked on was *A House in Tuscany* (*Ein Haus in der Toskana*) in **1989**. I'm not entirely sure how I got that job, but by that time I knew so many people in the German film world that someone must have put me up for it. This series was probably my most important work in film. I worked with them for most of **1989** then again for another year in **1992**. The director of the entire series was Gaby Kubach of Munich and we became very close friends.

Up until then, my work on films only lasted for a few months at a time. Now I had the opportunity to work for almost a whole year on one production. I worked long enough with many of the crew that we became like a big family. Since the shooting was going to last so long, the entire crew were given apartments in a small town in Tuscany called Massa Marittima. I had to stay in the hotel

A House in Tuscany, 1989.

where we put all the actors, so I could be available when they arrived and departed.

I will never forget one morning while I was working on this job. I was driving to the set with the makeup man early on the morning of **9 November 1989**. On the radio we heard the news that the Berlin Wall had just been opened. Everyone on the set was so excited. The news meant so much to my German friends and their families. Several of the actors and crew were shedding tears. I was glad I could be there with them that day to share in the wonderful news.

Production Managers typically try to save as much money as possible during filming. As a cost-cutting measure, I was informed by our manager that I would not be working through to the end of the film and I would have to return to Rome. I was upset, but what could I do? He was the boss. I packed my case, called a taxi and said goodbye to the few people who were around the hotel that morning. However, instead of a taxi arriving to take me to the train station, the Production Manager drove up in his car. He didn't look happy and I was quite sure it wasn't because I was leaving. He told me to get in the car and he drove me to the set. There I found the entire crew and all the actors having what seemed to be a picnic rather than shooting their scene. I was told they had decided to go on strike when they heard I was leaving. They refused to return to work until I was taken back. I was so touched. What a great feeling and what great friends. I became friends with so many of the actors and crew from *A House in Tuscany*. I loved every minute of that production. Whilst working on *A House in Tuscany*, I was able to cast Carmen in a small role as a nanny. The Music Master from St Stephen's also agreed to play a musician in the film.

When Carmen graduated from St Stephens in **1989,** she decided to continue to study acting on a higher level. She went on to study for six months at a private theatre school in Paris, which was run by Claudine Gabay. The school was in Pigalle, right by the Moulin Rouge and under Montmartre. That was the centre for all the prostitutes and transvestites in Paris. I was worried about sending Carmen to school there knowing she would be walking alone at night in the middle of that neighbourhood. Claudine assured me it was actually one of the safest places in the city for Carmen to be at night. She said the prostitutes on the street would come to recognise the young girls at the school and they would all watch out for their safety. The school was a wonderful experience for Carmen. She told me about her time there saying, 'Classes ended at 10.30 pm, so the women on the street were in full business when I got out. I had gone to Paris to practice my French and also prepare for my auditions for London, so between Molière and Shakespeare I had a full plate. Claudine was like a character from a novel. She had intense, wide eyes and constantly had a cigarette in her mouth. I loved living in Paris. It is an astonishing city. By the time I left, I knew every alley in the city and I had also learned all of Brel and Piaf by heart.'

More names on The List: Cookie Mueller and Vittorio Scarpati. Cookie and Vittorio were friends of mine who lived in New York, but came to Positano for a few months every summer. Cookie was a writer and actor, who had grown up in Baltimore along with John Waters, Divine and Mink Stole. They were all part of the group who acted in John Water's films, including *Pink Flamingos, Female Troubles, Multiple Maniacs* and *Polyester*. Scott had introduced me to Cookie one day when she was with the photographer Nan Goldin. Scott had met Cookie when they were both living in Provincetown, Massachusetts. Vittorio had come from a family from an area close to Positano. I adored Cookie. She was wild and fantastic and so much fun. Everyone in town knew her. Her son Max was close in age to Carmen and they became friends. Max even stayed with us for about a month one summer.

Once Cookie took Carmen and Max on a little day trip to Capri back when they were about 12 years old. Carmen remembers it as quite an adventure:

Cookie bought the three of us round-trip tickets for the boat to Capri and we set off. When we reached Capri, we met two of Cookie's girlfriends at the port. While they were all talking, Max and I heard that the last boat leaving the island would be at

Carmen

Cookie Mueller and Vittorio Scarpati.

a room?' Eventually she found a place which offered to give us one room for all five of us to share. Somehow Cookie even convinced them to give us dinner for free too.

Of course, Cookie and her friends went out that night. They were three beautiful women. They knew they wouldn't need any money to get drinks. Max wanted to stay in the room, but Cookie tried to take me with them. I looked older than 12, but not old enough for a club. Cookie took me to a perfume shop and sat me in a chair. Then, using all of the tester makeup in the shop, she made me up in her style. She always wore lots of heavy makeup. Cookie was enjoying it. She said now she could treat me like the daughter she never had. I loved it too. I was always into theatre and makeup and the way she did my makeup was way over the top. We went to the club, but even with

3.00 that afternoon. Max and I were little mischief makers then. We didn't want to go back that early, so we didn't tell them what we had heard. We spent the day at a pool and as the afternoon went on, Max and I kept asking if we could stay a little longer—just one more jump in the pool, just one more… We kept it up until it was after 3.00. Max and I were so excited that we had succeeded in getting them to miss the boat. Now we would be able to stay overnight! We didn't realise Cookie and her friends didn't have any money for a hotel, or food, or for the return tickets on the boat. The tickets we had were non-refundable.

Cookie was always very resourceful and was used to finding ways to get by. She took us around to all the tiny hotels and told them we had missed the boat and had no money. She would use Max and me to try to convince them saying, 'My children have nowhere to sleep. Could you please give us

Carmen, Carolina and Max Mueller.

the makeup, they wouldn't let me in. It was a rather heavy-handed, all-night club, so it was probably for the best that they refused to let me go inside. Cookie walked me back to the hotel and then joined her friends at the club. I'm not even sure the three of them came back to the hotel that night.

The next morning, they were all seriously hung over. The other two women went off on their own to try to get a boat to Napoli. Cookie took Max and me and we headed to the boat for Sorrento to see what she could do. When we got there, Cookie started waving our old tickets at the men by the boat trying to explain that we had no way to get back. She knelt down in front of them and dramatically started pleading, 'Per favore signore, for the children! Per favore!' Eventually they got tired of her begging and let us on the boat. We got to Sorrento, but we still needed to get

back to Positano, so we start hitchhiking. By that time, we were quite a sight. Cookie was hungover, her makeup was a mess and we all had the same clothes on for two days. We looked like a bunch of gypsies. An elegant old car pulled up and I was surprised to see they were people I knew—a couple who owned a jewellery store in Sorrento. They asked what I was doing with these other two. I gave them some type of explanation and thankfully they gave us a ride home. It was an incredible trip. I don't think Max and I ever admitted to Cookie that it had been our fault that we missed the boat that day.

I remember one year Cookie and I had signed our children up for a summer camp in Rome. The day we were to take them there, Cookie showed up in full makeup and wearing a tiny leather mini skirt. On the train to Sorrento, Max broke out in some type of rash all over his body. It caused Cookie and Max to turn back home. I was sorry for Max, but honestly I was a bit relieved for myself. I really didn't want to show up with Cookie at the camp. I didn't think she was dressed the way you should be to drop your child off at camp.

The last time I saw Cookie was in Positano at Bar de Martino. I had seen Vittorio outside. He looked awful and was perspiring like crazy. I asked Cookie what was wrong with him and she just said he wasn't feeling well. Thinking back, I'm fairly certain he already had AIDS. Cookie may have had it too by then. Vittorio died in New York on **14 September 1989** and Cookie passed way less than two months later on **10 November**.

In early **1990**, not long after the shooting was over for *A House in Tuscany*, I had a request from Sveriges Television, the Swedish national public television broadcaster in Stockholm, to work on a film for television called *Express*. Pelle Seth, the director, asked me how the shooting had gone in the locations where we had filmed *A House in Tuscany*. I told him it was the perfect place to film, so they decided to shoot a small part of *Express* in the same place.

The film was to be shot mainly in Sweden, but they wanted to use a few locations in Italy including Massa Marittma, Niccioleta and the train station in Civitella Paganico.

The Production Manager, Johan Mardell, told me my job would involve some casting, however he had no Production Manager Assistant, so I would have that position as well. That was another great job. It was quite short, but it was fun. I found it interesting to work on a non-German production for the first time.

Following *Express*, I was asked to work on another Swedish film titled *The Best Intentions*, which was directed by Bille August. The film was about the early years of the relationship between Ingmar Bergman's parents. We shot in and around a hotel in the centre of Sorrento and in Paestum with its magnificent Greek temples. We also shot a view overlooking Positano, where we waited for hours until the light was just perfect.

Carmen was home on holiday during this production, so she came along with me to Sorrento when I had to prepare all the beautiful costumes, which were in the style of the early 1900s. Carmen also came on set when we were doing some of the shooting. She ended up helping me on the set close to Bille August when I was blocking the roads. Bille August told me when this film was over he was off to Spain to shoot *House of the Spirits*. He

told me I could come and work on that film next, provided I could speak a little Spanish. It was such a pity that I didn't.

Working on *The Best Intentions* gave me another experience shooting with Swedes. It was quite different working with them than it was with Germans or Italians. The Swedes ate very little at lunch and absolutely no alcohol was served while we were working. They were all so very quiet on set. It was all very serious and professional, but when the day's shooting was over, we would all go off to the restaurants and then the drinking would really begin.

My work on *The Best Intentions* only lasted about three weeks, but it was the most well-known film I had been involved in. It won the Palme d'Or at the **1992** Cannes Film Festival and at that time, it was one of the most expensive Swedish films ever made.

Germany became a second home for me while I was working on the German productions. I travelled there frequently for work. In addition to János and Justus, I had many good friends in Munich so I felt quite at home there. I was also able to see many of the new friends I had made in the film business. Dieter Graber lived in Munich and he and I kept in touch for many years. I had heard that soon after he retired he and his girlfriend went on holiday to Phuket, Thailand. They

The Best Intentions.

were there when the terrible tsunami hit in 2004. I heard Dieter died in the storm. His girlfriend had survived but had been seriously injured.

During one of my stays in Munich I was invited to dinner at Justus' house. He had invited a few film people over whom he wanted me to meet. Towards the end of the dinner, János arrived with his friend Marion and a man called Gebhard, who knew Marion from boarding school. The four of us headed off to a bar, which seemed to be in the middle of the woods. Gebhard was very charming and right from the start there was powerful chemistry between us.

A few days later, Marion suggested we visit Gebhard at his house outside of Munich. His house was a beautiful mansion situated on a large property. Gebhard was very happy to see us and he asked us to stay with him for a few days. The few days somehow turned in to 12 mad and magical days. None of us had much money, so we ate boiled rice. Fortunately there was a good supply of wine, which we drank out of silver goblets. We entertained ourselves by playing Hide and Seek or Hide the Ring. Sometimes Gebhard would play the piano whilst Marion and I danced around the room like ballerinas. We would stay up all night and then in the morning we would all drive to a well-known pub nearby, where priests served us beer. I heard that Marco from the Poseidon happened to be in Munich, so we invited him out to join us at the mad mansion. Marco seemed to enjoy our weird life in the mansion. I remember hiding in a wardrobe together with Marco trying desperately not to giggle during one game of Hide and Seek. Then one day Marion and János stuck me on a train and sent me back to Italy. I realised they were both in love with Gebhard and were rather jealous of his growing attentions towards me.

Gebhard and I had many super little outings during that time. One time we took a trip to Herrenchiemsee on the lake of Chiemsee to visit the palace of crazy King Ludwig. We even thought about hiding there overnight to spend the night in the king's bed!

I often saw Gebhard when I went to Munich. He and I got on so well together that we continued to see each other whenever we could. Even now, after more than thirty years we are still very close friends. He eventually got married and I am now close to his wife, children and grandchildren too. I could go on and on about my friendship with Gebhard, but that would take too long. A friendship like ours can never be broken.

János in Life, in Death and in Dreams

I cannot tell you how difficult it is for me to write this section about János. As I wrote this, I kept making mistake after mistake and my computer kept playing up. I had the feeling that János was up to his tricks. I began to think he didn't want me to write about this time of our life because he knows it will still upset me.

János was in Positano for his 42nd birthday on **11 June 1991** and we decided to throw a big party for him in his favourite trattoria, the Grottino Azzuro. So many of his friends came to be with him on that evening that his party took over the entire restaurant. We all knew his health was getting weaker, which made it such a bittersweet evening. There was so much love, but also much sadness at the party. I will never forget what János said to me as we left to go home: 'Well, I made it to 42, but I'll never see 43.' I was afraid he might be right, but I still hoped a miracle might happen.

János returned to Munich for a while and then he called to say he wanted to come back to Positano to begin the illustrations for my book— for this book. We met in Naples so he could buy the art supplies he needed before we continued on to Positano. I didn't think János looked very well, but he acted as if he was fine. He didn't talk much about his illness, other than to ask me to give him injections every evening which had been prescribed by his doctor. I wasn't sure I could do that—the only shots I had ever given were to my dog. János said not to worry, he would put the needle in his arm just a weeny bit and then I would only have to push it in for him.

János and I would go out to restaurants or to Bar Internazionale with friends or the two of us

would just have quiet times at home together. He began work on the illustrations. The first drawing he did was of me as a little girl under a gum tree. I was holding a koala in my arms. After a few days, he began to look really ill. I called Justus and told him János had to go back to Germany.

When he returned to Munich, János was immediately put into hospital to begin treatment. As soon as I could, I went to Munich to be with him. I stayed at his apartment and would pedal a bicycle to the hospital each day to visit him. I was surprised and happy to see that after his treatments he looked so much better than he had in Positano. He hadn't lost weight and his skin was as smooth as satin. Deep inside I was still hoping for a miracle.

I had to return to Rome and by the time I could get back to Munich again he was out of hospital so I stayed with him at his house. He was busy working on a painting of Carmen and her boyfriend, which he gave to us. That painting still hangs in my house. His health seemed to be pretty good, so after a while he told me I should go back to Rome. He said he would let me know when it was time for me to come back again.

The next months are a blur of me going back and forth to see him and him going in and out of hospital. His health began to decline further. Then János went back into hospital one more time, but they sent him right home again. Apparently, there was no more that could be done.

When I heard the news, I flew to Munich as soon as I could. I was shocked when I saw János. He was down to only about forty kilos. He was still quite lucid, but he had caught the chicken

Carmen and János.

pox and it made his face itchy. He was continually scratching. It was a horror to see him suffer like that. Marco came from Positano to see him. I had warned Marco that he would be shocked at how much János had changed. He didn't believe me, until he saw János himself. He couldn't believe how thin he was. A group of us stayed with him and played cards that night. János insisted on keeping score. I could tell he was making mistakes in the scoring, but when I commented on it, he just told me to mind my own business. Carmen flew in from London to see him. She loved János very much and wanted to say goodbye. He continued to grow weaker and more frail. Eventually he lost his eyesight. More friends came to say goodbye. He was getting so bad that I began to pray or chant that he would die quickly.

Dream—3rd January 1992

I was dancing with János. He was strong like before and we were laughing. We were outside on a large terrace along with many other people. Music was playing loudly. János came towards me and we danced and danced. I think it was a tango. We were twirling and twirling around together. It felt wonderful and could feel the strength of his arm against the small of my back as he held me. It was such an exciting and emotional dream.

Karl, Jacques and Volker, three of his friends from Cologne, came to stay with János. They were there with us on the night of **4 January 1992**. His friend Jacques asked me if I would like to come into the bedroom and help him clean János' face. I went in and quietly asked Jacques what I should do. János was blind and weak, but he heard me and called out, 'Jennie, what is your problem now!?' That was such a János thing to say. We cleaned his face and went out to the living room where Justus was discussing the plans for the funeral. About ten minutes later, I went back into the bedroom to check on him. János was dead.

Justus sent everyone downstairs to his apartment, but he said that I could stay with János. I would have even stayed without his permission. János had been my best friend for 16 years. I simply could not believe he was gone.

When the ambulance arrived, I watched as two medics put János' body into a long plastic bag. As they closed the zipper —*zzzzzzzz*, I felt I had died too. I will always remember the sound of that zipper.

A couple of nights after János died, I dreamt about him again:

János was looking his beautiful self. I cried, but that was okay with him. He didn't yell or get angry. I wanted to ask him so many questions, but I decided to bury them with him. It felt like we were together for such a long time. We talked and talked just like old times. He was dressed in very dark colours, which was unusual for him. He had rarely dressed that way before. When I woke, I felt as though I had really had a visit from János. It didn't feel like a dream at all.

The funeral was a few days later. Naturally, Justus had János buried in the best cemetery in Munich. He had invited many film people. A few of János' friends in their blue jeans and leather jackets were there as well. I knew them all. A big part of my life vanished along with János, but he will always be with me in my heart.

Carmen loved János very much too. She and I both knew János had wanted to be cremated and not put in a box. She wrote a poem about that:

ODE TO A BOX
Shoved in a box
Flesh saturating with the bittersweet taste
of relentless steel
It is such an elegant way to dispose of the
deceased
'Oh, nasty business—let us put him in a
box. We have a large array of boxes;
marble metal wood, gold-rimmed, plain,
simple, lacquered, elegant, austere,
baroque, thick, thin, heavy, light, bright,
reserved, long, short, octagonal—and of
course, all lined with stainless steel.'
They call it the will of God
AMEN
Press the cork in a bottle's neck and it will
hold in a scream—
No one will hear it—it can never escape.
A scream for
All eternity.
Such civilized silence.
We shall dress him in his favorite suit and
arrange his lovely curls as we used to like
them—as he used to like them, of course.
A final touch of blush and jewellery—
Except the box was so—so terribly
expensive—the gold-rimmed one,
you know
—and octagonal of course, as he stiffened
in such an awkward position. We could
not bare to have his bones bro—yes well,
you know. Oh and you should see
the wonderful flower arrangement.
A grand farewell. Should silence any
scream.
Why can't you throw me into the sea, into
that never-ending viavai of life?
Pecked by a seagull, entwined by seaweed,
kissed by an octopus, devoured by a whale
drowned by music and laughter from a
distant ship

Segregated. Outcast by stainless steel.
Little boys are told to stand in a corner or
to apologize.
That's it! I've done something wrong—
something bad—if I just apologize the
steel will melt away.
Steel does not just melt. Designed to
endure all kinds of weather—
all kinds of lives.
Who lies in the box beside me?
BOX
Funny word—booox,bbbox,box
It echoes.
I can hear the life outside—but it cannot
hear me.
I can hear roots growing—sucking juices
from the earth—the moist warm earth.
Stainless steel. Shiny and clean. It blocks
out memory—blinds the senses.
I begin to forget.
A worm knocked into my box—I heard it
—he's mustering now—always laying
their construction in my way.
Yes! That's it. Like giving Mother Nature
a nose job.
Why can't I feed the worms or the roots?
How disgusting—worms crawling into
your eye sockets and eating your brain. We
shall be kept clean in stainless steel.
Disgusting style of life?
'It's not for us; shut up in a box instead.
Preserve us.'
Preserve us as we rot.
Beautiful cycle of life. I want my ashes to
fly through you and feed you over
and over.
Must I be barren and milk less too?
Must I listen to the creak of the decrepit
old woman as she rocks all day—she has
Fitted bars on every window—
she will not look out or let anyone in.
You are all so afraid of life.
Stainless steel.
Prison may be a life sentence—
this is a death sentence.

After the funeral, I was too upset to leave Munich. My friend Marion let me stay in one of her spare apartments. I would often visit the cemetery to chat to János. Each time I went, it seemed I could never find his grave and would have to go to the office and ask them where he was again and again. The film production of *A House in Tuscany* was organising for the second series and they had offered me a job. I didn't want to go to their offices. I really didn't feel like going anywhere, but I needed a job. I didn't know what to do. So, I asked myself what would János tell me to do. I knew what his answer would have been, so I went and got the job.

It was **1992** when I returned to Massa Marittima and back to *A House in Tuscany*. Gaby Kubach was still directing, but there was a new Production Manager, a new Camera Man and quite a few other new faces.

One day I went to work on the set and was told, 'We need prostitutes' and they wanted real ones. When I went to try to find some prostitutes, I didn't want to go alone, so I took Alex, the Assistant Director. We tried to talk to some Street Ladies, but their pimp showed up and put an end to that. Finally, we found one young woman who said she would help us. She took us to a boarding house where several of the prostitutes lived and we found some women who agreed to be in our film.

In addition to shooting at the actual house in Toscana, we were often on the road in Florence, Sienna and other interesting locations. Towards the end of the season, we were rather behind schedule. There was one big scene which they had planned to shoot in a hospital in Italy, but instead they transferred the scene to Munich. One day the new Production Manager told me they would be shooting in Munich and since I didn't speak German I would have to leave the crew. It took the Director only about a minute to tell him that if Jennie didn't go, then none of them would go. That was another victory for me!

In Munich, my first big job was to find a number of Italian extras. Where would I find Italians in Germany? Italian restaurants, of course. I scouted around to any restaurants I could find. I also found an Italian theatre group and then called any of my Italian friends who I knew were in Munich. Within a few days I was over crowded with Italians.

My work on *A House in Tuscany* lasted a year and it was wonderful. When the shooting was over, I went to the Berlitz School of Languages to see about learning a little German. They told me they had a teacher who could stay with me each day. We would have breakfast, lunch and dinner together whilst I learnt German. They told me I would be speaking the language quite well after eleven weeks. That all sounded too good to be true—until they told me the price. I nearly fainted. I was making good money in this profession, but not enough for that. I didn't know what to say, I think I asked them how much it would be if I didn't eat the meals and then I left with only the few words I already knew in Deutsch.

Carmen and I went to Vienna on holiday and both of us were continually dreaming about János. We decided to make a pilgrimage to Hungary in his honour. We knew János had never been able to return to his home, so we thought we would go for him. We wanted to bring him back to life, even if only in our minds.

We took a train from Vienna to Budapest. When we arrived, we went to a travel agency where we met a man named Tibor, who became our guardian angel for the trip. I told Tibor why we had come to Hungary and gave him a number I had for János' aunt in Sweden, so he could get some further information about János' early life. Tibor found us a room to rent in a private home owned by a woman named Ester. She was very kind and although she didn't speak any English we managed to get by with the help of some dictionaries she had on hand. We had two rooms, a bathroom and a TV set for very little money. That evening we toured the Centre of Pest on foot. I thought it was such a beautiful city. János and I had talked many times about visiting Budapest. It felt strange that now I was here without him. Ester insisted on cooking us bacon and eggs for supper and then we fell into bed early. We were exhausted and slept for twelve hours.

On **Friday 18 December 1992**, Ester woke us early and we went back to Tibor for more advice. He told us to take a taxi to the 14th district where we could find Okiz Labor, a clothing factory where

A House in Tuscany, 1992.

JANOS

János had worked many years ago. I knew János had worked as a model when he was younger. He may have been a model for this company. The people at the factory were a little suspicious of us. They had never heard of János Zsigmond. We showed them his photo, but everyone just shook their heads no. They wanted to know why we were looking for him. They thought perhaps he was in trouble. 'So, where is he now?', one man asked. When I told him he was dead, the man looked surprised and quickly hurried us out of the office saying he was very sorry.

Tibor had connected us to his friend Robert, a driver who spoke perfect English. Robert was willing to drive us anywhere we needed to go and he could act as our translator as well. On **Saturday 19 December 1992**, Robert drove us to Szabadegyhaza. We found the distillery where János' father, László Zsigmond, had been the director. We were presented to Ferenc Selmeczi, who introduced us to his seven brothers, all of whom remembered László with great admiration. When we departed, Ferenc burst into tears. I am sure Carmen and I were doing the same thing.

We visited an apartment building where János had lived back in the 60s with his friend Georg. It was a tall slum-like building with broken windows, bad smells and sad tenants. We knocked on every door and showed anyone we could find a photo of János, but once again we only had people shaking their heads no saying 'nem, nem nem. We never knew him.' We also met János' elementary school teacher whilst visiting his school. He promised to send me János' report book from his last year at the school.

That night I had a vision. There was a large window in our bedroom, so it wasn't totally dark. I was staring at an armchair close to my bed and I could see a man sitting there. When I looked at his face, I saw it was János. It seemed his face began to move closer and closer to me. I screamed and Carmen woke up. When she put on the light,

Top: Jennie, Carmen and Ferenc Selmeczi.
Bottom: Visit with János' aunt, Ilona.

us a cup of tea and showed photos of the family. This was the closest contact from János' past that we had come across. Ilona asked me what sort of man János was—if he was really a man… I knew what the aunt was insinuating. I told her János was one of the most special men I had ever known and I loved him very much. When I told her he had died of cancer, she immediately said, 'No, not cancer, AIDS.' Robert was translating all of this for us. I hadn't told Robert the whole story, just that János had died. Robert lived though two full days with us on this emotional journey. When I had first met him, I felt he was very sensitive and I was right. He was the perfect person to go through this drama with us. When we said goodbye to Robert, he had tears in his eyes. He told us, 'I like you both very much and this has been an adventure for me. I even liked the lapses of silence.' He was referring to the silence in the car each time we had discovered something or someone connected to János' past.

The night before we left, I saw a poster on a wall, advertising a concert with Blood Sweat and Tears. I was thrilled. They were one of my favourite groups in the old days. The concert was quite a long way outside of the centre of town and we only had enough money for the tickets, which wouldn't have left enough for us for transportation there and back, so we couldn't go. Later that night, Carmen and I were passing by an opera house which was having a free Christmas concert. We weren't at all dressed for an opera house, but we went just the same. It was a magical way to spend our final night in János' city.

I could see I had been looking at my shawl draped over the back of the chair. I think all those days of reliving János' past life were becoming a little too much for me!

Sunday 20 December 1992 was our last day in Hungary. We had found an address of one of János' teachers who was living in Rakosgsaba. When we arrived at the address, an old man opened the door. His wife was the teacher and she also happened to be János' great-aunt Ilona. She knew everything about János. She offered

The next morning we left Budapest for Munich. We went to the cemetery: Plot 94 – Row 7 – Grave 8. We wanted to tell János of our adventure. His friend Clause had put a veil of pine leaves over the grave along with two wreaths of pinecones and a red candle. We brought János some white tulips and mimosa.

A few months later I received a letter from Robert, our driver in Budapest. It was dated **15 March 1993**:

Dear Jennie,

I received your letter and pictures two weeks ago. Thank you very much. Forgive me that I answer so late, but I really had to find some quiet hours to answer. This is not easy, because reading your letter and staring at János' photo I have so many feelings and emotions that I am not able to write a short objective letter.

First let us talk about business. I am sending Mr Nemet's very kind card. The translation is as follows:

Dear Madam,

I found János Zsigmond, our former pupil's material in our register. The birth register contains exactly those data, which you told me. In the Yearbook of 1965 on pages 68 and 80, can be found his name and his results. Probably he finished the second school year already in September, but he didn't matriculate in the third year. Well, where he went and continued his studies, nobody knows on base of these documents. I send you the Yearbook of the school.

Sorry it is so worn and not aesthetic. Firm and frequent use and the book was made of weak paper. I wish you pleasant journeys and good health.
Yours faithfully,
Pal Nemet, teacher

When I am writing this letter, I have the picture in front of me. I learn more and more about Zsigmond János. I like this charming picture. But I don't feel anything emotionally about him, but I do about you. I tried to describe to you in the car, what I felt. (I don't know if I succeeded.) Meanwhile I have found the right phrase, cathartic. Those were two cathartic days in my life. It may sound strange, but I felt so happy in your company and every time I think of you, I feel cathartic happiness, dearness and belief I felt with you.

Let me finish this letter with some words about myself: I have been working in a Travel Agency called IBUSZ, for three weeks. My duty is to entertain foreigners, provide the accommodation, programs etc… This is a nonstop office, so once I work by day, once by night. I have many free time. As you know I went for skiing to the mountains, I had time for thinking. I found out a new theory; I divided people into two parts; animal-people and conscious-people. The main difference between them that the animal-people are driven by feelings and emotions, while the others by brain. I don't want to write long about this, because I am sure that you understand exactly what I mean, as you and Carmen and me, we are animal-people. I can admire or pay attention to conscious people, but not love. Love is for nature, animals, plants and of course animal-people. Forgive me for this meditation, but I felt a strong need to talk about this to you and hope that you are both all right.
Yours affectionally, Robert

Carmen wrote back to him, but she never received an answer.

A 'Girl Friday' at The Poseidon

Vern Lambert, my mentor and dear friend, died on **19 August 1992**. I hope he met up with János. I also hope János didn't have a jealous fit when Vern told him all the things we did together! Goodbye Vern. We will meet again one day.

Another name on The List: Piero Guanieri, my friend in Rome. Piero had been very dear to me during János' illness and death. Then a while after I lost János, Piero asked me to his house and told me that he was HIV positive too. Piero knew I had a friend in New York who was an AIDS researcher. He asked me if I could send his results to him and get his opinion. I could feel Piero's desperation, so of course I wanted to do what I could do to help.

Piero had a friend named Sandro who also had AIDS. They both wanted a break from Rome, so they went to Calabria to Sandro's mother. Piero asked me if I would join them there. The place was near a beautiful sanctuary that had water which many believed had healing powers. People would make pilgrimages there to drink the sacred water. Piero and Sandro decided to give it a try. After a couple of days of us driving there, drinking the water and driving back to where we were staying, I had an idea. I suggested that we take a *demigiano* jar and fill it up so we wouldn't have to make the trip each day. I thought it was a great idea, but no one else did. I guess that wasn't how the cure was supposed to work.

Shortly after we returned to Rome, both Piero and Sandro ended up in a hospital which had a large ward exclusively for AIDS patients. The ward was always filled with patients and their visitors. I found it an incredibly sad place to visit. I left Rome to move back to Positano and never saw them again. I heard Sandro had died first and then Piero about a year later. I continued to hope a miracle would happen to stop all these deaths.

On **6 January 1993** Rudolf Nureyev died of complications from AIDS. I suppose that means

he should be part of The List too. Later that year Federico Fellini died on **31 October**.

Carmen was now studying in London. After attending Claudine Gabey's school in Paris, Carmen had decided she wanted to continue to study theatre. In **1990** she and I travelled to London where she had an audition for the Guildford Theatre School. A few months later she went back alone for another audition to the Guildhall School of Music and Drama. She loved the Guildhall School and was so excited when she was accepted. She studied there from September **1990** through **1993**. Those three years at Guildhall were so full on for her. She wrote this about her time there: 'It was a vital and deep experience, where the deeper self struggled to emerge. I had many teachers from all over the world. I studied with Naohiko Umewake with whom I later trained in the Noh Theater in Japan. The Guildhall had an exchange with the Moscow Academy. I found the Russians to be the most remarkable teachers. They have a way of making theatre a riveting experience. And of course I could never forget Yevgenyi who would suddenly scream out while he was directing, "My fuck, you are genius!" At Guildhall we did everything: circus arts, singing, *commedia dell'arta*, radio, kitchen sink drama, Greek tragedy, Shakespeare and even imitating animals... We had to spend every weekend of our first semester at the zoo. The seeds of all my experiences there will bloom within me for the rest of my life.'

It was **1993** and since Carmen was now in London, I felt free to live wherever I wanted and Positano was my choice. I had no other film projects lined up for the immediate future, so I wasn't sure what I would do for work next. Marco asked me if I would like to do some promotion for the Hotel Poseidon. He wanted me to go on a promotion tour to London and Vienna. He must have known that would appeal to me. Carmen was in London and I had close film friends from *A House in Tuscany* who lived in Vienna. I went and must

have done a good job, because when I returned Marco offered me a permanent job as the PR manager for the hotel.

I already knew the Poseidon well. I was close friends with Liliana, Monica and particularly, with Marco and I had gone to many wonderful parties at their hotel. I remember their Black & Red party. Everyone had to come dressed in red or black. There was so much red that night the terrace looked like a field of poppies. The party was an auction to help the stray dogs of Positano. I certainly couldn't miss that. My friend Lisa Perugi was the Master of Ceremonies that night. I was surprised she was there. I've known Lisa for many years. She and her then husband Marcello Perugi used to throw fabulous parties at their villa. In all that time, I had never seen her with any of 'man's best friends'.

I started at the Poseidon in **November 1993** and I quickly discovered that working in a hotel

wasn't very different than working in the film business. Perhaps, I had wanted to think that at first. I missed running around a film set. I think deep down I hoped one day I would be able to do more of that work, but for now the Poseidon was a good substitute. You see, in a hotel you have the owners, who are like directors. The guests are like extras, either staying for many scenes or just passing through. The staff are like the film crew. Each are very important in their own way and each knows what they have to do to make the hotel run smoothly.

When I first started, I wasn't quite sure what I was supposed to do or maybe they didn't know where exactly I would fit in. I was in charge of PR, but I was also sort of a 'Girl Friday' or a trouble shooter. I would do whatever needed to be done. Even working in the gardens was be fine by me.

I was often rambling about in the gardens of the hotel, picking off dead leaves and flowers or tying up plants. I've always loved working with nature and have always been a bit obsessive about removing dead flowers and plants. I have to tell you a little tale I heard years ago, which I think is why I get so crazy about this. It's a true story about the Siamese twins Chang and Eng who lived in the early **1800s**. They had been brought around the world as a curiosity by a Scottish man named Hunter. Later they married two sisters and between the two brothers 21 children were born. Chang became an alcoholic (I cannot imagine being attached to another person who drank too much!) and his health grew worse and worse, until one night Chang died when they were both asleep. Eng died just three hours later. That is why I cannot bare to see dead leaves or flowers clutching onto live plants. They make me remember poor Eng having a dead alcoholic brother clinging onto him in bed!

I actually met one of our good clients when I was gardening at the Poseidon. Gisela was from Germany and she visited the hotel once or twice a year. On her first visit she was staying in Room No. 1, which was one of the rooms that had been part of the original villa before it had been turned into a hotel. Room No. 1 had a small balcony where Gisela would often sit and read in the sun. Below the balcony was a garden, which was only accessible to the staff and gardener.

While Gisela was staying with us, I noticed the walls outside of her room were rather weather stained and ugly looking. I decided to buy some *Vita Americana*, a common vine in Positano, which usually comes about three meters long. I knew it would immediately look as though it had been growing there for years and my wall problem would be over. I had two young boys from the nursery bring over meters of the vines and the three of us made our way to Gisela's balcony to attach them to the walls. We didn't realise the poor woman was sitting there in her chair in her birthday suit getting a little sun! What could I say? The vines had to be put up. I apologised, but

Ed Wittstein's postcard of Hotel Poseidon.

I didn't offer to leave. Gisela was very sweet about it. She stayed where she was. Fortunately she had been reading a very large book, which came in handy. She and I chattered away whilst the two boys attached the creepers to the walls. She must have thought, what a strange hotel to have a gardening crew which works on your terrace even though you are sitting there in the nude and they don't even ask if they should come back when it was more convenient? Actually, Gisela and I became good friends, as I did with a few thousand other clients who stayed with us.

There was so much to do around the hotel in those days. It felt like changing scenes in a film. I was moving furniture around, hanging paintings and putting fresh flowers in all the rooms whenever they needed it. As I walked around with bunches of flowers in my arms I sometimes felt like Eliza from *My Fair Lady*, but instead of selling bunches of violets, I was putting flowers into vases. By the end of the season, I must have carried thousands of flowers and hundreds of vases.

There was a small room at the hotel which never seemed to be used by any of the guests, even though it had glass doors which opened onto the terrace by the swimming pool. There was something about that room that made everyone think it was private. It had heavy blue drapes, which were nearly always closed to the view. Inside there were just two divans and a low table with a television set on it. I asked the owners if I could re-do the room and I was delighted when they said yes.

We covered the doors and window with curtains, so the clients wouldn't see what we were doing. We wanted it to be a surprise for them. The workers were using power tools and making quite a bit of noise. It was May, so there were already many clients in the pool area. Each morning I would apologise for the noise and tell them all their drinks were on the house. No one ever asked for a free drink. They were all just excited to see what was happening behind the curtains in the little room.

A new fireplace was installed and a marble bar was erected under the large window, which faced the living room. Bob and Ed wanted to lend a hand in decorating the space. Ed had designed menus and postcards for the hotel and now both of them wanted to leave their mark in the secret little room behind the curtains. They thought we should do it all in black and white to give it a completely new feel. We bought little white tiled tables, which could be used singularly or put together to seat larger groups and some black plastic chairs. Plastic in a classy hotel such as the Poseidon may sound ghastly, but it worked. There was a small black stand-up piano, which guests could play. Jono Coleman the Australian-English comedian and TV star used to come and stomp out jazz during cocktail hour. Jono was a frequent guest with his wife, Margot, and their children. He named the new space 'Jennie's Bar' and the name remained until I eventually left the Poseidon. The little bar has had so many new looks over the past years, but no matter if it is dressed up or dressed down, it always has a magical feeling.

The Poseidon had become the place for people to stop by in the evening for a drink or dinner. There were always interesting people there and something amusing was always happening. We organised many special events. We had fashion shows for up to 200 guests, who watched models display the latest designs on a little catwalk over the pool. We held many art exhibitions, where the guests would be given free drinks. The free drinks sometimes brought in more guests than the art. More than once I heard someone whisper as they left the exhibit, 'Oops. I forgot to look at the paintings.'

After my first year of working at the hotel, I was given the opportunity to rent an apartment on the premises. It was right under Marco's flat and Monica lived in a small villa close by. It was perfect for us. We worked such long hours and that way we didn't have a long way to get home.

Opening day for the season was always quite stressful, but also lots of fun. For the first few years, our work the night before the opening lasted into the wee hours of the morning. The hotel crew would be laying carpets on the main staircase from the top to the bottom all the way down the four floors. Others would be running around with buckets of paint, giving any last finishing touches to the walls. The cleaning ladies would be wiping off any traces of dust from the furniture and the reception staff would be carefully checking that everything was sparkling for the arrival of the first guests. As time went on, opening day became more organised, although there were always last minute things to do before the clients stepped into their rooms.

Watching the staff work together was a joy. They were a special group of people, always smiling, never overpowering and always at your service for whenever and whatever was needed. The pages of the hotel's Visitors Book were full of praise for the staff—of course, that was all due to the Aonzo family, who had chosen them.

After a few years at the Poseidon I began to feel as though I was working in *Faulty Towers*, the BBC production with John Cleese. You will soon see what I mean…

One time, we had a British tour group stay with us. They were all upper class and of a certain

The Hotel Poseidon #1.

age. They spent their days out touring the area and when they returned to the hotel one evening, one of the women said she wasn't feeling well. We called a doctor to check on her. Then she had a light supper and went to bed. At 6.00 o'clock the next morning, I was woken by my telephone. It was Monica. She asked me to go to the garden and cut some roses and then bring them to Room 27, because the woman had died. I went to the rose garden and cut a bouquet. A few minutes later, I was knocking on the door of Room 27. There was no answer, so I knocked a few more times. It didn't occur to me that the woman's husband had been transferred to another room and of course the woman couldn't open the door, because she was dead!

There were certain documents which had to be obtained before the woman could be removed from her room. Her poor distraught husband was taken back to England by a couple of his friends, who had been travelling with them.

Later that evening as I was checking on clients in the bar, a German man called me over to his table. He wanted me to look at his wife's face, which was covered in red spots. I knew this couple well and knew they were big beer drinkers. I was never certain when they were being serious or having fun with me. I looked at her spots and I was quite sure she had the chicken pox. I told them to finish their beers and go to bed. I would have a doctor in to see her in the morning. The next morning I went to their room, which was Room 28—right next door to Room 27. The husband let me in and as I went towards the bed, I let out a scream. The woman was lying there and her face was the most terrifying colour. Her husband told me to calm down. He said she had just put calamine lotion all over her face to ease the itching. The doctor came and confirmed it was chicken pox. He told her not to leave their room under any circumstances. I begged her not to leave the room too. I didn't want any of our clients to see her face like that, nor did I want them to catch chicken pox from her. So, we now had a corpse in Room 27 and a case of chicken pox in Room 28.

I telephoned the kitchen and asked the chef Gennaro to prepare a bowl of chicken soup and have it taken to Room 28. Gennaro was confused and said, 'I thought that woman was dead.' So, I had to explain that the dead one was in Room 27 and the chicken soup was for Room 28 where our client with chicken pox was staying.

The following morning I saw Madam chicken pox sitting on the divan near the front desk ready to leave. She had tied a scarf around her head so it covered most of her face. 'Where do you think you are going?', I whispered. She said she was getting out of there and going home. That was a relief. I wondered how she would have felt if I had told her there had been a dead person in the room next to hers!

After 48 hours, all the proper documents had been obtained and we were allowed to take the poor woman out of Room 27, but it had to be done without any of our other clients noticing. That wouldn't be easy due to the position of the room. We had to plan her exit carefully. We had a staff member on each of the staircases keeping a look out for any guests. Luigi Bozzo, the manager, and I were on the main part of the escape route with walkie talkies in our hands coordinating the move. It felt like I was back in my days on a film set blocking streets and working with extras. Somehow, we managed to get her out without notice.

In **1996**, Monica Aonzo became the Vice-Mayor of Positano. She would attend all the local ceremonies wearing her green, red and white sash. She had to spend much of her time in the Town Hall with the Mayor and his group discussing the problems of the town, organising special events and officiating at civil weddings. Most of the weddings were for foreign couples and sometimes I served as the official translator whilst Monica officiated.

For a while, Monica kept talking about a big wedding that was being planned in town. The couple was requesting all these special things, which were very expensive. They wanted to decorate the entrance and gardens of the Town Hall with all new plants. They requested that the stairs from the street down to the terrace where the ceremony would take place be filled with fresh bougainvillea. I must say, it did all look rather amazing. Monica had no idea who the couple was and she was concerned they might not be able to pay for everything. All she knew was that the groom couldn't get married in the church, because it was his second marriage. It turned out the groom was Tim Mondavi of the Napa Valley wine family in California. He was marrying a woman named Holly and his two young daughters were to be the flower girls.

On the day of the ceremony, the bride arrived in a carriage drawn by a black horse draped in white lace. She arrived more than an hour late, due to traffic. There were local musicians in costume playing music. The flower girls and the matrons of honour were dressed in pastel chiffons and held wands with chiffon ribbons flowing in the breeze. There were about 60 guests. Many of them were from California and were decked out in super clothes. Some of the biggest Italian wine producers were invited as well. When the service was about to begin, I felt a bit of stage fright as Monica and I worked our way through the crowd of guests on the terrace. I think we were both a little nervous. Monica started reading the service in Italian, but when she came to my part in English she kept reading. I dug her in the ribs and said, 'Whoa, its my turn now.' There were a few giggles from the audience, which made us relax. The wedding was a success and when the service was over, the two little flower girls ran over to their father, the groom, and gave him a big hug. It was the most important wedding Monica and I ever did.

Once after Monica and I had finished another wedding ceremony at the Town Hall, the groom asked me if we had two wine glasses, which we could give him. He said they needed to jump on the glasses and break them. I asked him if they were Greek. I had once been to a crazy Greek restaurant in Munich where you could break as much crockery as you wanted to. The service in the restaurant was so quick. The waiters hovered over everyone—trying to take the plates away immediately after your last mouthful, before you had the chance to throw them. The groom said no, they were Jewish and it was a tradition for good luck for the couple to break glasses at a Jewish wedding. Monica overheard the groom's request and immediately said, no. She knew there were only two good glasses in the Town Hall and she couldn't risk having them jumped on. The couple

seemed quite happy when she gave them two paper cups to use instead.

It was during my first years of working at the Poseidon that Luciano Nuovalare, Katinka's husband, died on **25 January 1994**. Katinka and I are still very close, even though she now resides in Berlin and only comes to Positano every now and then. Massimo Troisi died on **4 June** that same year. He was one of my favourite Italian actors.

On **12 September 1994**, Monica was in a clinic in Piano di Sorrento where she had just given birth to her second daughter, Liliana. Her first child, Margherita, had been born back in **1989**. The clinic Monica was in was either closing down or being renovated and she was the only patient there. She called me and asked if I could spend a night with her to keep her company. I was happy to go and meet her new little girl. Monica had had a caesarean and could hardly move. I knew just what she was going through, since I had felt the same way after my caesarean when I had Carmen.

In the fall of **1995**, Bob called me from the U.S. His long-time partner, Michael Sherrin, was very ill with cancer. They were planning to spend Christmas at Michael's home in Pennsylvania and Michael had asked if I could come over and be with them.

Bob and Ed had ended their relationship years earlier, but they remained friends and continued to share several houses together. Michael had become a good friend of mine ever since he and Bob began dating. I would see him often in Positano and I had also visited them in New York a few times. Michael was the Director of Music at the George School, a small elite Quaker school in Newtown, Pennsylvania. It is a very special school and I had even considered sending Carmen there when she was a teenager. Michael was also a painter and in the summer of **1995** we had an exhibition of his paintings in the Poseidon hotel.

I arrived at Michael's house on Christmas Eve. He had a beautiful little house in the middle of a field. There was a light snow falling and his large living room windows looked out over the field of snow. They sat me down with a glass of wine and as we started to catch up I began to hear music coming from somewhere outside. A large group

Bob Miller, Michael Sherrin and friends.

of Christmas carollers appeared outside their window. They were singing their hearts out to Michael, in the glow of the candles they held in their hands.

For the next week or so, I spent most of my time with Michael. He showed me old videos of his trips with Bob and chatted about the past. I remember Michael broke down in tears when we talked about János. Some of the teachers from the George School came by to visit and brought homemade goodies for us to share. One day his mother arrived with her partner. Michael quietly asked me to take him upstairs to his bedroom. I knew Michael loved his mother, but he just didn't want to speak to her or anyone anymore.

I usually got up early, but on the morning of **2 January 1996** I slept in. When I woke up, I went to Michael's bedroom and found Bob there. Michael had died in his sleep. Bob was distraught. He said he had tried to call family and friends to let them know, but he just couldn't. He asked if I could do it for him. There was a little service for Michael and many friends came down from New York. They came back to Michael's house afterwards to share a meal together.

There had been a warning that a big snowstorm was headed our way. They advised people not to

go outside, if possible. The guests left quickly after the lunch was over and rushed to the train station to get home safely, before the worst of the storm hit. It was a massive storm. Bob and I and the two dogs were barricaded in the house for four days. We had quite a problem trying to get the dogs outside when it was needed. I would open the door and let them go as far as their leashes allowed, while I held tight to the doorknob until they had finished what they had to do. One day we heard a knock on the door. It scared us both. Two men had come over on skis just to check if we were okay. When we heard the roads to New York had been cleared, we returned to Bob's brownstone in Manhattan. All the cars on the city streets were completely covered with snow. It was an amazing sight.

A while back, I had met the film director Paul Morrissey at the Poseidon Hotel. He had worked with Andy Warhol and had recently released a film called *Nico Icon* about Nico, the actress and singer from Velvet Underground. While I was in New York, Paul invited me to a party for the film at a hotel in Chelsea. I was a little worried about what I had with me to wear for such an event. I was going with my friend Elizabeth who always dressed beautifully. When we arrived, I found most of the men and woman were dressed as though they had just stepped out of the 60s, so I felt right at home.

Another person I had met at the Poseidon was Tom Foglietta, the American Ambassador to Italy under President Clinton's administration. When I mentioned to Tom that I was planning a promotional trip to the U.S. for the hotel, he said he would be happy to arrange everything for me if I wanted to come to Washington D.C. Tom Foglietta had introduced me to a woman who was also working for the Clinton administration. She met me in Washington and offered to let me stay in her house. She took me on a tour of the Capitol where I saw all the famous rooms I had seen in various films. She even took me to some places in the Capitol where most visitors are not allowed. She was able to get me an invitation to visit the White House. The invite was for two people, so I took Erica, a roommate of Carmen's from St Stephens who was now a lawyer in Washington. Outside of the White House there were life-size cardboard figures of Bill and Hillary Clinton set up for people to take photos. Of course I did, being sure a large brochure from the Hotel Poseidon was visible under my arm. When I went back to the hotel, I put the photo on the wall in my office—most of the staff believed it was real.

Another name on The List: Antonio Carbonetti died on **16 September 1996** in Rome. I cannot put down all my friends who died from AIDS. That list would be too long. However, I remember Antonio each day because I have a large painting of his in my house. He was a wonderful painter and his work had begun to be well known. Antonio had AIDS for 18 years before he died. I was amazed that he never seemed to be ill in all those years.

In **1996** when I was back at the hotel, we had a booking for a family from Riyadh, Saudi Arabia. It had probably been sent from the office of the Palace. It was the family of the Prince, one of the many sons of the King. We didn't know much about the booking before they arrived. People of that class make bookings all over the world, but not usually in a small four-star hotel. They could have afforded to book several floors for themselves at the Ritz in Paris.

We knew they would be arriving late, so we all waited around so we would be ready to greet them. I was sitting with the manager, Luigi, on the main terrace around midnight. Finally I saw a huge blue van pull up in front of the hotel, but I didn't think they would be travelling in a vehicle like that. It turned out the van was only for their luggage. Then I noticed a little movement in the

Jennie and friends in New York.

living room, so I thought I should go and see if any of our other clients needed something.

A good-looking couple appeared on the terrace. The attractive young woman was dressed in a long gypsy type skirt and a colourful blouse and the man was wearing a short-sleeved shirt and summer trousers. I welcomed them as usual, and offered them a drink. I wanted to get them settled in before the Nobles arrived. The couple smiled, but politely refused. I didn't know I was actually addressing the Prince and Princess themselves. I felt a bit foolish once I realised that. Of course they wouldn't drink alcohol; they were Muslim.

They had three male children with them. The eldest was about ten years old, the next about eight and a baby who was only a few months old, who was being held by an English nanny. There were also five other nannies from the Philippines.

A bit later, I went to the room where the two older boys were staying and I found them jumping up and down on the beds and zapping the television remote. I knew right away that we would get on well together and we did. They were super

Davide, Vanina, Jennie and Mario.

kids and they spoke perfect English. One of the nannies told me the children were hungry. That was a problem. It was after midnight so the kitchen was closed and the chef had already gone home. I suppose they were accustomed to staying in super deluxe hotels, where they could order at any time of night. All I could offer them was toasted ham and cheese sandwiches. Oops, another *faux pas*. One of the boys politely said, 'Please no ham, only cheese.'

I went to the room where baby Abdullah was staying with his English nanny. He was crying his head off. My first reaction was to take the baby out of the nanny's hands to try to calm him. She gave me a look which said I should give the little one back to her *immediately*. I turned and saw a bodyguard glaring at me, even more harshly. The nanny later told me it was forbidden for *anyone* to hold the royal baby except for the family or the nanny. I guess that was *faux pas* number three!

The following morning I had a telephone call from the English nanny, begging me to come to her room as soon as I could. She was very upset. She told me that the night before she had seen a bottle of beer in the mini bar. She hadn't had a beer since she had started working for the

family and she impulsively drank it. Drinking alcohol was completely forbidden. Now she was petrified they would find out what she had done when the beer showed up on their account. No problem. I took the empty bottle back to the bar and then took a full bottle wrapped in a *Herald Tribune* back to her room.

The Prince had his breakfast on the main terrace each morning with his two older boys. Then he would go to the living room to smoke a Cuban cigar. After breakfast they would all go down to the beach where a private yacht would be waiting for them at the wharf. The boys would always wave to me when I arrived at breakfast. One morning I went to their table and asked the Prince if he was enjoying his stay at the Poseidon. In his perfect English, he told me, 'I have to admit, it is quite different from where we usually stay, but I do feel very comfortable here.' I thought that was a very special compliment for the hotel.

The Positano Red Cross was having a campaign to raise money to buy the town its first ambulance. The hotel had a collection box at the front desk, hoping clients would leave a little of their change for the ambulance. I had heard Arabian nobility often donated to hospitals and other causes, so I decided to have a few words with the Prince's secretary. He told me I should write a letter to be presented to the Prince. I wrote a request for a small contribution towards the purchase of an ambulance, which would benefit the locals and the tourists. I wrote it on a sheet of beautiful, handmade Amalfi paper and tied it with a ribbon. It looked like a very important scroll. The secretary told me I was not allowed to present it to the Prince myself, since I was a woman, so I had to find the right person to do it for me. I chose Piccoletto, a wonderful waiter who always made people laugh. I had always thought he should have been an actor instead of a waiter. As he delivered the scroll, I was looking through the window of the terrace. I saw the Prince smoking his morning cigar. Then Piccoletto walked over to him and bowed as he handed over the scroll. It looked like a scene in a film.

The day of departure had come for the family. I had enjoyed their time with us and knew I would miss them all. That evening, my friends Gabrielle and Maria Mandara were having an exhibition at their gallery, Idee D'art. It was the final night for three Buddhist monks who were creating a Mandala out of sand. I didn't want to miss it. The two boys asked me where I was going and I told them about the monks and the Mandala. The children were curious and asked if they could come with me. I told them they needed to ask their father. The next thing I knew I was being dragged over to where the Prince was sitting. He nodded, but told them they had to ask their mother. The kids begged me to go with them, so off we went up to the parents' suite. The Princess greeted me with a warm smile and said of course they could go, but asked if she and her sister could come along as well. I told her I would be happy if they both joined us and we all agreed to meet in the reception of the hotel. I then went and called my friends at the gallery and told them to be prepared for a special group I would be bringing with me tonight.

We were quite a group as we headed down to see the monks. I led the line, followed by a security man at my heels. After him came the Princess and her sister with another bodyguard behind them. Then came the English nanny wheeling the little one in his pram. The two young boys followed with more security men bringing up the end. At the gallery, we watched the monks finish their sacred work and then we all went back to the hotel. I never saw the Prince again. That night the whole family were whisked away on a private yacht.

You might wonder what happened to my request on the scroll. The Prince left a very nice contribution towards the new ambulance. When it was purchased, I took a photo of the cheque being handed over to the Red Cross in front of Positano's new possession. I sent the photo to the Prince's secretary and thanked them once again for staying with us.

Francesca Sorrenti

In the spring of **1997**, I heard some horrible news from New York. Back in the early **1980s** my sister-in-law Francesca had separated from Ricardo and she took their three children, Mario, Vanina and Davide, to New York City. Francesca works as a fashion stylist and her children followed in her footsteps. Mario Sorrenti is a well-known fashion photographer. He took the photos for Calvin Klein's Obsession campaign which featured Kate Moss, who Mario had been dating at the time. Vanina became a fashion stylist and photographer and Davide also went into fashion photography. In the mid-1990s, the heroin-chic look was quite popular in fashion shoots. The style glamorised the look of young people strung out on drugs. It actually was a reflection of the heavy drug use which was common among those in the fashion business at that time. On **4 February 1997**, I had a call from New York telling me that my nephew Davide had died of an overdose. The news was devastating. He was only 20 years old. He had just begun his career a few years earlier and his first cover photo had just recently been published for the magazine *Detour*.

Over the next few months there were several articles in the New York papers about Davide's death and the change it was causing in the fashion industry. On **20 May 1997**, Amy Spindler wrote in *The New York Times*, 'After years of denial by the fashion industry that heroin use among its players had any relation to the so-called heroin-chic style of fashion photography that has become so prevalent, the fatal overdose of Davide Sorrenti, 20, a promising photographer at the heart of the scene, was like a small bomb going off... Magazine editors are now admitting that glamorising the strung-out heroin addict's look reflected use among the industries young and also had a seductive power that caused damage.' Soon after Davide's death, magazines began to tell their photographers they no longer wanted any heroin photos, but instead wanted images which had a healthy and positive look. After her son's death, Francesca became an outspoken opponent of the heroin-chic style, hoping something positive might come from Davide's death.

At the end of **1997**, I finally decided to go back to see my family and friends in Australia. I was very excited and at the same time a little scared. So much had happened in the past 34 years since I had left. My mother and father had both passed away, as well as my brother-in-law Les. I had no idea how much else had changed and wasn't sure what to expect.

Carmen and I travelled on to Melbourne where Joan met us at the bus station. I hadn't seen my sister for 34 years, yet it felt as though it were yesterday. She said, 'Hello Jennifer. How are you going?' That seemed so funny to me after spending many years amongst emotional Italians. Her greeting felt so casual and reserved, but that was fine. I was just so happy to see her again.

We stayed with Clem and Val Sauer, friends of my brother, Alan. They organised a big dinner party with my school friends. Most of my friends arrived with scrapbooks and photo albums under their arms. It was wonderful; within

minutes, I was back in the past and it seemed as if nothing had changed, even though many things had.

Joan travelled with us up to Port Macquarie to visit our sister Peggy and her family. On a huge rock down near the sea I painted, 'Jennie came here from Positano'. Years later when I went back, my message was still on the rock for all to see. This trip brought my past back to life. I saw everyone and everything I had wanted to see. I left Australia knowing I would be going back regularly from now on to visit, and I did.

Carmen had to fly back before me. She had a role in *Kevin's Bed,* which was scheduled to play for three months in the famous Abbey Theatre in Dublin. Katinka and I went to Ireland for the last night of the play, which was a great success. Carmen had continued her work in theatre and film. A few years earlier in **1994,** she had a role in a German production called *Blut an der Wiege,* which was shot in Munich. The following year she worked on another German production in Austria called, *Weihnachten mit Willy Wuff.*

She had joined the Theatre Mélange company in **1996** and toured all over England for a few years. It was phenomenal. The company was made up of actors from India, Denmark, Nigeria, China, the U.K., Ireland, Italy, Somalia, France and Macedonia. They travelled around and put on superb plays. Carmen was Philomele in Wertenbaker's *The Love of the Nightingale.* Theatre Mélange brought *Ondine* back to life in **1998** with Carmen in the title role. Jean Giraudoux Jr, the playwright's son, came from France to see the production. It was unforgettable theatre.

Frank Sinatra died on the **14 May 1998**. I still play his music today and always will.

Back at the Poseidon I found out there were plans to turn my apartment into a suite, so I started looking for a new place to rent. Looking across the valley from the hotel, one house always stood out to me. An impressive, yellow 18th-century villa with its name, 'Margherita', written in huge letters on the front. I learnt the Gaetani family owned the Margherita. Luck was on my side again. The Gaetani's were one of the first families I had met when I first moved to Positano. I spoke to Raimonda and Fausta and they said the top floor apartment could be mine. It was fantastic. There were two bedrooms, two bathrooms, a living room and the most amazing large terrace. The view was not to be believed. I could even see what was going on at the hotel. I suggested to Mimi, the Maitre D' at the hotel, that he and I should have a flag system across the valley, so I could signal when I noticed things happening at the hotel from the view of my terrace at home. For example, if I saw a piece of cutlery fall from a guest's table, I could wave a red flag. A white flag could be waved when the service was going smoothly and a black one when the service is really bad.

My former apartment in the hotel was converted into a charming junior suite. Often when I took new clients to that room, I would tell them they were sleeping in my living room and would be hanging their clothes in my kitchen. The Aonzo's were always trying to do things to improve the Poseidon. Around this time Marco's wife, Laura, decided to open a spa in the hotel. Laura had great taste and she made sure the Poseidon had a wonderful spa. After the opening, you would see clients walking around the hotel in their white bathrobes. The hotel also had an excellent gym, which was used by outsiders as well as the hotel clients.

It was helpful having one of the owners of the Poseidon be the vice-mayor of the town. In **August 1999**, the German Chancellor, Herr Schroeder came to Positano with his wife and

Top: Jennie came here from Positano.
Bottom: Peggy, Jo, Carmen, Joan and Jo's children.

daughter. Monica invited them to the Poseidon for dinner. I hadn't been told they would be coming, so I was a bit surprised to see the staff all madly cleaning that evening as I was doing my early evening rounds in the bar and restaurant. Tables were being shined, the leaves on the terrace were being swept and everything was being tidied and organised. I asked Marco what all the fuss was about and he told me the German Chancellor was coming to dinner in about twenty minutes. Then Marco and the rest of his family raced off to their rooms to dress for the occasion.

While I was alone on the terrace, I heard the voice of Angelo at the reception desk. He was explaining the history of the hotel to some guests in a very formal way. Angelo led them to the top of the stairs and he turned to me and said, 'This is Miss Jennie, our PR Manager.' Suddenly I found myself in charge of greeting the Chancellor, his wife and their little daughter. There was a tall young woman with them, who I presumed was the nanny. Later, I found out she was a plain clothes security guard. Behind them were about ten bodyguards. I shook hands with the Chancellor, his wife, the 'nanny' and patted the little girl's head. I then proceeded to shake the hands of each of the ten bodyguards. I welcomed them all, which I now know I wasn't supposed to do. It was a long line of, 'Buona sera' here and 'Buona sera' there. The Chancellor must have wondered why I was being so friendly to his bodyguards. What might I do next? Invite them all to the bar for a drink?

The bodyguards immediately began their inspection of the terrace and the surrounding area and then placed themselves in position to oversee the evening. Before dinner, cocktails were served with the Aonzo family and other officials from Positano. By the time dinner was served, everyone was in a festive mood. I was taking care of our other clients and at one point I went to check the woman's toilet to make sure everything was clean and in order. When I got there, I found the tall 'nanny' standing on guard outside the loo. Inside were Mrs Schroeder and her daughter. The three of us started chatting about Positano and their holiday. As the evening wore on, the party became louder and livelier. When it was time for our guests to leave, I went to say farewell. As I approached them, Monica began to introduce me to Mrs Schroeder, but the Chancellor's wife interrupted Monica saying, 'Oh, I know Jennie. We've already had a chat together in the toilet.' Monica didn't know quite what to make of that. Mrs Schroeder's reply sounded as if she had known me for a long time.

I helped Monica with another wedding, which was a very special one for me. My niece Andy, who is one of Alan and Barbara's daughters, married Neil Ash on **15 October 1999**. A small reception was held in the Poseidon and most of my family were there. It was so wonderful having them all in Positano.

On **24 May 2001**, another politician came to stay with us at the Poseidon. Ehud Barak, the Prime Minister of Israel, along with his wife and two of their friends. When the booking was made, the hotel was nearly full, but Monica promised them she would see what she could do. There were rooms for their friends and the three bodyguards, who would be travelling with them, but no suites appropriate for the Prime Minister and his wife. Monica's mother, Liliana, offered to let them stay in her beautiful apartment on the lower floor, while she moved in with Monica for a few days.

During their stay, the hotel was completely blocked off. No cars were allowed to park nearby and police were on patrol day and night. There were dozens of Italian police in uniform and also in civilian clothes. My first job was to accompany two Italian policemen to the apartment where Barak would be staying so they could check it thoroughly for security purposes. Then, I was told to take one of the Israeli bodyguards to do more or less the same thing. Nothing seemed to escape this young man's sight. He seemed to have eyes in his ankles. As he was checking the apartment, he kept talking, but I couldn't understand what he was saying. I asked him to please look at me when he spoke and to speak in a louder voice, but he didn't reply. Then I looked again and realised he wasn't talking to me, he had been talking into a microphone tucked under his shirt.

I was a bit worried about how the other clients felt during this intrusion at the hotel. There were police everywhere around the clock. There were even machine guns laying around on the terrace near the room where Barak was staying. Some of our clients were thrilled to have the Prime Minister there and were asking for autographs, however others were a little un-comfortable. All in all, the four days went well. As they were being driven away, Mr Barak called

out of the window of the car to say, 'We will be back. *Shalom!*'

Most of our guests at the Poseidon were wonderful, but there were a few who were difficult. I remember one particularly difficult client who stayed with us. Mr Smith was an Australian, who had booked a room for ten days. By the time he left, those ten days seemed like ten years! It was in the middle of the season and the hotel was very full. Mr Smith was travelling alone and often when we had single clients I would offer to eat with them myself or to introduce them to other guests whose company I thought they might enjoy. I offered to dine with Mr Smith on his first night. I just wish the barman had told me Mr Smith had already had ten vodkas before I met with him in the dining room! He sat down and promptly ordered a bottle of wine to have with his meal. The next thing I knew, he pulled up his shirt and started drumming on his chest. *Oh my God!* I thought, *What have we got here?* He turned to a table near to us, where a quiet middle-aged German couple were dining. He asked them how they were doing as he continued thumping on his bare chest. I asked him to please stop and leave the couple in peace. 'Aw, I'm just trying to be nice.', was all he said. Soon, after his food arrived I had the feeling he might pass out and end up with his face on his plate, so I had to ask two of the waiters to take him up to his room.

That was the beginning of a ten day battle. The days were quiet enough, but the evenings were warfare. After a couple of days, I told him, that for his own sake, I would have him locked up in his room. I wasn't joking. I tried to tell him he would feel much better after his 'cure'. The next two days were much more peaceful; we didn't see or hear from him. He ate in his room and I checked with the barmen that he hadn't ordered anything from them. He seemed to be behaving. I thought my cure was working, although I was rather surprised to hear there were a few times people had complained about him shouting things that weren't very nice down to the clients in the restaurant below his terrace. Mr Smith had quite a mouth on him once he got to drinking. He needed his mouth washed out with soap—lots of soap! Why was he shouting now if he wasn't drinking? Then,

I checked with the women who cleaned his room and found out what he had been up to. Apparently he had finished everything in his mini-bar and had it all replaced multiple times!

During the day when he was sober, Mr Smith was quite charming and intelligent. Some of our guests found him rather amusing. However, the evenings were becoming a nightmare for me. I never knew what he would do. The worst evening was the night of a concert by The Positano School of Classical Music. The school had been founded by Eileen Huang. Her daughter Shungza is a well-known pop star in China. Her students were all gifted young musicians from Asia. Their concerts were lovely formal affairs. The little girls wore white dresses and patent leather shoes and the boys were in white shirts and dark trousers. We had organised their annual concert on the terrace. It was the perfect setting for the magical evening with an amazing view of the sea and coast stretching out below.

I arrived to make sure everything was set up perfectly for the concert and found Mr Smith sitting at the front bar on the terrace. He was only about eight meters away from the students. I knew that would never work. I politely asked him to move to the back of the bar until the concert was over, but he didn't budge. Once the music began, he started whistling through his fingers and shouting after each number, until I eventually had to have him physically removed from his seat.

When his ten days were over, Mr Smith said he wanted to extend his stay. No one wanted him there any longer and the staff at reception decided to tell him the hotel was completely booked. Everyone was tired of dealing with his outbursts and the waiters were tired of carrying him up to bed every night.

There were quite a few stories about our drinking clients and the fun they had. We once had a group of Japanese painters staying with us. None of them spoke any Italian or English. They were all very polite and went to bed very early. Their guide, who was Japanese but spoke Italian well, would stay up late each night to draw portraits for the guests. While he was drawing he would be drinking—a lot. He would mix everything from wine to vodka to tequila. One evening he was so drunk, I had no choice but to get him up to his room by myself. I more or less dragged him to the lift. I pushed him in, trying not to let him fall. He wasn't very tall; he only came up to my shoulder, so the only way I could hold on to him was to put one arm securely around his neck as my other hand pushed the button. I was afraid I was going to strangle him, especially since he was in sort of a semi-coma state and just dead weight. On the way up to his room in the elevator, I truly felt like I was working at *Faulty Towers*.

Another time we had a a group from a fashion magazine who wanted to shoot some photos on the terrace. The man in charge was French and his Australian girlfriend was there with him. After the session was over, they all went off to their rooms. A little while later I had an urgent call from someone in the group telling me the Australian woman was losing her baby. She had locked herself in the bathroom and wouldn't let anyone in. Losing her baby!? I didn't even realise she was pregnant! I ran down to the room, but she refused to open the bathroom door for me either. I called for Doctor Michele Fiorentio to come help. Finally the woman allowed the doctor in. Michele told me the woman had a miscarriage and had aborted her child. She had to go to the nearest hospital immediately.

I asked Pino, the hotel driver, to prepare the Poseidon's bus to serve as an ambulance. By the time I got down to the garage, the little bus was made up with a bed in the back. I was very proud of our staff that day. They were always so competent, no matter what was thrown their way. I guess there were no complications for the woman, because the next day I was in Amalfi and I bumped into that same couple. They were fine and having a drink at a bar.

In **2001** Liliana Aonzo was not feeling well. I went with her to Rome for a couple of weeks, while she was having a series of medical tests for cancer. Eventually she moved out of her beautiful apartment below the pool and into Monica's house upstairs so she could be more easily cared for. As her health began to get worse, the pain set in. When I would visit Liliana, I found it upsetting to see how much pain she was in. After one of my visits to her, I went down to the terrace and started

picking dead leaves and flowers off the plants, which usually helped me calm down. As I worked, two young men came over to me. I recognised one of them as a friend of Liliana's, Tonino Ottaviano, a plastic surgeon from Rome. He was travelling with his friend Marco Morosino on holiday. I told him about the pain Liliana was suffering and asked if he knew of anything we could do to help her. It was as if Tonino had been sent from heaven that day. He made a call to a doctor in Rome and was able to order some morphine for her. We were grateful. Liliana never suffered again. Doctor Tonino and Marco have both become very close friends of mine.

Ferragosto is a national holiday in Italy which is celebrated on the **15th of August**. That day Liliana felt so well that she insisted on being taken down to the terrace for the big Ferragosto party in the hotel. She wanted to watch the fireworks display and listen to the brass band as they followed the religious procession from the church down to the beach. Liliana had always been a very attractive lady who dressed well. That night, even though she had to be taken down in a wheelchair, she insisted on wearing a red dress for the party. It was a wonderful night.

Then just six days later on **21 August 2001**, Liliana decided to leave us. She didn't seem to be in any pain and she was surrounded by family and friends. She just said a few words and quietly left us. I always admired Liliana and enjoyed her company. It was very sad to lose her, but I could tell it was her time to go. The funeral was the day after. We all went up the many stairs above the town to the cemetery to lay her to rest. The Positano cemetery has the most unbelievable view. It is a view to die for, as we say.

Just a few weeks later it was **11 September 2001**—everyone remembers 9/11. When I arrived at the hotel that day, I was told to go to the office immediately. All the office staff were crowded around the television set. None of us could believe what we were seeing on the screen. It was too unreal. Everyone on the staff was upset, but I went into a fit. Carmen was staying with her father in New Jersey. I knew she was frequently visiting New York City and her cousin Mario was living quite near the World Trade Center with his wife

Ed Wittstein's drawing of the pool at the Poseidon.

Mary and their two children. Monica told me to telephone Carmen immediately. I didn't have her number on me so I had to have one of the drivers take me home. Thankfully I got through to her and she was safe. That was such a relief. Three days later it was Carmen's birthday. She went to spend the day with her friend Martin di Martino in the West Village in New York. She told me that on the subway everyone—even people who didn't know each other—were holding onto each other in grief. Carmen wanted to return home, but couldn't. All non-military flights within the United States had been cancelled for several days, while they tried to make some sense out of what had happened. Even once flights resumed it took a while for the airline schedules to get back on track.

29 November 2001 George Harrison died and his ashes were thrown into the Ganges River in India. I hope he and John are together again.

At the Poseidon, we had planned several 'Slow Food' evenings featuring various cuisines. On **17 November 2001,** we had a very special pairing from two cultures. It was a group of chefs from Israel and Palestine who called themselves 'The Chefs of Peace' and they prepared a menu titled 'Food from the Holy Land'. Ehud Gol, the Israeli Ambassador in Rome, came with his wife. The Ambassador gave a moving speech about the uprisings between the two nations represented there that evening. Watching them all, I wondered why they couldn't make a lasting peace in their own countries the way the people in that room were doing right then. They all stayed a few days with us afterwards. I felt as though I learnt so much from them and it was not at all about cooking.

Marco Aonzo threw some smashing parties at the hotel. He always invited great guests. Special clients would mix drinks for us at the bar and even the dogs would jump into the pool with us late at night. There were always interesting people passing through. The American actor David Keith, his wife, Nancy, and their daughter, Presley, stayed with us a number of times. I loved him in *An Officer and a Gentleman* with Richard Gere. David was great to have around and for many years he sent me Christmas cards with photos of their family.

There was one night when I was in the bar talking to clients, when I noticed four new people arrive. It was a cool night and we had a fire in the fireplace. The group sat themselves down near the fire. I was curious to know who they were, so I went down to the reception and checked their booking. The woman was Carol King! I love her music and knew that Marco had a CD of hers. I raced into the dining room, where Marco was eating with some of our very good clients, and asked him to get me his Carol King CD. He brushed me away saying he was busy and would get it for me later. I insisted I had to have it *now*, because Carol King was sitting in the living room. As soon as Marco heard that he jumped up and a few minutes later, I had her CD *Tapestry* in my hand. I put the music on and I walked over to her group. I told Carol I couldn't resist putting on her music and hoped she didn't mind. I spent the next few hours chatting with them and we had a lovely time.

About a year later I had to leave the Poseidon. I was very sad. It was the end of an era. I had met so many wonderful people during the 12 years I had worked there. We had amazing guests from all over the world and I worked with a fabulous staff. I have such fond memories of my time working at the Poseidon.

After I left the hotel, I began to do some freelancing, organising events and weddings. I organised a large exciting wedding for the TV and film actor Peter Weller and his fiancé Sheri Stowe. Peter is well-known for his starring role in the *Robo Cop* films. Peter and Sheri have a house in Positano not far from where I was living at the Margherita. They

Jennie with kangaroos.

were married in the main church in town on **24 June 2006**. Afterwards, all the guests were taken by boats to the reception at a restaurant down the coast. We celebrated Peter's birthday that night as well. It was a week of celebrations. I had organised the event out of a little room in my apartment, which I had turned into an office complete with a sign on the door which said 'Weller Wedding'.

Another big wedding I worked on was for my friends from Melbourne, Roger and Chrissy Kimberley, whose daughter Camilla married a man named Gus. Once again, the celebrations went on for about one week with over one hundred guests celebrating with them. Later, I helped set up a fashion shoot for Capri Cigarettes with Deborah Turbeville, a famous photographer from New York. I always managed to find interesting jobs to keep me busy.

Karol Wojtyła, Pope John Paul II, died on **2 April 2005**.

I returned to Australia many more times since my first trip back in **1997**. I usually would go around Christmas and then stay for a few months. I was able to travel around quite a bit each time I was in Australia. I saw many parts of my country which I had never seen before and I met up with other family and friends along the way. Some were friends from my childhood, others were people who I had met elsewhere, but now lived

Joan, Peter and Tony.

in Australia. Each time was another trip down memory lane.

I would always spend time in Adelaide with my sister Joan and my brother, Alan. I love Adelaide. It has a wonderful climate, amazing fauna and flora and much of my family is there. Back in **1997**, Alan's wife, Barbara, had passed away. It was especially sad because it happened when Barbara and Alan's daughter Di was in London where she married Jason on **30 July 1997**. She and Jason were heading to Rome to stay with me after their wedding when they got the terrible news about Barbara. They changed their plans and immediately flew back home. Di and Jason lived in Adelaide and I would always visit them along with their children, Ky and Taj. My brother eventually began seeing Pattianne, a woman I had known from school. That turned into a long-term relationship and they are still together. Peggy's daughter, Jo and her three children live in Adelaide as well. My sister Peggy and her husband Max live in Port Macquarie and in the middle of this small town

there is a huge park by the sea. Late one afternoon, we took a walk down there. We were there for a few minutes when I saw a small group of bats flying overhead. Then gradually, the sky began to darken as though night had set in. An enormous black cloud of bats was moving across the sky. I was told the bats took flight each evening and returned to the park a few hours later. The noise they made when they returned to the park was ear splitting. Then, once they had settled down in the trees, there was only silence. The next day the newspaper said there had been about 35,000 flying bats that evening!

Whenever I stopped by Mildura, my old school friends often gathered together for a lunch or dinner as a welcome home for me. Of course, I always visited my mother's grave whenever I was in town. Then in Melbourne I visited my niece Julie, another of Alan and Barbara's daughters. I also spent some time with my old friend Wendy in Melbourne. We travelled around the city visiting all the places we used to go when

Above: Jennie with Jenny Kee in Sydney.
Right: Jennie with Vali Myers in her studio in Melbourne.

we were young. We even went by the 'Virgins Retreat', the very first place we had lived when we had left Mildura together. I visited Vali Myers while I was in Melbourne. She had moved back to Australia from Positano and had a studio in Melbourne. I often spent time with two friends I had met at the Poseidon, Christine and Martyn Pickersgill, who lived in Black Rock, outside of Melbourne. They are avid dog lovers and Christine is very involved with the world of dog shows. I always get to go to a few shows when I visit and I love taking their dogs for walks on the dog beach. It's a beach just for dogs, which makes it very amusing. I travelled out to Phillip Island to stay with Barbara and Dennis, two

Above: Peter, Lex, Jennie, Anna and Michael.
Right: Jennie at her father's grave.

other friends I had grown up with in Mildura. I went to Sydney to stay with my nephew Peter, his wife, Julie, and their children, Amelia, Michael and Edward. While I was there, I also spent time with Jenny Kee. Jenny has always been very smart and talented. She had moved back from London and had gone on to become a leading fashion designer in Australia. Finally, I travelled up to Queensland to see my three half brothers Lex, Tony and Peter and to visit my father's grave.

On my way to or from Australia, I often stopped over in other countries for a quick visit. I visited Singapore, Bangkok, Dubai and Hong Kong. I loved all my trips back to Australia. Being able to reconnect with my family and friends back home again was like a waking dream.

On **25 June 2009**, Michael Jackson died, then a few weeks later on **11 July 2009**, Joan Bell my sister died. I miss her so much.

My New Family on Via Cristoforo Colombo

It was around **2010** when I moved to a new house at 169 Via Cristoforo Colombo. After living for ten years in the Margherita, Raimonda and Fausta asked me to leave. They had decided to rent my apartment only for the summer months rather than by the year as they had been doing with me. Fortunately, they did have another house that was available to rent by the year. It was a small house which was attached to their villa. That house turned out to be perfect for me—and it still is. It is more central and on the main road. The rooms of the house are set back from the road, which makes me feel as though I'm living in the countryside when I'm inside. I have a small terrace, where I can sit and watch the world pass by—literally the whole world seems to pass by my house. Tourists come from all around the globe just to take photos of the magnificent view in front of my house. The

house was built in the late 17th century, before the main villa was added on. In my living room there is a large cupboard with a beautiful old wooden door. It was once a door leading into the main house. Perhaps in the old days, this house was used as the servants' quarters or to keep the horses for the villa. Now it is just my wonderful home.

When I first moved to my current house, this end of Via Cristoforo Colombo was rather quiet and out of the way. As the years passed, new restaurants and shops appeared and now I feel it is one of the most interesting streets in Positano. The people along my street have become another family for me. Starting a few doors down is Dipinti e Terracotte, the gallery of Paolo Sandulli. I had met Paolo when I first came to Positano back when he was a young painter and before he went to Paris to study. Now he sells his paintings and sculptures

219

both here and in Praiano. The next shop heading up the hill is Ivi Gioielli, which is owned by Marco and Yolanda. Marco makes exquisite jewellery and I always love seeing their beautiful dog, Oscar, lounging on the floor between the jewellery cases. Next to them is Nando who runs a touristy shop called Positano Souvenir. My house comes next, followed by Luigi, who we call 'O Capitano'. Luigi has an antique shop where he displays his wares on the street and hangs interesting old objects on the wall of my house each day. Being between Nando and Luigi I am squeezed between the new and the old, which I like. Next we have Antoinetta who makes wonderful *granita di limone* that her family sells from a little cart in the centre of town. The next shop is Profumeria di Positano, which is owned by dear Gennaro and Filomena Barba. They make wonderful natural perfumes and scented soaps and their business has been in Gennaro's family since **1922**. Finally, the last shop to open in this area is Ceramiche Parlato, which sells beautiful ceramic pieces made by Berenice, Ferdinando and their children, Giovanna and Crescenzo.

Just above and below these shops are two wonderful restaurants. They are both just a few minutes walk from my house, so it's like having a bar and restaurant in my living room. At the top of the street is Li Galli Restaurant, which was opened in **2010** by Giuseppi Irace and Ciro Caso from Praiano. On the opposite side of me is Ristorante Bar Bruno, which is lots of fun. The food in both restaurants is so good and they always treat me like family. Everyone on my street is like family. They all look out for each other and they mean so much to me. I suppose I have always created families for myself all over the world. They never replace the ties I have to my real family, they just add on to it. If more people did this, maybe there would be less sadness and depression in the world.

I should mention another 'resident' of Via Cristoforo Colombo… In my house, I have a large bedroom with a very high ceiling and a small terrace with a marvellous view of the town and the sea. One very dark night in **2015**, I opened my eyes and saw something incredible. Around my bed there were tall slim trees swaying to and fro as if there was a slight breeze. It was like being in a dream, but I knew I was definitely not asleep. It made me rather frightened. The room was filled with beautiful bushes all sparkling in silver, gold and bronze and there was a hazy, misty substance in the air that began to move towards me. I reached out my arms and gently pushed it away from me. I found I could push the substance back and forth

with my hands and I started playing with it. As I did, I felt as though my arms and hands were covered with a fluffy sort of mist that made my skin feel smooth.

The next night the same thing happened again, only this time everything was a bronze colour. Even my writing desk was heaped with a mountain of gleaming bronze. I was so awake that time that I reached for my cell phone to try and take a photo to prove it was real. However the minute I pressed the button, it all vanished.

I soon realised I wasn't frightened by these visits anymore. I began to think of them like visits from friends. I got into the habit of calling my spirit friends back whenever I wanted to see them again. I never told anyone about them. They would have thought I had completely flipped out, so I kept it to myself as a sacred secret. I spent many nights with them. Some visits were short, other times they stayed longer. The nights were full of movement and colour. One time, I saw an abstract and not so beautiful face in the midst of the glitter. The face reminded me of the faces in paintings by the Austrian painter Egon Schiele. That was the only time I actually saw a face in the room. It was also the longest evening I ever spent with them. I played with my friends until three o'clock that morning. I was talking and even singing to them

until eventually I was so tired I had to gently say, 'I have to leave you all now. I'm so tired, but please come back again another night.' I turned on the light and they all disappeared.

I could bring them back whenever I wanted. I would just have to concentrate in the darkness and it would only take a few minutes before it all started up again. I finally told Carmen about it. She believed what I told her, so one night she agreed to come into my bedroom and stay with me. She could hear me talking to my friends and see me moving my arms, but she couldn't see anything herself.

After about two years of these visits, I decided to write to my psychic in Australia who often helps me resolve my problems and make decisions. I asked her about my spirit friends and she sent this reply:

Jennifer, you are being visited by the spirits. What you have seen is where they are and how they live in the spirit world. It is amazing! But I have to warn you to be very careful how often you visit them. We live in the physical world and too much time spent 'travelling' to the spirit world can interfere with our own reality. Even I do not spend too much time there, as it can impact the way I feel about

RISTORANTE BAR BRUNO

our sometimes mundane reality. You have a beautiful gift, it has been shown to you, but please, just visit every now and then. Know they are always around you, even if you aren't 'tuned in' to them specifically. They are still there in the other planet of existence. It's your proof, if you like, of what there is after we pass over.

In **October 2017**, I wrote again:

My dear friend, for over two months now I have stopped calling the spirits in. However last night I decided to try and see if they were still around. Within minutes of my staring into the blackness of the night, they appeared just like before. The dazzling colours were not there anymore, instead they came all in white mixed with silver sparkles. They sort of looked like tiny snowballs or what I would call white wattle or even popcorn! I let them stay for about 15 minutes and then turned on the light. I will try not to call them back as you told me to be careful.

The house I rent is very old. In 1942 a young man died here, probably in my bedroom. He died in agony and was buried in the cemetery in Positano. He was a writer and was a very complex and interesting person. I do not want to go into too many details about his life out of respect. Do you think he has anything to do with the spirit friends I see at night?

I was quite shocked by her answer to me:

Dearest Jennifer, He is the LAST PERSON I would want near you. In fact, if I were near you, I'd be on your doorstep cleansing your house and you now. His 'essence' or spirit is not good; he's what I would call a 'psychic vampire' and would drain the energy right out of you. PLEASE PLEASE, get yourself an AMETHYST

crystal pendant and wear it at all times. Sage every room in your house while repeating, 'I banish all negative spirits from my home.' If you cannot do that, you need to find a reputable psychic medium over there to do it or get a priest or minister to bless your house. This man's energy is not good. I feel he is somehow 'linked' to the spirits you are seeing. I keep getting the same word over and over again in relation to him, 'deception'. He will show you what you want to see to drag you in and then use that energy to suck the life out of you. I think this is already happening. I do not want to alarm you, but PLEASE, go and get some sage and burn it in your house NOW. Sending you love and healing energy.

After I heard this, I told Marco at the jewellery shop next door what she had said. He gave me a

small amethyst pendant to wear on a chain to help keep the ghost away from me. I wear it around my neck every day. I also have a large bowl of sage which some friends bought me and several large sage smudge sticks I use to purify the house. I even had a local priest come bless the house.

I am sure most people will not believe my spirit story, but it is true. I had promised I would never enter that world again, however on the night of **30 March 2018**, I was naughty and decided to have a quick look to see if the sage and the priest's blessing had done their job. Within a few minutes the white mist appeared on the ceiling and began to drift lower towards my bed. My writing desk and wardrobe were completely covered in a whitish beige mist. Then I noticed the bookshelves pulsating with a very dark brown mist. I began pulling the brown colour towards the bed to mix and swirl the light and dark together, so everything didn't seem so dark. Again my arms and face felt much smoother than usual when I put them into the mist.

I will do more swabbing with the sage and I have never taken the amethyst from around my neck. I am desperately trying to get Him to pass over to the other world and leave me in peace.

I have tried very hard not to have the spirits visit me anymore, but something strange happened when I was in Berlin on my birthday in **July 2018**. I slept over at a friends house and as soon as I got into bed, I was amazed to find the spirits there with me so strongly. I had thought they were only in my bedroom in Positano, but this made me think that either the ghost has nothing to do with my spiritual life or maybe he is following me around. Who knows...?

János

Over the Rainbow

Since moving to my current home, my life seems to have fallen into a pattern. I usually spend my winters in Australia or elsewhere and my summers are always in Positano. When I'm home, I enjoy sitting on my terrace and watching the world walk by or I spend time visiting with friends along my street and throughout town. My house is often full of friends who visit from around the world, many of whom return each year. Bob and Ed usually came for a few months during the summer along with Ed's partner Juan. I have many other frequent visitors such as Helen Romain, her daughter Samantha and her husband, Roy, Maura Tessiere, Rod Cowling and David Timney from London, Pat and Barbara Senatore from California, Kate Bagley from Australia and so on and so on.

Ed Wittstein

Of course, Carmen comes to visit as well. She has been living in Rome for some time now. Carmen continued acting for a few more years. In **2000-2001** she worked on the film *Gangs of New York* with Leonardo DiCaprio, Cameron Diaz and Daniel Day-Lewis. It was directed by Martin Scorsese. Then in In **2004** she was in *Secret Passage* with John Turturro. It was set in Venice in 1492 and directed by Ademir Kenovic.

Around **2005**, Carmen took several transformational workshops with Alejandro and Cristobal Jodorowsy, but she decided to move away from acting and focus on her art work. She developed a world of mythical painting culminating in the creation of the Pholarchos Tarot. She spent many years in research for the deck, making her studio into an alchemical laboratory of sorts. She studied at Liz Greene's Centre for Psychological Astrology and is certified in dream work with Scott Sparrow at the DreamStar Institute. Carmen is a member of the International Association for the Study of Dreams (www.asdreams.org) where she presents papers on dreams and the contemplation of images in line with the Western mystery tradition. She also leads workshops on dreams, Talismanic Art and Tarot and is writing the companion book to the Pholarchos Tarot. I'm so pleased to read the wonderful reviews which have been written about her Tarot cards and to hear how well they are being received.

In **2011** I lost my friend Ed Wittstein. He had been ill for quite sometime. The last time Carmen visited him in New York, she told me he was too ill to go out and was being cared for by Juan at home. Ed and Bob fell in love with the sea, the mountains and the people of Positano and in return they were loved by the town. Ed had always been sketching in his own distinct style filled with poignant humour. He had his first exhibition in

Carmen in The Gangs of New York with Cameron Diaz, Leonardo DiCaprio and Daniel Day Lewis.

Trail of Wings

Trail of Spirals

WRITTEN IN BLOOD & EARTH

Trail of Coral

Cards from Carmen's Pholarchos Tarot.

Trail of Sparks

Ace of Spirals

Ace of Sparks

Top: Ed and Juan.
Bottom: Carmen's graduation from St Stephens.

Ed and Bob had both been like family to me for so many years. They were always there for me and Carmen. I remember once I was quite ill and they flew over from New York just to check on me. When Carmen graduated from St Stephens, they were there for the graduation ceremony. Years later, they flew to London to see Carmen in her first role in the theatre production of *Odine*. Bob had said he hoped he would be able to see Carmen get her first Oscar. He was joking of course, but I know if she had, he would have found a way to be there with us.

Bob and Ed are also the reason I decided to write this Diary. When I used to tell them stories of my past, they suggested I put my stories down on paper, so I began writing my notes. Without their advice I would have never even thought about writing my Diary. It hurts me to think I am now doing what they wanted, but they will not be around to celebrate it with me. When I first started writing my notes, Bob read them and said, 'I love what you've written. It's just like you're sitting down and talking to me.' I'm sure he meant I wasn't a writer, but rather just chatting away. I thank both Bob and Ed for starting me on this project and I hope someday somewhere in the cosmos we can all meet again and discuss the past.

On **23 July 2011**, Amy Winehouse died at the young age of 27, five days before Ed.

Just about two years after Ed passed away, Bob Miller died in New York on **10 August 2013** after

Positano at the Gargiulo Gallery, followed by shows at the Hotel Palazzo Murat, the Idee D'arte Gallery and the Ristorante Mediterraneo gallery of Enzo. Everyone in Positano loved Ed for his humour, generosity, kindness and the wonderful way he depicted the town and the people in his sketches. Ed died in New York on **28 July 2011**, but he will always be remembered by the people he met in Positano and around the world.

quite a long illness. He was the kindest person and he was fun too. Late in his life Bob became a wonderful oil painter and also began doing collages. We shared such a close friendship, which lasted for so many years. Bob truly was like a family member to me. I believe it was after Bob died that I began to go down physically and mentally. I fell into a deep uncontrollable sadness, which I have never fully gotten over.

2014 was another tragic year when I lost several more of my close friends. Justus Pfauer died early that year. Francesco Maione, one of my closest friends since Carmen was about four years old, died on **14 February 2014**. Marina Iello, a young woman from Praiano who was like another daughter for me in some ways, died on **5 June 2014**. Francesco's long time partner, Adriana Sandrini, died on **16 July 2014** in Argentina. John Moss, my friend from Rome, died on **23 December 2014**. The final death date I'll give is for Kirsty, the daughter of my friends Christina and Martyn in Australia. On the evening of the **3 July 2017**, as I was celebrating my birthday in a restaurant with Carmen and Katie Wasiak, my friend from Australia, I didn't feel well and wanted to go home. The next day I heard that Kirsty had died the night before. She was young and left behind two small children. It sent shivers down my spine. I had felt that something bad had happened during the night. I know it is rather morbid of me to include so many death dates, but these people were all

important to me, even the entertainers and actors whom I never met. They all influenced my life in some way.

On **25 December 2017**, Christmas Day, I found myself counting down the days until **2018**. In Italy the number 17 is very unlucky and the year **2017** was one of the worst years I have ever had. When I heard I had to have an operation on my foot, I made sure I did it in **2017** so my bad luck would be over. I was in Rome laid up for a couple of weeks after the operation. I've had a few health problems over the past few years and also have been dealing with the ghost in my house, so life hasn't been easy for me. I was not at all well for the past year. My doctors couldn't put their fingers on the cause of the problem. My neurologist put me on some medicine for depression and panic, but nothing seemed to help. At one point, I thought I was going to die. I wasn't scared, but I was aware I still had things I wanted to settle before I left, so I decided to see a new neurologist. He changed my medicine and the morning after my first dose, everything was better. It worked so fast. I felt incredibly good for the first time in a couple of years. I feel I'm growing, I'm changing, I'm evolving. I am coming out of my chrysalis and soon I will be flying! I began to feel that on **1 January 2018**, I would be reborn. I was sure **2018** would be a good year for me in many ways. I spent that New Years Eve alone for the first time in my life. I heard the fireworks outside, but

preferred to stay in with the cat I was looking after in Rome since she was so scared of all the noise.

On **14 February 2018**, Valentines Day, I had been laid up for nearly two months waiting for my foot to heal. At least it gave me lots of time to write with my computer on my tummy, despite the pain in my foot. I continue to get my body back into shape and think positively about the future once again. I am getting to the end of my Diary. When I look at the list of dates remaining, there seems to be so little to write about anymore, especially anything which would be of interest to you—or even to me, for that matter. I must have done something in these past few years other than go to Australia, paint and clean my house, have dinners or small parties with friends and write my Diary. When I was small I thought getting older would mean sitting in a rocking chair on the veranda watching the people pass by. However I cannot see myself ever getting to that stage. I couldn't wait for my foot to heal so I could return home again.

30 March 2018, I have decided it is nearly time to close my Diary. It is not my end, just an end of a very full life. There are still so many people I would like to mention in this book, but if I tried to name them all it would never end. So I decided to make some collages of my friends instead. Throughout my life, I have made collages as gifts for friends, for each film production I had worked on and for The Poseidon Hotel. I am continuing that tradition here as I look through all my old photo albums to find pictures of as many of my dear friends as I can to fill these final pages.

3 April, 2018, the older I get, the more I have tried to work out for myself the questions of life and death. I've stopped believing in heaven and hell in the way I had been taught in my youth. I have begun to believe that our destinies are allotted to each of us when we are born and we will never really know why certain things are decided for us. I love life and it makes me sad when I see how many people never have the chance to live theirs in full. I am not afraid of dying, but I don't want to be sick and suffer. I just want to fly away.

Recently, I had a thought. If there is no heaven or hell, what is there? Then I remembered the song *Over the Rainbow*. I have loved that song ever since I first heard it when I was four years old and my sister Peggy took me to see the movie *The Wizard of Oz*. I have now decided that when I die I want to go Over the Rainbow and be surrounded with little fluttering bluebirds. I hope all my friends from my past and present will be heading that way too. I know we will never be able to see, hear, touch or feel each other again, but I'm sure our energies will be able to come into contact. We will be able to talk and laugh about the past. This vision of mine may seem like a wild dream, but I hope it comes true and I hope we can all go Over the Rainbow and meet up again one more time.

János

Postscript

I dedicate this Diary to my dear friends Bob Miller and Ed Wittstein. I would never have considered putting my stories down on paper without the encouragement and support they gave me years ago. Without them, this Diary would have never come into being.

I also would like to thank Chris Wisniewski who travelled from Cape Cod, Massachusetts to help sort through all my notes, stories and photos and turn them into this Diary. I had been working on this project for so many years that I was afraid I would never finish it. I really could not have completed it without her help.

I would also like to thank Katie Wasiak for helping me as I was nearing the end of my Diary and Gennaro Barba for his help whenever I had computer problems. I could go on forever thanking people for their friendship and kindness, but same old story, no place and no time!

I want to apologise to any of my friends who were not mentioned in this Diary. I have never forgotten any of you, but it would have taken a few more hundred pages to write about everyone I have known. I hope you will forgive me. At this time of my life, I do forget many things, but each and every person who has filled my past is still with me and always will be.

Love and Light,
Jennie

November 2018

38871732R00137

Printed in Poland
by Amazon Fulfillment
Poland Sp. z o.o., Wrocław